PC Magazine Guide to Linking LANs

PC Magazine Guide to Linking LANs

Frank J. Derfler, Jr.

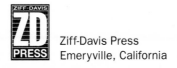

Ziff-Davis Press
Emeryville, California

Development Editor	Eric Stone
Copy Editor	Glen Becker
Technical Reviewers	Tom Jones and Lee Maybaum
Project Coordinator	Sheila McGill
Proofreader	Lysa Lewallen
Cover Design	Ken Roberts
Cover Illustration	Cherie Plumlee Computer Graphics & Illustration
Book Design	Paper Crane Graphics, Berkeley
Technical Illustration	Cherie Plumlee Computer Graphics & Illustration
Word Processing	Howard Blechman and Kim Haglund
Page Layout	Sidney Davenport and Anna Marks
Indexer	Ted Laux

This book was produced on a Macintosh IIfx, with the following applications: FrameMaker®, Microsoft® Word, MacLink®Plus, Aldus® FreeHand™, Adobe Photoshop™, and Collage Plus™.

Ziff-Davis Press
5903 Christie Avenue
Emeryville, CA 94608

ISBN 1-56276-031-9

Manufactured in the United States of America

10 9 8 7 6 5 4 3 2

———————————————————————

To the staff of and visitors to the PC Magazine LAN Labs. Beyond the beautiful water and the white sand beaches, remember the things we did before anyone else!

■ Contents at a Glance

■ Table of Contents

■ Acknowledgments

I acknowledge and sincerely appreciate the help of Steve Rigney, who contributed text, ideas, sweat, and tears to this book. Lee Maybaum and Tom Jones helped keep us on track. Eric Stone provided stabilization and Glen Becker provided style. Kaare Christian helped develop ideas on interoperability. The hard work of Howard Blechman, Sidney Davenport, Kim Haglund, Ted Laux, Lysa Lewallen, Anna Marks, and Cherie Plumlee helped make this book a good-looking success.

■ Introduction

It's typical. You learned a little something about DOS subdirectories and wrote a batch file, so somebody made you a network manager. You learned how to set up shared files and printers, solved some problems with networked applications, and got an electronic-mail system running, so they gave you a couple more networks to run. Now, somebody (maybe you!) had the bright idea of linking the LANs in your organization together so you can quickly and efficiently share information among your operating locations. This book can help.

Whether you need to link networks this week, maintain an already installed inter-LAN network, or plan for the future, I've created a book that you can use as a tutorial, technical reference, and vendor guide. Throughout the book, my constant goal is to make the material available and easy to understand.

As in *PC Magazine Guide to Connectivity,* the first book in the Ziff-Davis Press Connectivity Series, I included thumbs-up/thumbs-down lists to summarize the advantages and disadvantages of different technologies, approaches, and techniques.

Both books also give you the benefit of the decision matrix charts I developed for *PC Magazine.* These charts, present in several chapters of this book, guide your decisions about techniques and product types by helping you work through a series of yes-or-no questions. You might not always like the recommendation the charts provide, but you can clearly see how to change the conditions that lead to that recommendation.

In this book I've also supplied periodic "hints" that explain a piece of especially good advice or a trick I've picked up along the way.

If you need a broad overview of the techniques and options you can use to link LANs, the first chapter provides points of reference and definitions, while Chapter 2 guides you through the buzzwords of inter-LAN connections and describes how the terms interrelate.

The third chapter explains the full-time, high-powered LAN-to-LAN connection devices: bridges and routers. I specifically describe the functions of each type of device and tell when to select one or the other. The products on the market are complex, and this chapter gives you a guideline to make sense out of competing claims and designs. Chapters 4 and 5 take you into greater depth and provide checklists for selecting products.

Chapter 6 opens the doors to the more flexible techniques you can use to move information between LANs, including electronic mail. This chapter is a tutorial describing how you can economically link LANs using electronic mail—without the expense or technical challenge of bridges or routers.

But electronic mail often can't meet all your needs for moving information between LANs. E-mail is not invisible, and it requires specific actions by people on both ends of the link. Chapter 7 describes how other devices—including products I've dubbed wide-area information transfer systems (WAITS) and the well-known electronic bulletin board systems—can move files between LANs automatically and economically.

While Chapters 3 through 7 describe the devices that act as portals between LANs, the remaining chapters in the book deal with the important and potentially expensive inter-LAN links. Chapter 8 describes the technical details you need to know about serial ports and multiplexers—the vital intermediate links between the devices on the LAN and those of a telephone company or private carrier providing the inter-LAN circuits.

Ordering telephone-line services between LANs is an art. The monthly recurring costs can quickly overshadow any up-front equipment costs. Chapter 9 describes dial-up and leased telephone-line services. I tell you who provides local and long-distance services, list the positive and negative aspects of different types of service, and show you how to order services. The chapter carries you from simple dial-up lines through ISDN and switched multimegabit circuits. Chapter 10 gives you the same type of detailed information for the important X.25 and frame-relay packet-switched systems.

Chapters 11 and 12 round out your education with important information concerning two problems you face when you link LANs: network management and interoperability. Whether your network covers a building, campus, continent, or hemisphere of the globe, you need to control its resources carefully. Chapter 11 describes the tools and techniques of network management. When different LANs are connected, they can't always talk, so Chapter 12 introduces the concept of interoperability and provides some advice on making different systems work together.

At the end of the book you'll find a complete glossary of terms associated with networking and telecommunications. You'll also find a list of vendors that market products for LAN-to-LAN connectivity in the appendix. Of course there is an extensive index, too.

Throughout this book I've tried to avoid techno-babble and yet provide you with the practical information you need to make smart decisions. Good connections!

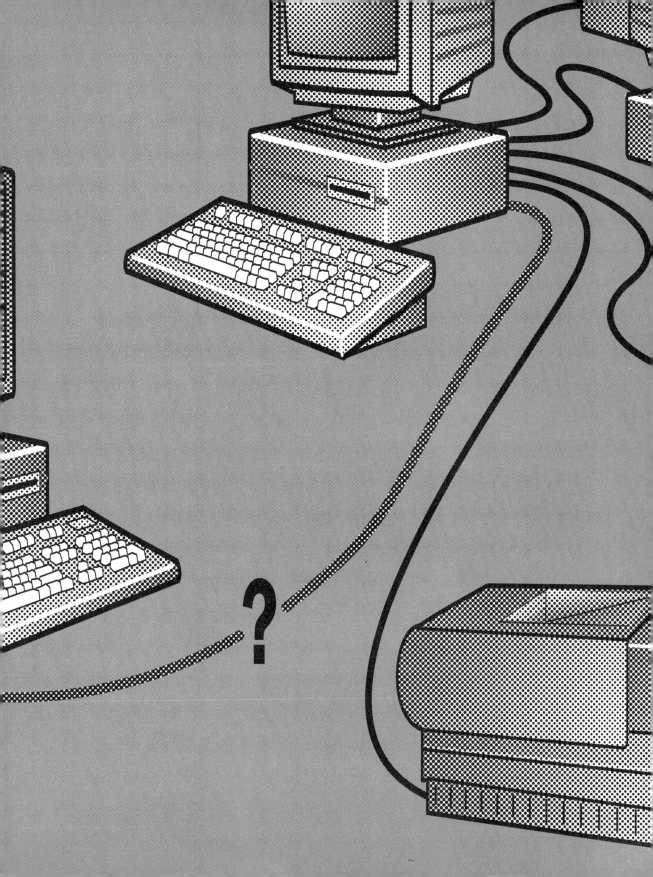

Linking LANs:
A Way of Business
for Modern
Organizations

- The LAN Side

- The LAN Part of LAN-to-LAN

Relatively few organizations do business in just one place. The owner of a retail store dreams of establishing a franchised chain. Service organizations open outlets in other neighborhoods and cities. The life cycle of business is the familiar pattern of nature: Grow and divide.

In organizations that rely on networked PCs, managers and workers establish new LANs when they set up shop in new locations. Then they quickly find that they need to link those LANs in some way to support the corporate business.

Studies of the traffic on internal corporate telephone systems show that the classic 80/20 rule applies: 80 percent of the calls are made within a local office, and 20 percent go to distant corporate offices. The division of traffic on data networks is typically about the same. Modern organizations that do business in more than one place move a lot of data within each office or building, but the people in the organization also need to connect their networks and move significant volumes of data among the different business locations.

The type and volume of data that people need to move vary widely, so companies in the LAN interconnection business have fielded products that make many levels of inter-LAN connectivity available. In this book, I'll use the resources of PC Magazine LAN Labs and my own experience to explain the techniques, problems, possibilities, and costs of LAN-to-LAN connectivity.

I'd like to underscore that my emphasis is on linking LANs (local area networks). In the 1980s, wide-area networks predominantly carried data between terminals and mainframe computers. During this period the wide-area networks took on a life of their own and became the center of a great deal of development work. The wide-area network became as important as the devices it serviced at the ends. But in the nineties the center of balance has shifted. Local area networks, typically heavily populated by personal computers, are the workplaces for people in the 1990s. My consistent focus in this book is on LAN-to-LAN connectivity because that's what people in modern organizations need.

LAN-to-LAN connectivity options range from relatively simple, informal arrangements using dial-up telephone lines and modems to technologically complex devices that examine every Ethernet packet or Token-Ring frame and make sophisticated decisions on its disposition. The costs for inter-LAN connections range from practically nothing to many thousands of dollars a month. Creating effective inter-LAN communications systems is a challenge that can have an impact on the bottom-line effectiveness of an organization or business.

Linking LANs is the modern way to do business. Office LANs support local workgroups, but linked LANs support an entire organization.

■ The LAN Side

PC Magazine Guide to Connectivity, also published by Ziff-Davis Press, provides detailed descriptions of local area network technology, along with lists of companies marketing LAN products, plus valuable programs on diskettes that you can use on your LAN. The goal of the book you have in your hands is to describe how to link the LANs described in the *Guide to Connectivity*. At the same time, it's worth taking some time here to provide a quick overview of LAN technology and practices. In this chapter I'll review a few fundamentals, with special emphasis on how a LAN permits sharing resources. The next chapter contains a more detailed look at the buzzwords and terms used in LAN interconnection systems.

The New LANs

There are three reasons for the significantly improved performance and features available from modern local area network systems. The first driving factor is competition. Companies like Artisoft, Banyan Systems, Digital Equipment Corp., D-Link Systems, IBM, Invisible Software, Microsoft Corp., Novell, Performance Technology, and U.S. Sage are in heated competition for business in the LAN market. Competition has spurred innovation and technical quality. Today's LANs are more flexible, expandable, and interoperable than any minicomputer system. Companies have given up the strategy of trying to snare and hold accounts with proprietary technology; they are relying instead on performance and service to win customers.

The second reason for the performance improvement in these products comes from the continually growing power of the PC hardware. Today's affordable computers based on 80386 and 80486 processors have processing power and memory to spare. In fact, a lot of their power goes to waste if they aren't networked. Inexpensive and powerful PCs are the building blocks of networks.

If you have strong and inexpensive building blocks, you need some equally high-quality way to mortar them together. The third reason for the improvement in the power and quality of LANs comes from advances in the architecture and execution of networking software. Programs running in networked client computers and in network servers use a combination of code written in the C programming language and in assembler, so the programmers can create features using powerful C libraries, update the software frequently, and still maintain fast throughput. Writing fast code for LAN operations is an arcane art; the best programmers now have libraries of proven routines, and they know a variety of techniques for improving performance and maintaining interoperability. The community of programmers knows about LANs and has the tools to produce excellent LAN software.

LAN Operating Systems

In the phrase *network operating system,* the emphasis must be on the word *system.* A network operating system includes many pieces of software that run in various computers attached to the network cable. Later in this chapter I'll describe some of the functions of these pieces of software and how they communicate.

Some LAN operating-system products come with a significant suite of features, including electronic mail, LAN remote control, and management utilities. All of these features can use or be useful for LAN-to-LAN connection. We'll describe LAN-to-LAN e-mail, remote control, and management considerations in later chapters.

When you link LANs, security is an important consideration. Often, people who send their data across an inter-LAN link don't need full access to all of the resources of the distant LAN. The LAN administrator who allows everyone to have free reign on the network will at best run out of resources like disk storage space, and could suffer a loss of data from mischief or human error.

A LAN software package typically uses one or more of three types of file-security plans. The first plan gives each shared resource on the network a "network name"; a single name can designate a whole shared drive, a subdirectory, or even a file. You can associate a password with a network name and limit the read/write/create capabilities associated with that password. This scheme is used in networks based on the old Microsoft MS-Net model. The network-name architecture makes it easy to protect the shared resources, but one user might have to keep track of several passwords. And security is easily compromised when password management is a constant headache. This type of security system is particularly difficult to administer in a multi-LAN environment.

The second security plan assigns specific rights to a specific user and provides a password to identify that user. This scheme works fine in small organizations, but customizing the rights of each user quickly becomes an administrative problem in larger networks.

The third security architecture uses the concept of groups: Each person belongs to one or more groups, and each group has specific access rights. This architecture, popularized by Novell's NetWare, makes each person responsible for only one personal password and lets the LAN administrator easily move people into different groups as they change jobs or leave the organization. However, administrators in multiserver environments must still ensure that the correct security information is available on each server.

All of the security architectures typically permit an administrator to allow or deny individuals or groups the ability to read, write, create, delete, search,

and modify files. For example, you might want to give data-entry clerks the full
ability to modify accounting files but no ability to modify other types of files.

Modern network operating systems are moving to global naming services that make it easier to administrate a network with multiple servers.
Banyan Systems has led the way in its network operating system VINES.
Each resource, such as a disk drive, special program, or printer, has a very
specific three-part network name. VINES servers automatically interact with
each other over any available communications links, and they update a common database of user names and access rights that covers the whole
extended network.

When you plan to link LANs, the question of administration might not
be high on your list of considerations, but it should be. Details like the
names you give to servers, the log-on names people use, and the names you
assign to resources such as printers all have an effect on the efficient use of
the extended network. If you use simple naming schemes, then the person
using a log-on name of Tom and trying to log on to a server named Accounting to use a printer named Laser might run into a problem on a nationwide
network populated by dozens of Toms with separate accounting depart-
ments, each equipped with a laser printer in each district office. Keeping control of names and resources is a major challenge when you link LANs.

HINT. *Linked LANs can offer many benefits, but you'll need to consider a
scheme for naming resources and people across the entire extended network to
simplify management and avoid conflicts.*

LAN Pieces and Parts

Let's run through the ingredients we mix together to produce a LAN. In
many cases the devices I'll name are not specialized products, but merely typical PCs and other computers acting in a specific role—for example, PCs acting as *servers* of various types and PCs acting as *clients* to the servers. To
confuse the issue, a computer can often act as a client and a server at the
same time.

Each networked computer needs a device—typically a printed circuit
board like the Artisoft adapter shown in Figure 1.1—that goes into an expansion slot to make the electrical and mechanical connection between the computer and the network cable. These network-interface cards (NICs) or *LAN
adapters* determine the type of wiring or *media* the network uses and how
the nodes share the access to that media. The term *media-access control*
(MAC) will recur many times in this book. It simply refers to the strategy
the LAN adapters follow to provide orderly control of the nodes' transmissions into the network.

Figure 1.1

This Artisoft AE-3 LAN
adapter has connections
for unshielded twisted-pair
wiring and thin coaxial
cable, and a multipurpose
interface that can link to
special transceivers for
fiber-optic or thick coaxial
cable.

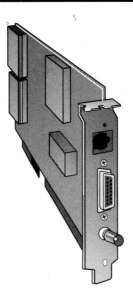

Finally, there is the cabling itself. Today buyers have many options for LAN cabling. The choice is influenced both by what might already be installed and by the electrical environment of the building.

There Are Servers, Servers, and Servers

Networks are for sharing. The devices that share their resources over the network are called *servers*. People typically think of a server as a computer that stores files and has shared printers attached. But in modern local area networks, many different kinds of devices act as servers. The three general categories of servers are file servers, print servers, and communications servers.

File servers hold files for the client computers while special software in the client PCs makes the file servers' hard disks, CD-ROM drives, or other storage resources appear to be local drives on the client computers. *Print servers* make printers available for sharing across the network. *Communications servers*, the richest group of all (and largely the subject of this book), make off-LAN communications links available to people using the LAN.

HINT. *There are three types of servers: file servers, print servers, and communications servers. The category of communications servers includes many different devices for LAN-to-LAN communications.*

File Servers

Like most concepts in this industry, these categories don't hold still for easy labeling. Advances in technology continue to change and shape how we categorize products in the LAN market. Before 1989 we had two fundamental architectures for network server software, and therefore two neat categories of file servers. One architecture, called the *client/server* model, requires dedicating a computer to the role of file server. The other architecture, called *peer-to-peer* networking, allows any PC on the network to act both as a client workstation and as a file server.

The product classification was simple because the dedicated server products used a unique file-management system such as Novell's NetWare, and the peer-to-peer systems used DOS. Then Novell gave NetWare the capability to use a PC as both a server and a client station, and Microsoft Corp. introduced LAN Manager, a networking product with peer-to-peer capabilities running over the multitasking operating system OS/2.

Today, the only product classification that makes sense for file servers is distinguishing between those using DOS and those using any other operating system. The "any other" class encompasses OS/2, dozens of flavors of Unix, hidden versions of Unix like those in NetWare and VINES, and other unique operating systems such as Digital Equipment Corp.'s VMS.

People in modern organizations often need access to file servers on distant LANs. Application programs as diverse as database-management programs, accounting programs, and electronic-mail programs can reach across inter-LAN links and update files on remote file servers. File transfer and sharing is the prime reason for linking LANs.

Print Servers

Similarly, the only definition of a print server used to be a computer with perhaps as many as five printers attached and accessible to other computers. In this definition, the computer runs special software that makes the printers available for sharing across the network. Client computers send print jobs to the print server. The print server queues the jobs, usually on a local hard disk, and then sends them to the printers in an orderly manner.

This model for a print server is still the most common, but in 1990 Intel introduced a small module—about the size of a VHS videocassette—containing all the processing power needed to act as a print server. In 1991, companies like Digital Equipment Corp. and Hewlett-Packard Co. introduced printers with their own internal print-server capabilities. So today you can share a networked printer across a LAN without having a separate computer acting as a print server. The print server is often literally in the printer instead of being an attached computer.

It is often handy to be able to send a print job to a print server on a distant LAN. It's easier to send the electronic message than a stack of paper, and the distant printer can play the same message-delivery role as a fax machine, but with very high-quality output. Remote printing is another excellent reason for making LAN-to-LAN links.

Communications Servers

I'll tackle the subject of the various types of communications servers more thoroughly in Chapter 2, because these engines of communications come in a variety of shapes and sizes and perform a number of different jobs. The name *communications server* implies a variety of functions, but all of them involve moving data aggregated together into Token-Ring *packets* or Ethernet *frames* between the high-speed network cable and some slower long-distance communications system. The nature of the packets or frames and the characteristics of the long-distance communications system dictate the type of communications server you use.

The category of products we call communications servers includes computers acting as gateways to mainframes or as asynchronous communications servers, access servers, bulletin board systems, electronic-mail servers, bridges, or routers. A networked PC can act in each of these roles, and many companies market specialized standalone devices to act as bridges and routers.

If you want to provide people working at client PCs with access to programs on an IBM mainframe computer, you can install hardware and software in one networked PC that turns it into a gateway that can communicate between the LAN and IBM's unique 3270 Systems Network Architecture communications scheme. The gateway translates between the different data alphabets used in the PC and mainframe systems, and between the different communications signaling and cabling schemes.

If you want people to be able to dial into your network and run application programs, then you need a type of communications server called an *access server*. I'll describe how access servers work and tell you about specific products in Chapter 7. In the same chapter I will discuss bulletin board systems that allow people to dial into and withdraw information from a LAN under strict control, and wide-area information transfer systems (WAITS) that move data automatically. In Chapter 6 I'll describe how electronic-mail systems link LANs.

Bridges and routers are complex devices with a single simple task. They are the gatekeepers for communications between LANs. They decide when to forward and relay data and how to do it. These devices are fully described in Chapters 3, 4, and 5.

You must evaluate the roles played by file servers, print servers, and communications servers on the various LANs when you plan your linking strategies. As Figure 1.2 depicts, modern computers can play several different network roles simultaneously, and people working across LAN-to-LAN links often need specific kinds of services from the remote LAN.

Figure 1.2

A PC in the 80386/80486 class can run software that lets it simultaneously act as file server, print server, and client to other servers. Modern network operating systems provide flexible methods of serving in different roles.

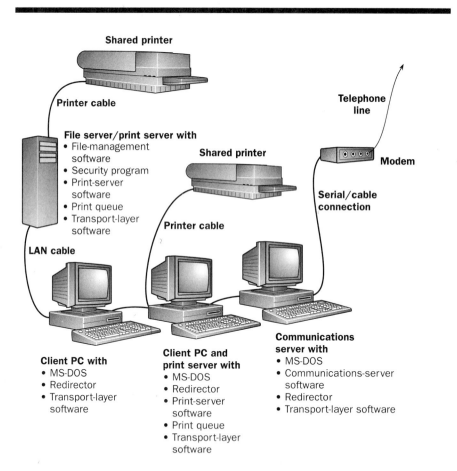

Shared printer

Printer cable

Telephone line

File server/print server with
• File-management software
• Security program
• Print-server software
• Print queue
• Transport-layer software

Shared printer

Modem

Serial/cable connection

Printer cable

LAN cable

Client PC with
• MS-DOS
• Redirector
• Transport-layer software

Client PC and print server with
• MS-DOS
• Redirector
• Print-server software
• Print queue
• Transport-layer software

Communications server with
• MS-DOS
• Communications-server software
• Redirector
• Transport-layer software

LAN Adapters and Media-Access Control

LAN adapter cards translate between the low-powered electrical signals moving data in parallel streams inside a computer and the more powerful serial data flowing in the LAN cable. Because the adapter cards are made with specific types of connectors and electrical transceivers, the decision you make about the type of LAN adapter you buy also determines the type of cabling and signaling you use on the network.

The IEEE has established a set of standards for LAN cabling, signaling, and media-access control: the IEEE 802.3 standard, generically referred to as Ethernet (although the original Ethernet standard is different enough to be incompatible), and the IEEE 802.5 standard, for Token-Ring networks. The 802.3 standard denotes a signaling speed of 10 megabits per second using a carrier sense multiple access (CSMA) media-access scheme. Variations under the standard allow for the connection of thin coaxial cable (thinnet), thick coaxial cable, and fiber-optic cable. In 1990 the IEEE approved an 802.3 specification called 10BaseT, establishing a standard for running Ethernet over unshielded twisted-pair (UTP) wire—in more common terminology, telephone wire. The common types of network media are shown in Figure 1.3.

Figure 1.3

The major types of network media or wiring are (from left to right): thin coaxial cable with a BNC connector, fiber-optic cabling and connectors, shielded twisted-pair wiring with an IBM Token-Ring connector, and unshielded twisted-pair wire with a modular connector attached.

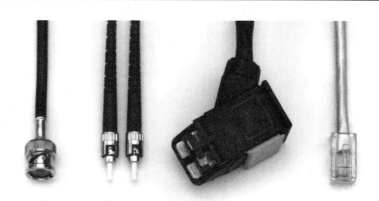

The CSMA media-access protocol operates on a listen-before-talking principle. The network adapter card listens to the network traffic on the cable before transmitting. If it hears a signal, it waits. In turn, the collision-detection feature ensures that if two or more nodes transmit simultaneously over the idle network cable, the other nodes are alerted by a *jam signal* and do not attempt transmission until the line clears, or until after a random period of time.

The IEEE 802.5 standard defines a network wiring scheme using shielded or unshielded twisted-pair wire or fiber-optic cable. The media-access control scheme uses a method of passing a message carrying permission to transmit; this message is called a *token*. The token-passing scheme stands in contrast to the contention MAC scheme used in 802.3. The 802.5 networks use signaling speeds of 4 and 16 megabits per second.

ARCnet, a MAC, signaling, and cabling scheme that never received IEEE approval, operates at 2.5 kilobits per second over coaxial cable, fiber-optic cable, or unshielded twisted-pair wiring. ARCnet is inexpensive, effective, and widely installed.

Several companies—including Artisoft, DCA 10NET Communications, and U.S. Sage—market adapters using relatively unusual MAC, signaling, and connector architectures as low-cost alternatives to their products that meet the faster and more widely supported industry standards. I don't recommend using LAN adapters that fail to follow the latest standards, although they might be only two-thirds the price of the standard adapters, for the simple reason that you could wind up with a network of orphan adapters. If the vendor goes out of business or stops supporting those nonstandard adapters, you'll have no options for expansion except to throw away the orphans and start all over. Adapters that meet the industry standards are reasonably priced and widely supported, and they provide top-notch performance.

The types of wiring, signaling, and media-access control schemes used on the LANs are important when it comes to planning the inter-LAN links. For example, if you plan to link one 802.3 LAN to another, you have a large set of options. If you want to link an 802.3 LAN to an 802.5 LAN, then you have fewer choices.

In many cases, particularly when you order specialized products like stand-alone bridges and routers, you must order devices equipped to connect to the specific type of wiring and signaling system used on each LAN. Often you must also specify the type of LAN operating system, because many communications-server products such as access servers and routers are designed for specific operating systems.

Envelopes Within Envelopes

If you're going to understand LAN-to-LAN connectivity, you must understand how packets or frames of data move across the local area network. The best analogy for data transport across a LAN is the way that people in formal society handle wedding invitations. There are many envelopes within envelopes, and the envelopes shuttle back and forth carrying messages. Network communications also consist of messages wrapped in envelopes and then wrapped again in envelopes.

HINT. *The concept of a single data packet contained within multiple envelopes for transmission is key to understanding LAN and LAN-to-LAN communications.*

Application programs running in networked computers don't need to be specially configured for network operation. They send requests to the computer operating system—typically DOS (possibly with Microsoft Windows), OS/2, or Unix—without caring whether the computer is networked or not. But in networked computers a special layer of networking software, the *redirector*, intercepts each request and moves it to another group or *stack* of small programs responsible for communications across the network. Thanks to the redirector, distant resources such as files, printers, and communications devices appear to the computer user and to the software as if they were attached directly to the computer.

The network communications programs contained in every networked node encapsulate requests from application programs, or data from network file systems, inside an envelope of bits that identifies its own source, destination, function, and size in terms understood by the network operating system. When this packet of data arrives at its destination, the network operating-system software can handle it efficiently and route the data to the correct file or program.

Typical network communications protocols include Novell's Sequenced Packet Exchange (SPX), its more commonly used subset the Internet Packet Exchange (IPX), the combination of the Transmission Control Protocol (TCP) and the Internet Protocol (IP), and the Network Basic Input/Output System (NetBIOS) used in many network operating systems.

When the redirector routes a request from an application program to the software conforming to a protocol like IPX, the IPX software adds bits to the beginning and end of the message received from the application. Then it passes the newly configured IPX packet to the networking hardware. The hardware's specialized processor wraps the IPX packet in another envelope conforming to a standard like Ethernet, ARCnet, or Token-Ring. This envelope also contains source and destination information, along with other data used for checking the accuracy of the received data.

Like the multiple envelopes in a wedding invitation, packets of information nestle within each other as they move across and between local networks. The relatively simple diagram in Figure 1.4 shows a classic Ethernet packet (not conforming to the slightly more complex IEEE 802.3 standard) wrapped around an IP packet, which in turn shelters a TCP packet.

The information in the Ethernet packet tells any Ethernet adapter the identity of the source and destination stations. Bridges read the source address in each Ethernet packet and use it to build a table of information showing the locations of network nodes. They read the destination information to determine whether to pass the packet out to the inter-LAN circuit. If the bridge is attached to an X.25 network, it will encapsulate the entire Ethernet packet in the X.25 envelope and pass it over the network. The receiving LAN must use the Ethernet format, although it can use any type of wiring. The bridge pays no attention to the contents of the *data field* in the Ethernet packet.

Figure 1.4

This diagram show how data packets are packaged within successive envelopes, each with its own specific addressing and data-identification information.

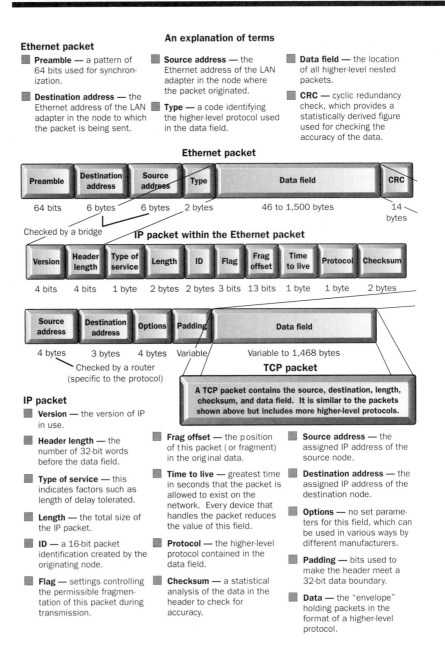

Ethernet packet

An explanation of terms

- **Preamble** — a pattern of 64 bits used for synchronization.
- **Destination address** — the Ethernet address of the LAN adapter in the node to which the packet is being sent.

- **Source address** — the Ethernet address of the LAN adapter in the node where the packet originated.
- **Type** — a code identifying the higher-level protocol used in the data field.

- **Data field** — the location of all higher-level nested packets.
- **CRC** — cyclic redundancy check, which provides a statistically derived figure used for checking the accuracy of the data.

Ethernet packet

Preamble	Destination address	Source address	Type	Data field	CRC
64 bits	6 bytes	6 bytes	2 bytes	46 to 1,500 bytes	14 bytes

Checked by a bridge

IP packet within the Ethernet packet

Version	Header length	Type of service	Length	ID	Flag	Frag offset	Time to live	Protocol	Checksum
4 bits	4 bits	1 byte	2 bytes	2 bytes	3 bits	13 bits	1 byte	1 byte	2 bytes

Source address	Destination address	Options	Padding	Data field
4 bytes	3 bytes	4 bytes	Variable	Variable to 1,468 bytes

Checked by a router (specific to the protocol)

TCP packet

A TCP packet contains the source, destination, length, checksum, and data field. It is similar to the packets shown above but includes more higher-level protocols.

IP packet

- **Version** — the version of IP in use.

- **Header length** — the number of 32-bit words before the data field.

- **Type of service** — this indicates factors such as length of delay tolerated.

- **Length** — the total size of the IP packet.

- **ID** — a 16-bit packet identification created by the originating node.

- **Flag** — settings controlling the permissible fragmentation of this packet during transmission.

- **Frag offset** — the position of this packet (or fragment) in the original data.

- **Time to live** — greatest time in seconds that the packet is allowed to exist on the network. Every device that handles the packet reduces the value of this field.

- **Protocol** — the higher-level protocol contained in the data field.

- **Checksum** — a statistical analysis of the data in the header to check for accuracy.

- **Source address** — the assigned IP address of the source node.

- **Destination address** — the assigned IP address of the destination node.

- **Options** — no set parameters for this field, which can be used in various ways by different manufacturers.

- **Padding** — bits used to make the header meet a 32-bit data boundary.

- **Data** — the "envelope" holding packets in the format of a higher-level protocol.

The *type field* in the Ethernet packet can tell network nodes that the data field is formatted for AppleTalk, DECnet, IP, IPX, VINES, or any one of many other protocols.

Figure 1.4 also shows the breakout of an IP packet contained within the data field of the Ethernet packet. A router—a node specifically addressed in the *destination address* field of the Ethernet packet—is programmed to look into the IP packet for the address of the destination node. The router then consults its own internal tables and examines variables such as the status of communications circuits to determine how to send the IP packet on its next hop toward the destination. Each router typically specializes in handling one type of packet format, although multiprotocol routers are becoming increasingly common.

In a public data network, the router would discard the Ethernet packet information and encapsulate only the IP information into an X.25 envelope or into a new type of envelope called *frame relay* for its trip across the wide-area network. When the IP packet arrives on the other side, the receiving router can insert it into a packet in Ethernet, Token-Ring, or some other appropriate format.

Figure 1.4 also shows how a TCP packet would nestle within the envelope of the IP packet. In turn, the TCP packet will hold other packets created in a format specific to an application program or to a service such as the Simple Mail Transfer Protocol (SMTP).

The concept of moving data within envelopes within more envelopes is central to some LAN-to-LAN communications techniques. Some LAN-to-LAN connection devices sort and take action on traffic based on different envelopes. For example, bridges typically look at the envelope created by the network hardware—the media-access control packet. Routers look inside the MAC-layer envelope and read the addressing information contained in the packet on the layer of network communications (such as IP or IPX).

■ The LAN Part of LAN-to-LAN

The LAN technology involved in LAN-to-LAN communications is important and interesting. The technical details of the LANs you must link will affect many decisions you make about how to link them. In later chapters I'll include some decision matrix charts to help you evaluate the alternatives. When you make LAN-to-LAN linking decisions, it pays to stay focused on the LANs at either end and to choose alternatives that will provide the best support for the LANs.

CHAPTER

2

The Most Important Buzzwords

- Imagine, If You Will . . .

- Invisible Movements

- The Medium Carries the Message

- Making Selections

The business of LAN-to-LAN connectivity is saturated with many unique terms and buzzwords. Knowing the buzzwords eliminates about 50 percent of the fog and uncertainty surrounding the buying decisions you might make. The other 50 percent is harder to clear up, and that's what the rest of the book is about! This chapter is specifically designed as a vocabulary-building exercise. My goal is to link words and acronyms to concepts. I'll explain the concepts well enough to put you in the ballpark, so you can read and understand the remaining chapters without constant reference to the glossary.

The basis of the chapter is a diagram bound into the back of the book that illustrates a LAN-to-LAN connection scenario and shows how the various pieces and parts fit in the overall scheme. On this basis, I'll provide the big picture before breaking it down into its component parts in later chapters.

■ Imagine, If You Will . . .

Take a look at the bound-in diagram in the back of this book, and imagine an organization with headquarters in New York and branch offices in Chicago, Dallas, and San Francisco. Each operating location has its own network of PCs. New York, Chicago, and Dallas use Novell's NetWare as their LAN operating system, but the network in the San Francisco office was inherited as part of a corporate merger, and it is based on Microsoft's LAN Manager. All four networks run over Ethernet.

In our scenario, the branch offices need to move data to the headquarters throughout the business day, but they also regularly need to exchange some data with one another. In our examination of public data networks in Chapter 10, we will expand this scenario to get some idea of the cost of this corporate intercommunications system.

Remote-Access Service

Perhaps the easiest way to exchange data between LANs is through remote control of a networked PC over a telephone line and modem. The remotely controlled PC performs in the role of an *access server* providing remote access for callers; this is represented by an *A* in the diagram. The calling PC can run programs on the called PC, and only keystrokes and screen images pass over the relatively slow modem link.

The modem remote-control software market is well established, and there are many competitive products. Unfortunately, remote-control systems don't work as efficiently under Microsoft Windows or the OS/2 Presentation Manager because the graphical user interface used in these environments is so detailed and changes completely with each click of a mouse.

BUZZWORD. Access servers *are networked PCs that are available for remote control by distant computers calling over telephone lines and modems. They provide a way to run any application on the LAN remotely.*

To apply modem remote-control LAN-to-LAN links to our scenario: One PC on the Dallas network could use normal dial-up telephone lines to call a modem attached to a networked PC in New York. Once they are connected, the modem remote-control programs running on both PCs provide an efficient way for someone in Dallas to make entries in a database, use electronic mail, or copy data files on the New York networks.

The software typically includes data compression and error control to get the best benefit from the telephone line. Modern V.32 modems can signal at 9,600 bits per second, and the compression protocols in the remote-control software can increase throughput to over 30 kilobits per second for certain kinds of files.

Remote-access service:

👍 **Provides the ability to run programs on a remotely controlled PC and see the results**

👍 **Allows fast unassisted file transfers**

👍 **Requires only modems, the networked PC, and some relatively inexpensive software**

👎 **Loses efficiency under Windows or other environments with a graphical user interface**

👎 **Is not invisible; special actions are needed to establish the link**

When a PC is set up to be remotely controlled, an authorized user calling from any location can access the full power of the network. The caller can run programs, use printers, access a mainframe computer through a network gateway, and otherwise act as a full member of the network. Modem remote-control programs don't care what network operating system or network adapter cards you use, so these packages can easily span the different LAN operating systems described in our scenario.

A remote-control connection is effective, but at some level of activity it will become uneconomical to keep individual networked PCs always ready to receive dial-in calls. When remote control of a networked PC becomes a frequent event, it's wise to establish a separate computer system as a full-time access server that can handle many incoming calls simultaneously. I provide a detailed description of such access servers in Chapter 7.

Almost all of the access servers we have reviewed at PC Magazine LAN Labs can provide shared calling resources such as modems for people on the network making outgoing calls. Such a device is represented in the diagram as *A/M,* for "access server with modem-server capabilities."

Although the price of V.32bis 9,600-bit-per-second modems is dropping, they typically still cost between $600 and $1,000. It makes economic sense to share modems among as many people as possible. Access servers acting as modem pools can share these devices, but you have to use certain techniques to link communications programs running on networked PCs to the shared modems. Specifically, you must either use hardware in each PC to redirect the communications across the LAN to the modem pool, or else use programs that can address the IPX or NetBIOS LAN protocols.

BBSs for Protected Access

Bulletin board systems:

👍 **Allow controlled access to files with excellent security**

👍 **Provide electronic mail**

👍 **Are easy for callers to use**

👎 **Typically do not allow users to run programs remotely**

👎 **Are not invisible to users**

A similar scenario for gaining entry to our LAN, although with different goals and a different lineage, would use the well-known *bulletin board system* (BBS). A bulletin board system, represented as *BBS* in the diagram, consists of software running on one networked PC that can simultaneously handle multiple incoming callers (typically four). The callers are greeted with a menu of messages and functions. They can easily read and post messages or upload and download files, but always under the tight functional control of the BBS software.

A modern BBS typically does not provide the intimate access to network operations you get from a modem remote-control system. The BBS software insulates the network from the callers, and prevents the BBS user from running programs that might crash the BBS computer or change important files on the file server.

BUZZWORD. *A bulletin board system or BBS provides tightly controlled network access over modems and telephone lines.*

In our scenario, PCs running BBS software on all the LAN segments would provide an excellent way for customers and suppliers to post orders, receive orders, and generally interact with the elements of the organization without gaining full access to the network. The simplified format of the BBS menu also makes it easy for members of the organization who are on the road to exchange information without mastering the intricacies of network operation.

BBS systems have also become the choice for both hardware and software vendors. Many corporations see the BBS as a practical alternative to voice dial-up technical-support lines. Most computer corporations offer their customers a BBS dial-up line for use in downloading hardware drivers and upgraded software, or as a forum for discussing problems. Novell offers a powerful alternative to voice-based technical-support lines in the form of LANANSWER, a BBS offered free to all Certified NetWare Engineers, or for an annual fee to any NetWare user.

BBSs provide an economical and flexible way to give people calling from anywhere in the world access to specific information on a LAN while protecting the LAN from unwanted intrusion or unintended disruption.

WAITS

Another category of products, which I dubbed *wide-area information transfer systems* (WAITS), automates the BBS concept—although many BBS packages are capable of running sophisticated program scripts of their own to act as WAITS software. Because of their overlap with BBSs, WAITS PCs are not shown separately on the diagram.

PCs running WAITS software on each LAN segment will automatically communicate with PCs running the same software on other LAN segments. If they use dial-up lines, the WAITS PCs will dial the calls. If they use other types of circuits for inter-LAN links, the WAITS can take whatever actions are needed to communicate.

After establishing communications, the WAITS PCs will transfer queued files, update files according to specific criteria, and take other actions based on files and commands they receive during their calling activity. The programs can make repeated phone calls until they succeed in their tasks, and they can relay files between LAN segments. They don't care about network operating systems or the type of cabling and signaling each segment uses.

Wide-area information transfer systems:

👍 **Completely automate file transfers between LANs**

👍 **Offer excellent security**

👎 **Are not invisible to users**

BUZZWORD. Wide-area information transfer systems *(WAITS) are networked computers running software that automates the tasks of moving files between networks. Computers running WAITS software can satisfy all the LAN-to-LAN connectivity needs for many organizations.*

Through the use of a computer running WAITS software, the various offices in our scenario can exchange files at any time without human action. Because these systems require only a modem and a PC that is capable of running the software at each end, they usually prove more cost-efficient than the use of relatively expensive hardware such as bridges or routers.

Linking Through E-Mail

Once the use of electronic mail reaches a critical mass in an organization, people wonder how they ever did business without it. Sending an e-mail message is often a substitute for making a telephone call, but electronic mail also takes on a life of its own. People find they can coordinate large projects involving many colleagues and resources more efficiently through electronic mail than in any other way—including face-to-face meetings.

Mature electronic-mail systems are not limited to a single LAN segment. Electronic-mail gateway programs running on networked PCs, as represented by a *G* on the diagram, can automatically dial each other to exchange and collect e-mail messages. They can operate on a regular schedule or make calls only when the volume or priority of messages warrants taking the action.

BUZZWORD. Electronic-mail gateways *can move messages and attached files between dissimilar or identical LANs.*

E-mail gateways can do more than simply link identical electronic-mail systems. Because gateways can move mail between different message systems, modern e-mail programs can allow each person on the network to use a personal favorite electronic-mail package while still communicating throughout the network. This extreme situation would not be very practical, but it would work!

Products like Novell's Message Handling Service can translate between different electronic-mail programs located on a local LAN segment or on very different networks, including those based on mainframe computers. The e-mail packages are not limited by differences in LAN operating systems or cabling schemes, although some packages offer specific management features under operating systems like NetWare that they don't have when running with other LAN operating systems.

Because you can attach binary data files to electronic-mail messages, e-mail can be an excellent way to carry on a great deal of your LAN-to-LAN business. When the San Francisco office computes the closing sales figures at the end of the day, the branch sales manager can attach a spreadsheet or database file to a message addressed to the corporate sales manager in New York. If the San Francisco office did especially well, a copy to the Dallas office might be in order. At a time established by the software, the e-mail gateway PC in San Francisco connects to the gateways in New York and Dallas and transfers the messages as files. The managers must take actions to attach each file and to save the attachment when it comes in, but this is simple and helps them keep track of the activity.

Electronic-mail gateways:

👍 Can move mail and attached files between LANs

👍 Don't require expensive equipment

👎 Don't give applications access to files

👎 Can require a complex installation process

■ Invisible Movements

None of the LAN-connection alternatives described so far move data invisibly. People operating on one LAN segment must run specific programs, make connections, attach files, or give directions in order to make LAN-to-LAN communications happen. It takes training and experience to make these connections, and except for remote-access service, they don't happen in real time. But many organizations need real-time invisible connections so that people on one network can run the software they typically use and allow it to draw information from, enter information into, print on, or make connections through other LANs.

The devices that make these full-time connections are called repeaters, bridges, and routers. We will explore the significant and insignificant differences among these products in Chapters 3, 4, and 5.

Repeaters:

👍 **Provide an inexpensive way to extend the high-speed network cable**

👍 **Don't require much setup; they are essentially plug-and-play devices**

👎 **Can allow a heavy traffic load to degrade the operation of two LAN segments**

Repeaters

One basic interconnection device not depicted in our scenario is the repeater. A repeater regenerates a signal so that it can traverse a longer distance.

Repeaters operate at the level of cables and electrical signals, and there are limitations to the distance they can extend a high-speed LAN. For example, an Ethernet repeater is limited to connecting two or three LAN segments, with the total cable length not exceeding 1,500 meters. Because of this, the repeater is normally used to interconnect LANs within the same building or campus. While repeaters typically connect network segments using the same media-access-control and signaling schemes, some specialized repeaters are capable of connecting LAN segments using different cabling and media-access-control schemes; for instance, linking Ethernet to Token-Ring.

BUZZWORD. Repeaters *regenerate electrical signals between cables to extend the potential distance of transmission. The world of repeaters lies between approximately 500 and 1,500 meters of cable.*

If you need a quick connection between similar LANs, a short distance apart, a repeater is a lot cheaper than the more complex and sophisticated interconnection devices available today, and makes a lot more sense.

Bridges:

👍 **Provide an efficient way to extend the LAN cable**

👍 **Can isolate LAN segments so that traffic does not pass between them unnecessarily**

👍 **Do not require expert skills to install**

👎 **Can only link similar networks— Ethernet to Ethernet or Token-Ring to Token-Ring**

Bridges

Moving up in our scenario, both in complexity and price, our diagram shows a LAN-to-LAN connection made with a network *bridge*, represented by a *B* in the diagram. Bridges look at data that the LAN adapters have arranged into packets or frames. They read destination and source addresses in the packets or frames and make decisions on whether to pass each packet or frame on to the inter-LAN circuitry.

BUZZWORD. Bridges *link network segments over local or long distances. Unlike repeaters, they read the addresses in packets or frames and make decisions as to which ones will move over the link.*

The bridge keeps a list, called a *routing table*, of all known source addresses; it refers to that table every time it receives a new packet. If the packet contains an unknown source address, the bridge looks at the new address and stores it in the routing table for future retrieval.

Bridges are totally transparent to other devices on the network, and various LANs interconnected by a bridge form a single logical network. Bridges also have the capability of connecting networks with disparate transmission media; for instance, linking coaxial cable to fiber-optic cable or to twisted-pair wiring.

Routers:

👎 **Can move data between networks with different types of media-access control and signaling**

👎 **Use the inter-LAN media efficiently**

👎 **Require expertise to install**

👎 **Can only handle operating systems with the same network communications protocol—IPX to IPX or NetBIOS to NetBIOS**

Routers

A *router* is the most advanced and capable device used in our scenario for LAN-to-LAN connectivity. A router, represented by an *R* in the diagram, is more intelligent than a bridge in its ability to handle several levels of addressing. Instead of looking at every packet or frame and making a decision like a bridge, a router receives specially addressed packets or frames from networked devices. The router opens each packet or frame, reads detailed addressing information inside, and, after determining the destination, chooses the best path for the data packet to get there. Routers use special addressing information conforming to high-level protocols of the packet or frame addresses read by bridges.

BUZZWORD. Routers *make sophisticated decisions on how to move blocks of data between LANs. They read highly specific addressing information, and might strip off the Ethernet packet or Token-Ring frame to move the internal block of message data across the inter-LAN link.*

Routers can link LANs using different media-access-control and signaling protocols like Ethernet and Token-Ring, but the linked LANs typically must use the same complex transport-layer addressing software, such as Novell's IPX or the IP layer of the TCP/IP protocols.

Bridges Versus Routers

In a nutshell, both bridges and routers examine packets or frames as they go by and decide whether to pass them through the communications circuits linking the LANs. The two different types of devices use different criteria to make their decisions, and each is efficient in different combinations of LAN software and hardware.

In our scenario, the fact that the LAN segments use different network operating systems becomes significant in the choice between bridges and routers. Because NetWare and LAN Manager do not use the same transport-layer communications protocols, our multi-city system needs a *bridge* to move complete Ethernet packets across the inter-LAN link. If the LANs all used the same software—either NetWare, LAN Manager, or some software supporting a popular protocol like the Internet Protocol portion of the TCP/IP packet—then a more discriminating *router* might have been appropriate.

Note, however, that the only role of the bridge is to move the packets across from LAN to LAN. Some program or process on the originating side must convert the request for file or print service contained in each packet into a proper format for the network operating system at the destination. Neither a bridge nor a router resolves LAN incompatibilities, as the previously described techniques such as e-mail gateways and BBSs do—and that is an important difference.

◼ The Medium Carries the Message

So far, I've described the devices that function on each LAN segment to move files, messages, or packets on and off the LAN. But when you need to link LANs there is another important and potentially expensive layer of decisions waiting for you: what kind of circuits to use to make the inter-LAN connection.

Dial-Up Telephone Lines

Dial-up telephone lines:

👍 **Are widely available and flexible**

👍 **Have low installation costs, or none at all**

👎 **Can become expensive compared with other alternatives when used for several hours a day**

Most people are familiar with modem communications over dial-up telephone lines, but it is unlikely that dialed calls will be the most economical link between LANs if you have a lot of data to move. You are billed for dialed calls on the basis of seconds of connection time over the actual distance between the locations, and the costs add up quickly. Other connection alternatives such as leased lines and packet-switched networks provide pricing schemes that are more economical for long-duration connections. On the diagram, access servers, modem servers, bulletin board systems, and e-mail gateways all use dial-up lines. PCs running WAITS software can also use dial-up telephone lines for connections.

BUZZWORD. Dial-up telephone lines *are those you dial yourself over the public telephone network. Network switches create a temporary point-to-point connection that is broken down and reallocated when the call ends.*

Leased Lines

Leased lines:

👍 **Are available quickly and at reasonable prices, particularly in the U.S.**

👍 **Provide relatively economical service when used to carry traffic several hours a day**

👎 **Can require expensive termination equipment**

The first alternative to dial-up telephone lines that you should consider is the use of what are commonly called *leased lines*. Although modern telephone technology threatens to undermine the definition, leased lines are thought of as full-time connections that are billed at a flat monthly rate. The rate increases with the distance of the connection and with the speed of the data you want to send over the leased line.

Leased lines are available for regular analog voice or fully digital service. If you want to send data over analog lines, you need a device called a *modem* to convert the digital computer signals to analog tones. Digital leased lines carry data in digital form, but they still require interface devices called *digital service units* (DSUs) to connect the computer equipment and the digital channel.

ISDN:

👍 **Will provide fully digital telephone service to every desktop**

👎 **Has been slow to arrive, but should be largely in place in the U.S. by 1994 or 1995**

Satellite systems:

👍 **Can economically link many locations over long or short distances**

👍 **Avoid the complex interactions between different telephone companies needed to arrange leased-line service**

👎 **Usually are economical only for networks with many locations or with operations in rural locations**

👎 **Involve an undesirable delay in interactive speech and data exchanges due to the long transmission path from ground to space to ground**

Although people still order them, the low-cost high-speed modems for dial-up lines are making analog leased lines obsolete. Typically, leased lines are ordered for digital service at a speed of 19.2 kilobits per second or greater. In our scenario, the various operating locations are connected by digital leased lines in a configuration providing redundancy and alternative routing.

BUZZWORD. Leased lines *provide full-time connections for a flat monthly fee. They typically include high front-end installation costs.*

ISDN

In Chapter 9, I describe your options for making the communications link between LANs, and how you go about tackling such tasks as ordering leased lines. Chapter 9 also provides information about using a service called the Integrated Services Digital Network (ISDN), which is emerging in cities around the world.

BUZZWORD. *The* Integrated Services Digital Network *(ISDN) is a plan to provide two 64-kilobit-per-second channels over digital telephone lines to desktops worldwide.*

ISDN service will deliver two channels of 64-kilobit-per-second service to every desktop. These channels can handle any combination of digitized voice and computer data. Bundled packages of the basic-channel services provide high-speed facility-to-facility connections. ISDN has gotten off to a slow start, but it holds great promise for worldwide digital connectivity in the mid-1990s.

VSATs

Very small aperture terminals (VSATs) and other satellite technologies provide very flexible LAN-to-LAN links for organizations with many operating locations spread over considerable distances. In an oversimplified scenario, you order an Earth terminal from any of a dozen companies, have the company install it on a rooftop or in a parking lot, arrange for satellite transponder time, hook cables up to your network communications devices, and move data between your locations. There are no local telephone companies involved in the ordering or installation process, and the costs are insensitive to distance. In our diagram, a VSAT service is represented by a satellite linked to a router.

BUZZWORD. VSAT *systems combine ground stations with a digital transponder in an orbiting geostationary satellite to provide flexible inter-LAN circuits across short or long distances.*

Satellite systems, used either alone or in combination with other types of inter-LAN circuits, can provide flexible and economical links between LANs.

Public Data Networks

In Chapter 10, we will consider the services offered by *packet-switched* networks. These long-distance services use a packet-handling protocol called X.25 to control the routing and insure the reliability of data on the networks. The connectivity diagram shows the public data network as a cloud that hides the complex computers acting as data switches.

Public data networks (PDNs) use packet-switching techniques to move the data of their subscribers across cities and countries and around the world. Organizations can also establish their own private packet-switched networks. The cost of public data networks is insensitive to distance and connection time but very sensitive to how much traffic you send. Chapter 10 also describes new technologies like frame relay and switched multi-megabit data systems that threaten to displace today's X.25 PDNs before much time passes.

BUZZWORD. *Packet-switched* networks *contain switches that examine each packet and can choose among alternative redundant routes. They potentially offer reliability unmatched by other inter-LAN alternatives.*

■ Making Selections

Designing an inter-LAN communications system is very much like ordering from a menu in a Chinese restaurant. You can combine choices from a list of network devices with choices from a list of connection alternatives. You must blend bridges, routers, repeaters, and other network portal devices with the best circuit alternatives to match your needs, budget, and management philosophy. Some of the choices will be expensive, and others can be very economical. The information in this book will help you make the right choices for your organization's needs.

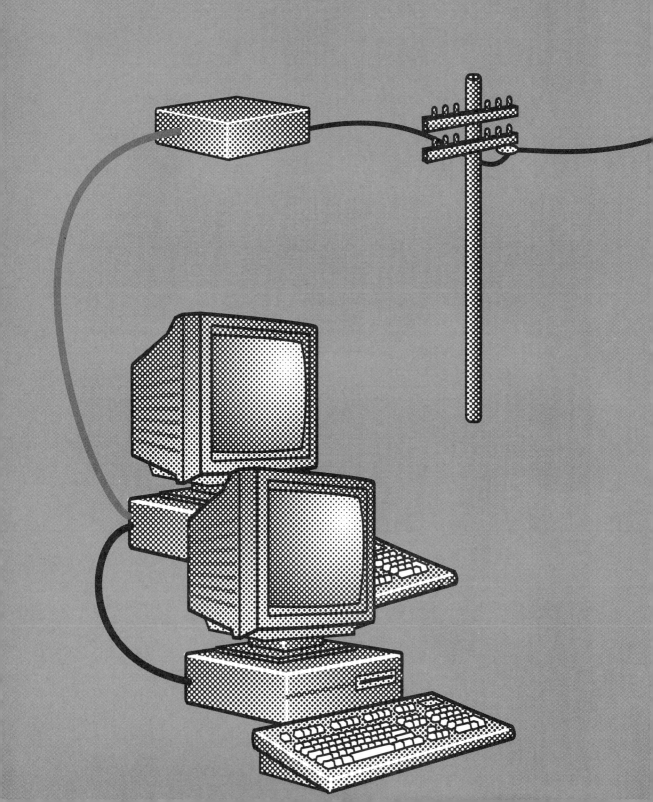

Repeaters, Bridges, and Routers: The Full-time LAN Portals

When you put together a system to link LANs, you need some device on each network segment to act as the interface between the high-speed LAN cable and the typically slower long-distance link. This interface device includes:

- The hardware needed to translate between the different electrical signaling techniques used on the two connection systems

- The software to look inside the transiting Ethernet or Token-Ring frames to check them for validity and perhaps for destination

Since you're likely to pay hundreds or thousands of dollars per month for the long-distance circuits you use to link LANs, it makes sense to buy the right interface equipment so you can make the most efficient use of the inter-LAN links.

This explanation seems simple, but the interplay of options, costs, reliability levels, and user needs has driven the industry to develop many different types of LAN-to-LAN interface devices. Some of these devices, such as access servers, wide-area information transfer systems (WAITS), or electronic-mail gateways, operate on an as-needed basis. They connect over the inter-LAN circuit long enough to do the required job of moving data, and then they disconnect. These part-time devices typically are not completely invisible to the people using inter-LAN links. Often, people must specifically address or connect to the part-time access portal—although devices like e-mail gateways or computers running WAITS software do perform without human intervention. I'll describe the gateways and other part-time devices in depth in Chapters 6 and 7.

But many organizations need full-time LAN-to-LAN services. When you must update and interrogate databases, handle a high volume of messages, or move large files such as graphics, drawings, or other types of imagery, it's practical to make full-time inter-LAN links with full-time portals. Some applications, like programs that allow you to enter orders or check inventory, require a full-time invisible connection between the computer running the program on one LAN and the file server on another.

Three different categories of interface devices—repeaters, bridges, and routers—provide full-time invisible connectivity. Each category of products has specific capabilities, costs, and architectures associated with it. This chapter focuses on the technology of the 24-hour LAN portals, and Chapters 4 and 5 describe product features and considerations.

In addition to the classifications already implied—full-time versus part-time and visible versus invisible—these portal devices are also categorized as internal and external, and sometimes as local and remote. The terms *internal* and *external* simply indicate whether the product resides inside a PC or in an external standalone box. The external devices typically include their own processors, power supplies, and cabinets. The terms *local* and *remote* describe whether the product connects local high-speed LAN segments— within a few thousand feet—or sends the signals over a long-distance line to a remote site, a few miles or a few thousand miles away.

HINT. *Look at the possibility of installing part-time connection devices like e-mail gateways or WAITS before going to full-time systems. The part-time systems can meet many needs and save money.*

■ Telling the Categories Apart

The definitions of repeaters, bridges, routers, and gateways are entwined with the concepts of the layers of network functions and the handling of packages of data. (BBS software, access servers, and WAITS software can be lumped with e-mail gateways and other types of communications servers into the gateway category.) The International Standards Organization (ISO) has developed a reference model for network operation that describes the jobs of different functional layers in the network, as shown in Figure 3.1. Some-times pieces of hardware perform the functions defined in the reference model—often at the higher layers. But often the hardware is controlled by internal *firmware* programs contained in memory, and these programs per-form the functions described in the model.

Figure 3.1

The network reference model developed by the International Standards Organization describes seven conceptual layers of network operation. While not all network architectures can be divided in exactly this way, the model provides a handy and consistent method of describing how the pieces and parts of any network function.

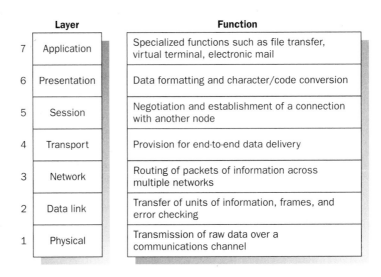

Layer		Function
7	Application	Specialized functions such as file transfer, virtual terminal, electronic mail
6	Presentation	Data formatting and character/code conversion
5	Session	Negotiation and establishment of a connection with another node
4	Transport	Provision for end-to-end data delivery
3	Network	Routing of packets of information across multiple networks
2	Data link	Transfer of units of information, frames, and error checking
1	Physical	Transmission of raw data over a communications channel

Many real networking products don't follow the model slavishly. Networks from companies like Digital Equipment Corp. and IBM have network architectures that predate the model and are difficult to map into its neat boxes. But repeaters, bridges, routers, and gateways do fit the model cleanly. The reference model makes a good way to contrast their different functions.

Repeaters operate at the physical layer of the ISO model. They are relatively simple hardware devices that pass all traffic in both directions between the LAN segments they link. Repeaters deal with data organized into *frames* for transmission over the LAN cable. Each frame has a clearly defined beginning and end, and contains a number of packets; such packets are generated by programs conforming to specific communications protocols.

Repeaters don't discriminate; they use specialized processors and some programming in ROM to relay everything they receive. They don't have the processing power to interpret the 0's and 1's that make up the frames; they merely recognize the point where one ends and the next one begins. Repeaters can't handle the addressing or network-control information put into the packets by software operating at the higher layers.

The function of a repeater is to extend the network cable beyond its normal limits. For example, a repeater will allow you to create an Ethernet network of several thousand feet—much more than the typical limit of less than 1,000 feet—because the repeater retimes the packets and reinserts them into each cable segment. But it's important to note that a repeater doesn't provide any isolation between the LAN segments; everything that comes along goes across.

Bridges can read station addresses and make decisions based on those addresses, so they are said to operate at the media-access control (MAC) sublayer of the data-link layer of the ISO model; thus the phrase *MAC-layer bridge* is common. A bridge contains both hardware and ROM-based software, but the software is much more complex than that used to control a repeater. The software allows the bridge to provide some discrimination over which packets pass between the LAN segments.

Routers contain even more powerful software that allows them to discriminate among frames based on information within the data they examine. The addressing data read by a router conforms to specific protocols, operating at the network layer of the ISO model. The router-control programs decide what paths the packets will take as they flow between LAN segments. Routers gather the information needed to make these decisions by reading elements within the packets and even keeping track of the performance of the alternative paths between LAN segments.

LAN *gateways* translate data formats and open sessions between application programs, so they operate at the highest layers of the ISO model. Electronic-mail gateways form a common type of LAN-to-LAN portal, operating at the session through application layers of the model. Another common type of gateway links the LAN to a device using a completely different data alphabet and signaling system, such as IBM's SNA communications system for mainframe computers.

While these are the classical definitions of repeaters, bridges, routers, and gateways, companies have created products with features that surpass the definitions and confound those who like clean classifications. For example, later in this chapter I'll describe a *brouter*, which combines the features of a bridge and router in certain installations.

■ Repeaters

Typically you would choose a repeater to link LAN segments when there isn't much traffic on either segment, when any link between the segments is very fast, and when equipment cost and not connection cost is the primary consideration. Because of these factors, repeaters are almost always local devices. As Figure 3.2 shows, you normally use one repeater to connect two high-speed LAN segments directly, instead of using two repeaters to connect two LAN segments over a slower long-distance line.

With costs ranging from just under $1,000 for simple Ethernet equipment to well over $2,000 for Token-Ring devices, repeaters are generally less expensive than other linking devices and easier to install. They're useful because they can interconnect different types of physical media such as coaxial, fiber-optic, and twisted-pair cables. Note that repeaters cannot translate the frames between Ethernet, ARCnet, and Token-Ring networks, but they can move Ethernet frames, for example, between different types of cabling. On the downside, all the traffic generated on each LAN segment connected by repeaters appears on all LAN segments, so the network segments can become very busy, and certain kinds of problems on one segment, like malfunctioning adapters that send out improperly formed frames, can impact all segments.

HINT. *Relatively low cost and easy installation make repeaters an attractive way to extend local network cable segments, particularly when the individual LAN segments are not heavily loaded.*

■ Bridges

You select a bridge when you need to link LANs, either locally or remotely, and you are concerned about loading each LAN segment with unnecessary traffic. Bridges discriminate among frames, moving only frames that are addressed to nodes on the other LAN segment. As Figure 3.3 shows, if you use remote bridges, you need two devices to translate between the slow long-distance inter-LAN circuit and the fast local area network cables. But if you use a local bridge between LAN segments, you need only one bridging device.

Figure 3.2

Repeaters move all the MAC-layer frames they receive between the LAN cable segments without reading the contents. They retime and reinsert frames into the adjoining cable segments, thus getting around electrical limitations on cable length.

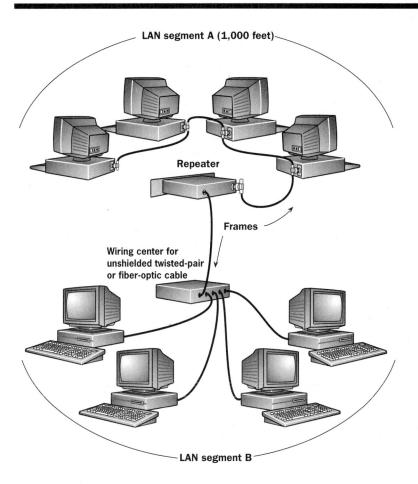

Like repeaters, bridges can move frames between different kinds of media, and similarly, this action is invisible to anyone using the network. The client PCs don't need any special software or hardware to benefit from the actions of repeaters and bridges. But unlike repeaters, bridges can link an Ethernet LAN segment to a Token-Ring segment, for example, as long as the networks use software conforming to the same network communications protocol (IP to IP, NetBIOS to NetBIOS, IPX to IPX, or DECnet to DECnet) inside the MAC-layer frame.

Figure 3.3

If you use a local bridge to link two LAN cable segments directly, you only need one device. If you use remote bridges, you need two devices to handle the conversions between the LAN cable and the slower long-distance link.

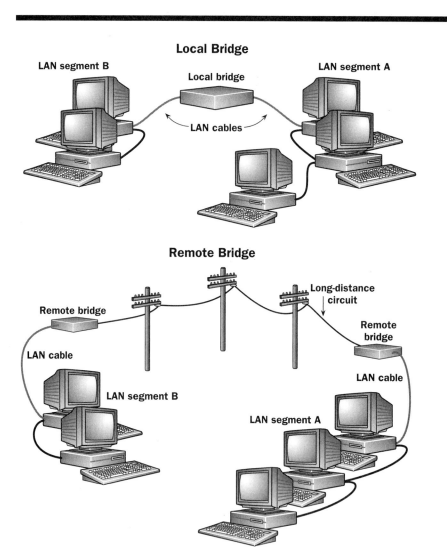

Specialized bridges are available that can strip from the transmission frame the packets generated by one of these protocols and reinsert them into a frame of a different type. Since these devices don't read the addressing within the packet, they operate on the MAC frame level and are true bridges. As I'll describe shortly, routers achieve the same end of crossing different LAN types, but through a different means.

Bridges learn. Their software sends out a broadcast message that generates a reply from all network nodes. The bridge software reads the source address of each frame and associates source addresses with LAN segments.

This action limits the traffic crossing between LAN segments and practically prohibits problem packets or adapters on one LAN segment from affecting the other connected segment or segments.

If the bridge receives a packet or frame for an as yet unidentified destination node, it forwards the packet or frame until the destination replies. This is known as *forward-if-not-local* logic. Later we will compare this logical operation with the techniques used in routers.

Modern bridges are important network management devices. Because they monitor the traffic so closely, special software in the bridges can provide information on traffic volume and network errors. But bridges are busy devices, and they must evaluate packets on the fly, so if you combine bridge activity with a lot of reporting, you typically need hardware with its own on-board communications processors to handle the load efficiently.

HINT. *As your network grows, management of the key portals such as bridges, routers, and wiring centers will become increasingly important. Plan to buy products with management capabilities. See Chapter 11 for more information on network management.*

The learning bridge works well for linking two LAN segments, but the process becomes more complex when multiple LAN segments are linked together, either directly in local connections or remotely through long-distance circuits. If multiple LAN segments are connected through bridges, either across a *backbone* or in a serial *cascade* (both shown in Figure 3.4), then extraneous traffic must pass though one or more segments as it moves to its destination. This puts an unnecessary load on the intervening segments.

The possibility always exists that somehow multiple LAN segments will be connected by more than one path—perhaps through a dial-up connection, a maintenance connection, or a wiring error. When this happens, it's possible for frames to circulate continuously among the LAN segments, a situation called a *data storm*. There are several established techniques to handle data storms; the most common technique, adopted by the IEEE 802.1 Network Management Committee, is called the *Spanning Tree Algorithm*. Software conforming to this algorithm can sense the existence of multiple paths and shut one down. Products supporting this algorithm are primarily local bridges. Spanning Tree features aren't as valuable in remote bridges, because they conflict with techniques used to move data over more than one of the slower long-distance circuits.

You'll also hear about techniques called *source-level routing* and *protocol-transparent routing* used by remote bridges. This use of the term *routing* in the context of bridging products is confusing, but common. In source-level routing, used primarily in Token-Ring networks, the bridge sends a test message to a destination station. Source-routing bridges along the way add their own addresses. The destination station then sends a message back to the source station providing a full list of all the intermediate bridges. The bridge servicing the source station uses this information to build a map of the interconnected network and determine the fastest path between source and destination nodes. Protocol-transparent routing uses the forward-if-not-local logic described above.

Figure 3.4

Backbone bridge installations (right) isolate each LAN segment and keep inter-LAN traffic on a backbone. Cascade installations (facing page) use fewer bridge devices, but they load a great deal of data on intervening LAN segments.

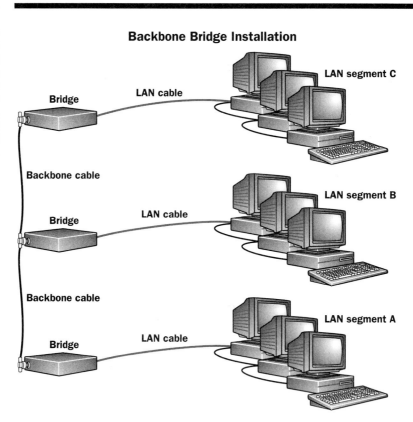

Backbone Bridge Installation

■ Routers

Bridges are smart but relatively single-minded. They either pass the traffic or ignore it, and they can only handle data in homogeneous packets like those carrying IPX or NetBIOS addressing information. Routers are smarter and more discriminating. The software in a router reads complex addressing information and makes decisions on how to route the data across multiple internetwork links.

Figure 3.4

(continued)

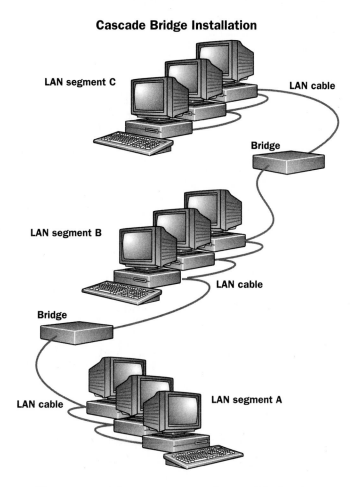

Cascade Bridge Installation

The programs in some routers always pick the shortest path between two points; these are known as *static routers*. Because the routing information is entered manually, static routers require a lot of attention from a skilled manager. The more sophisticated products, *dynamic routers*, make packet-by-packet decisions based on the information they glean from other routers and network devices about the efficiency and reliability of different routes between the source and destination nodes.

Because routers read only those network packets that are specially addressed to them, they don't work as hard as bridges; therefore, they put less of a load on the host CPU. Because they allow only specially addressed packets to pass between LAN segments, routers also put the lowest stress on the inter-LAN links, without passing any bad data. I described bridges as using forward-if-not-local logic. Routers use a logic best described as *forward-only-if-known-remote*. They pass traffic over the inter-LAN link only if the network address is known and shows that the data is not destined for a local node.

Long-distance inter-LAN links are expensive, so it's worth noting that routers use the links more efficiently than bridges. That's because routers strip off the MAC-layer address information before they send a packet across an inter-LAN link. If you pass a lot of short packets across the inter-LAN link—keystroke entries, for example—the MAC-layer address can take as much as 50 percent of each packet.

Some routers, including those from Eicon Technology Corp. and Newport Systems Solutions, use a compression algorithm in their software to improve the throughput further. On-the-fly compression is tricky. In general, compression is useful in slow or very crowded communications circuits, but if the circuits are fast, then it takes longer to run the compression software than to send the data across without compression. In inter-LAN links, companies like Eicon Technology believe that circuits with speeds over 64 kilobits per second do not benefit from compression.

HINT. *Consider buying routers with built-in compression as a way to get up to four times as much data over the internetwork link without paying for faster service or modems.*

Routers don't maintain tables describing each node and associated LAN segment as bridges do. They only know about other routers that are identified by subnetwork addresses. The routers don't care what format a packet or frame is in; they merely read the subnetwork address, decide on the route, and perhaps wrap the packet or frame in an appropriate envelope, such as an X.25 or frame-relay packet. But the data packets or frames sent to the router must conform to specific network-layer protocols. Vendors sell routers conforming to the DECnet, IP, IPX, OSI, and XNS protocols, and many others.

Companies like Cisco Systems, Proteon, and Wellfleet Communications sell multiprotocol routers that allow you to combine protocols like DECnet and IP in the same network. The Wollongong Group sells an effective router combining the NetWare IPX protocol and the IP portion of the TCP/IP protocol. However, there are no standards for these multiprotocol routers, and interoperability between products from different companies could be a problem.

■ Brouters

In an effort to differentiate their products, some companies such as Halley Systems market devices with the attributes of both bridges and routers, known as *brouters*. Typically a brouter performs the full routing function for one protocol, like IP or XNS, and acts as a bridge for all other frames on the network. Obviously, such products are useful in organizations that combine packets of different types on the same integrated network. Typically you would consider using brouters when you try to mix several homogeneous LAN segments with two very different segments.

Note that there are other less precise uses of the term *brouter*. Some vendors of bridges use the term for enhanced bridges that don't really route. The term *bridge/router* is a clearer statement of what was originally meant by the term *brouter*.

■ Selecting an Architecture

Repeaters, bridges, routers, and gateways are complex products, and every installation is different, but there are some useful precepts for selecting among them. Primarily, remember that the communications line is an expensive and limited resource. Do everything you can at the equipment end to limit the traffic on the long-distance line. This usually means using a router on long-distance inter-LAN circuits.

If you're connecting LANs using high-speed links within a building or across a campus, then the choice is not as clear. The architecture decision is based on how much isolation you need for each LAN segment, and on the "culture" of the organization. If the organization is highly structured, then you'll probably choose routers or even electronic-mail gateways because of the way they clearly define each LAN segment as a subnetwork. Routers provide managers with some degree of privacy and isolation for the LAN segments serving their functional workgroups. But if you have an "open" organization structure and have invested in your own high-speed local circuits, then bridges or even repeaters might meet your needs.

The LAN-to-LAN decision tree, Figure 3.5, walks you through the practical aspects of choosing among the various network connection devices. While you must choose between routing and bridging, the other choices are not mutually exclusive; you might have two or more of them on the same network segment, possibly along with a bridge or router. For instance, all of your offices might not be networked, but you might want to use e-mail gateways to link those that are, while using BBS software to maintain communications with those that are not.

As you look at Figure 3.5, notice that you will choose a router when you don't require MAC-layer hardware on both sides of the connection—and also when you do, if you need to route packets based on network addresses.

A WAITS system should work fine in organizations with a specialized need to transfer files automatically across LAN segments. If your organization relies on an e-mail program for communications in each operating location, you might be interested in LAN e-mail gateways. These devices—essentially PCs running special software—connect to distant LAN segments to exchange messages and their attached files.

Figure 3.5

This decision tree helps you choose among the different LAN portal alternatives.

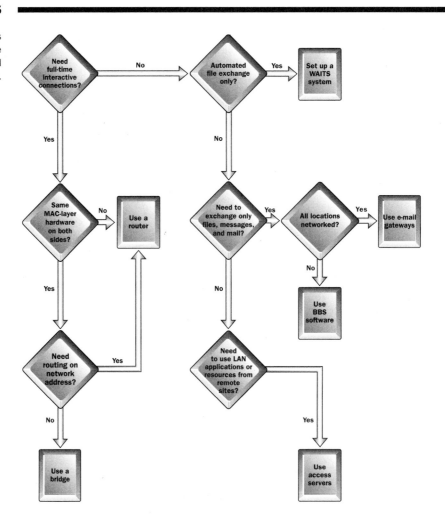

Bulletin board systems are likewise good choices when you want to transfer messages as well as files. Like most e-mail programs, they provide private mail and public conference facilities. BBS programs also facilitate communications with your employees who use PCs out in the field or when they work at home.

An increasing number of organizations are faced with the problem of how to link their LAN segments. Repeaters, bridges, routers, and gateways are the portals for inter-LAN connectivity. Chapters 4 and 5 provide more detailed information on bridges and routers. Chapters 6 and 7 describe the other LAN portal alternatives.

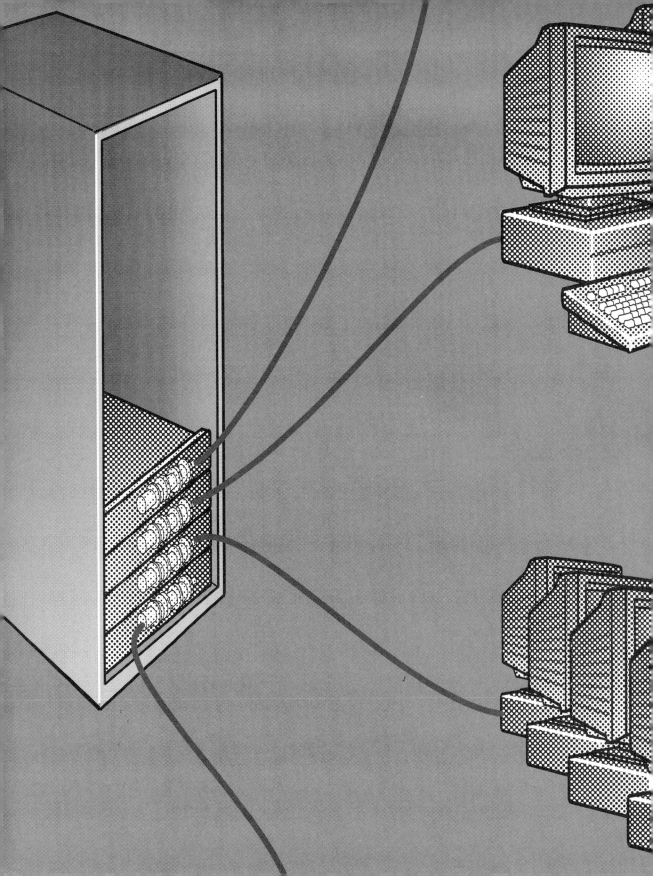

Thirteen Critical Questions

- Local or Remote?
- Internal or External?
- What Type of LAN Connections?
- Which Long-distance Circuit Connections?
- What Transmission Speeds?
- How Many Link Ports?
- Data Compression?
- Size of the Address Table?
- Load Balancing?
- Type of CPU?
- What Type of Network Management?
- Price?
- Whom Do You Trust?

This chapter explains the different architectures, features, and capabilities you'll find in repeaters, bridges, and routers. In effect, it provides an annotated checklist you can use when you research and buy these devices. This list is not exhaustive; your final purchasing decision may be affected by factors as simple as front-panel diagnostic lights and as tangential as the leasing plans for the equipment. But this list of critical items to consider will serve as a safety net for your decision-making balancing act. The next chapter discusses some of the more arcane technical topics that are unique to routers.

Only a few of the factors that are detailed in this chapter apply to repeaters. Because bridges and routers are relatively complex devices with more features, more of these decision factors apply. I will indicate when a factor typically applies to only one category of product, but keep in mind that the manufacturers of repeaters, bridges, routers, and brouters refuse to let you put their products into neat categories. These companies continually evolve and modify their products in order to differentiate them from the competition. In fact, some companies, such as Cisco Systems, Vitalink Communications Corp., and Wellfleet Communications, incorporate both true routing and true bridging in the same box. Evolution is a powerful and wonderful force for progress, but it's tough on people trying to pin specific labels on specific products.

■ Local or Remote?

Some products merely connect one high-speed LAN cable to another, with no intervening slower-speed long-distance circuit. Because they operate only within the local area network, they are called *local* devices. Repeaters typically operate as local devices. Although it is technically possible to have a pair of remote repeaters operating over a long-distance circuit, and companies do sell such products, that arrangement puts a great load on the slower intervening circuit because repeaters do not exercise any discrimination over the data they pass. Remote repeaters are practical only when you don't have much data moving on either LAN segment and you have very low costs for the inter-LAN circuits.

You'll find both local and remote bridges on the market, but because the capabilities of a router are often wasted when it's set up locally, you typically find routers installed as *remote* LAN portals. There are, however, two major exceptions to that statement: Local routers exist in LocalTalk networks, and in very complex campus and industrial local area networks.

Local routers are very important in the world of networked Apple Macintosh computers. The Apple LocalTalk networking system uses such a slow signaling rate that it is easily overloaded by just a few active nodes. So, as Figure 4.1 illustrates, LocalTalk networks evolve into complex systems of short LAN segments with multiple interconnections between the segments. Each short LAN segment can carry the traffic generated by its own nodes. The interconnections between segments provide the extended connections that people using computers on each segment need to communicate across the organization. This design results in what is termed a "meshed" architecture, in which there are multiple possible paths between any two LAN segments. And this complex meshed architecture requires local routers to move and control the flow of data.

Figure 4.1

LocalTalk networks are often made up of short cable segments, with a few nodes each, connected by local external routers. In this diagram, there are two ways for LocalTalk packets to get from cable segment B to cable segment D. Only networks with routers can offer multiple alternative paths.

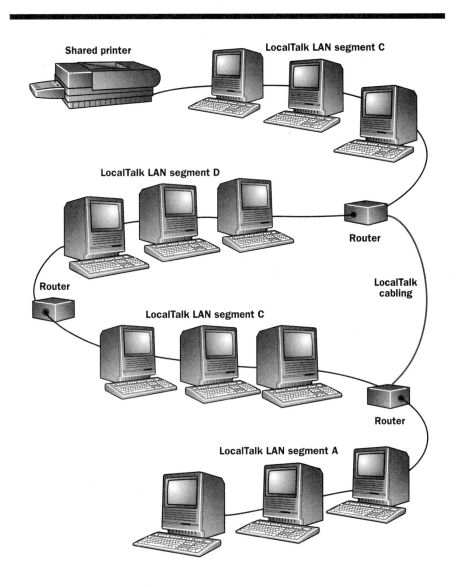

Similarly, large network installations on campuses and in industrial facilities can use local routers to control the traffic on the multiple interconnections among the many LAN cable segments. As I explain below, NetWare LAN file servers often contain local routers.

■ Internal or External?

Repeaters, bridges, and routers can take on many physical forms. It helps to sort them into at least two groups: internal and external. Devices installed inside a PC are called *internal* devices. Often the PC can continue in its normal operational role while providing power to the adapter board that constitutes the repeater, bridge, or router. The *external* devices typically come as standalone units in their own cabinets.

The word "typically" should be a giveaway by now. There are many exceptions to these simple descriptions. For example, the wiring hubs used as a central point in the wiring of many modern Ethernet and Token-Ring network installations can also house repeaters, bridges, and routers in the form of slide-in circuit-board modules designed for the wiring-hub cabinets. Such devices are internal to the wiring hub, but we would still classify them as external because they are outside of a networked PC.

Other external products have been designed with physical shapes ranging from something that looks like a plain white pizza box to bulky cabinets with rows of flashing lights and liquid crystal displays to indicate status. An external repeater might be as small as a package of cigarettes, while an external router might have its own disk drive and reside in a cabinet as large as a typical desktop PC.

One of the most common locations for an internal router is inside a server running Novell's LAN operating system NetWare. The NetWare package includes a software module called ROUTEGEN that provides a system administrator with a method of linking as many as four LAN adapters together as a local internal router. As Figure 4.2 illustrates, in this configuration there is no separate router hardware. Each LAN segment has a LAN adapter in the server. Novell's router software moves IPX packets among the adapters as needed. Releases of NetWare after Version 3.11 also include the ability to route IP packets.

I strongly recommend taking advantage of NetWare's internal routing capability to break apart busy NetWare LANs into separate cable segments, each with its own LAN adapter in the server. Modern PCs and servers with 80386 and 80486 processors can easily overload a single Ethernet or Token-Ring segment. Breaking the segments apart to accommodate more network traffic and then joining them together again under the control of internal router software running in the server is a very smart idea.

Figure 4.2

Novell's NetWare contains a software router that can move IPX and IP packets among as many as four separate LAN segments. Each cable segment functions as part of the total LAN. The four adapters plus the Novell software constitute an internal local router.

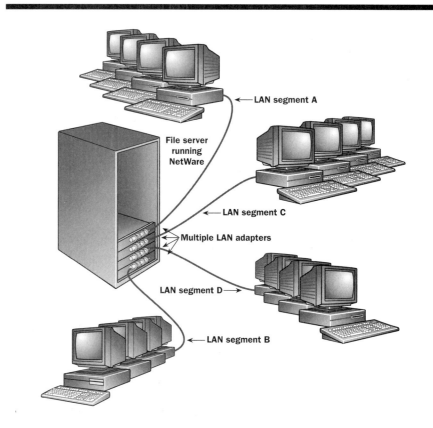

■ What Type of LAN Connections?

It's obvious that you should choose your LAN portal devices carefully to match the LAN adapters and cabling you use on the LANs you need to link, yet even this advice isn't as simple as it seems. Some portal products, both internal and external, come with their own LAN attachments, while others let you supply the LAN adapters. But be cautious; even products that allow you to supply your own LAN adapters often require you to choose from a short list of specific makes and models.

Also, it isn't enough to specify Ethernet or Token-Ring schemes. Each of these categories of products offers different cabling choices ranging from shielded wire to unshielded twisted-pair wire to fiber-optic cable. External transceivers are available to convert, for example, between Token-Ring's shielded twisted-pair wiring and unshielded twisted-pair wiring, but using external transceivers is not as desirable as using internal LAN adapters with the appropriate cable connections, because the transceivers add cost and complexity.

■ Which Long-distance Circuit Connections?

While you often have some flexibility in choosing the LAN adapter connections you need in each portal device, you have no flexibility when you specify the type of connector you need for the long-distance circuit termination equipment. You'll have to make sure that you order your remote repeaters, bridges, or routers with connectors conforming to the appropriate RS-232C, RS-449, V.35, or other circuit interface standard. Chapter 8 provides more information on these connection options.

The rising popularity of fiber-optic media creates another area for connection confusion. At least four different cable-and-connector combinations are used to provide service under the "standard" Fiber Distributed Data Interface (FDDI). Companies like AT&T and IBM have different FDDI implementations using fiber-optic cable of different sizes operating in different modes. While you might want to take advantage of FDDI's 100-megabit-per-second signaling capacity to move data farther than you can in the typical Ethernet or Token-Ring installation, you must carefully choose the fiber-optic cable interface, or *applique*, for your portal equipment.

When ordering FDDI-capable equipment you'll be faced with choices like selecting 8.3-, 9.5-, and 10-micron single-mode fiber or 50-, 62.5-, 85-, or 100-micron multimode fiber. (Note that 62.5 microns is the FDDI standard for multimode fiber, but some companies still support nonstandard products.) To add to the confusion, new evolving standards provide ways to use the 100-megabit-per-second FDDI signaling scheme over shielded and unshielded twisted-pair copper wiring—although for shorter distances than the true fiber systems permit.

Ordering the correct interface requires careful consideration of the long-distance connection service you'll use initially as well as how your need for faster service will evolve. Since the faster long-distance services you might need in the future could require different connections to the circuit termination equipment, you must plan carefully. As Chapter 8 describes, the V.35 interface is widely used and is a safe choice for most installations.

■ What Transmission Speeds?

The type of connector you need for the long-distance termination equipment is closely related to the speed of the long-distance circuit. Not only must you order equipment with an interface meeting an appropriate physical and electrical standard, but the interface must have a fast enough signaling speed to meet present and future needs. For example, you might order internal router circuit boards with V.35 connector and wiring interfaces, but with a signaling speed limited to 128 kilobits per second. Another model of the same product might use the V.35 interface with signaling up to 1.544 kilobits per second or more.

■ How Many Link Ports?

Some bridges and routers can handle multiple connections. A router might simultaneously connect one LAN segment to several other segments or long-distance circuits. So when you order a router you should plan carefully for the required number of connections and, if you'll want to add connections later, buy a device with expansion capabilities.

There is more to this consideration than just physical port connections. Routers and bridges that connect over X.25 and frame-relay packet-switched networks, described in Chapter 10, can engage in multiple virtual sessions across the packet-switched networks. As Figure 4.3 shows, these virtual sessions allow nearly simultaneous communications among several LAN segments with only one physical connecting port on each device. The number of virtual sessions available is controlled by the software in the device and the type of connections made to the packet-switched network, so if you plan to use X.25 or frame-relay connections you should note how many virtual sessions the device can support.

■ Data Compression?

The long-distance circuits used to link LAN segments can cost many thousands of dollars per month, so it makes economic sense to get the most out of them. Circuits designed to support faster signaling speeds typically cost more than those for slower speeds, so it also makes sense to maximize the use of slower circuits. *Data compression*, available in some bridges and routers, is a technique that can move more data through the circuit than the signaling system would otherwise allow.

Data compression transforms a set of data into a smaller representation of that data, a kind of shorthand notation, in order to save space and transmission time. Data-compression programs try to reduce the amount of redundant information in a stream of data by substituting one short character or symbol for repetitive strings of characters or blank space. Spreadsheet files particularly lend themselves to compression.

Figure 4.3

Packet-switched networks, described in Chapter 10, provide reliable long-distance connections between LAN segments separated by any distance. The bridges or routers using these connections can communicate over more than one virtual circuit at a time. The number of virtual circuits a device can use is limited by its internal software and the configuration of the network.

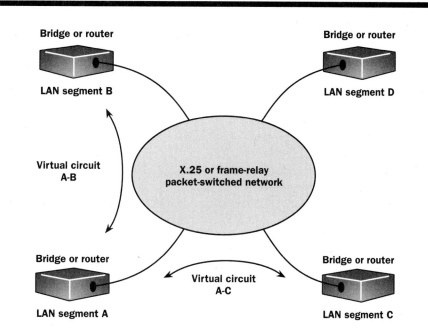

It isn't unusual for data-compression systems to achieve an average compression ratio of 4:1 for certain kinds of repetitive data such as text. In other words, if you used data compression over an inter-LAN circuit with 9.6-kilobit-per-second signaling, you could move data at an effective throughput rate of 38.4 kilobits per second. Data compression can allow you to install or lease inter-LAN circuits that are a fourth or a third of the speed you might otherwise need. This lower speed requirement typically shows up as a substantial monthly savings.

Like all things that seem too good to be true, data compression has some drawbacks and limitations. First, compressing on the fly requires a substantial amount of processing power. Devices using these compression techniques typically must have their own Intel 80286 or Motorola 68010 processors devoted to data compression and decompression. This heavy-duty hardware adds to the initial cost of installing a bridge or router.

Second, data-compression techniques typically become impractical at speeds of 64 kilobits per second and faster. The data exchanged between LANs typically consists of small blocks—files the size of print jobs or a few characters in database entries. Data compression works best with big blocks of repetitive data. When the long-distance circuits operate at 64 kilobits and faster, they can take away the data in small blocks at least as fast as the bridge or router can compress it, so in some cases compression can add to the overhead instead of reducing the costs.

If you have networks of computers running typical applications like word processors, databases, and spreadsheets, then compression might lose its benefit once you invest in connecting circuits of 64 kilobits per second or faster. But if the computers on your LAN segments are running applications such as graphics or imaging that typically involve large files, on-the-fly compression in the bridge or router might be beneficial to you at even higher speeds. Note that some graphics files are already tightly compressed by the programs that create them and cannot benefit from further compression during data transmission.

A word of caution: In bridges and routers, unlike modems, compression techniques are unique to each specific company. There are few opportunities to mix and match products from different companies when you deal with repeaters, bridges, and routers in general. But especially in the case of products using data compression, they must be matched in pairs over the data communications circuit.

■ Size of the Address Table?

The maximum size of the address table used in a bridge is important. If the address table is small, then the bridge must constantly broadcast to locate device addresses, and that slows it down. If the table can have many thousands of entries, the bridge will be able to operate more quickly and efficiently. However, with thousands of entries, it will take longer to find a match for filtering. You should be able to configure a bridge to meet the size and needs of your network.

A MAC-layer bridge automatically decides whether to forward a packet based on its source and destination addresses. The network manager can often set a number of other parameters for filtering as well. These might include forwarding all traffic from a specific source address, forwarding all traffic marked as containing certain higher-level protocols, and even changing the logic used to forward packets.

Typically all bridges forward a packet if it is not local, but a few bridge products will forward packets only if they know the destination device is remote, thus further reducing traffic on the inter-LAN circuit.

■ Load Balancing?

Sometimes you want to make two long-distance circuits look like one. It's not unusual to have more than one circuit available between two points. Ideally, the repeaters, bridges, or routers you buy can use these circuits in parallel so that they provide the sum of their data-handling capability and their very important redundancy to improve reliability. A technique called *load balancing*, typically used in bridges but also found in routers and repeaters, allows the portal devices to make the best use of redundant circuits.

As in compression, the techniques used in load balancing vary among products from different manufacturers, so plan on using identical products on each side of the interconnecting circuits if you want to use load balancing.

■ Type of CPU?

You can make a rough judgment about the processing horsepower—and hence the effective communications capabilities—of a bridge or router by asking what type of processor the device uses. The older Intel 80186 processor and its NEC equivalent, the V50, provide the minimal level of processing power for a bridge or router. Devices powered by these processors typically can't handle on-the-fly data compression, network-management reporting, or load balancing. The Motorola 68000 processor is somewhat more powerful than the 80186, but products with this processor all have about the same level of performance.

For internal bridges and routers, the type of CPU in the computer you use to host the bridge or router hardware makes little difference. The bridge or router hardware and CPU, not the PC's CPU, does the communications work. At most, the PC's CPU runs software that moves packets or frames between LAN adapters in local bridge or router systems. In remote devices, the host computer's CPU is generally available for other processing tasks and has little or no impact on the operation of the bridge or router.

If you want full features, look for products with an Intel 80286 or 80386 processor or a Motorola 68020 processor. It is not unusual to find a bridge or router with two or even three processors, each handling a special task such as compression or network management.

■ What Type of Network Management?

Chapter 11 deals exclusively with network-management systems and options. That chapter describes three different major network-management plans, and each plan uses different means to capture data about performance, network operations, and malfunctions. Because repeaters, bridges, and routers sit on the crossroads of the LAN and inter-LAN links, they are uniquely placed to gather this information. If you have an interconnected network of more than a dozen nodes, you should consider including network-management and reporting capabilities in your portal devices.

Many companies offer products that use proprietary techniques for gathering management data. I strongly advise that you consider only products that implement one of the standard nonproprietary techniques described in Chapter 11: SNMP, CMIP, or NetView.

■ Price?

Be prepared to pay $2,000 to $5,000 for an internal bridge or router with sophisticated capabilities, and several thousand dollars more for similar external devices. Keep in mind that an investment in the right type of portal communications equipment can pay large dividends by reducing the monthly cost of leased inter-LAN circuits. On the other hand, if your inter-LAN circuit costs are low, perhaps because your organization owns the microwave or fiber-optic cables carrying the data, then the less sophisticated and less expensive equipment might serve you better.

■ Whom Do You Trust?

Often, the brand name of the product you buy is less important than whom you buy it from. While your organization might develop internetworking expertise among its employees, your local dealer or supplier will be your first level of technical backup. The checklist of important factors in this chapter—and indeed this entire book—is aimed at helping you make the right buying and installation decisions in conjunction with the dealers and distributors of internetworking products.

CHAPTER

5

Router Basics

- The Operational Concept

- Routers March On

If you think of the topic of this book, LAN-to-LAN connectivity, as a major field of study in college, then Chapters 1 to 4 took you from the freshman to the sophomore level. This chapter, dealing with routers, their unique operating concepts, and their large bag of buzzwords, takes you to the junior year of study. After this chapter, we'll talk about more practical applications of products.

This junior-year course isn't as much fun as those that went before or those that will come after, but if you are going to talk to salespeople, consultants, or your boss about routers, you'll need to know the buzzwords. Read this chapter the night before a meeting and you'll be able to hold your own in a discussion of routers with any sales rep or consultant.

■ The Operational Concept

Picture a router as a PC sitting on a network. In addition to its LAN adapter card, this PC is loaded with communications adapters that give it the ability to send and receive data over two leased telephone lines simultaneously. It also runs special software to inspect the data packets it receives over the telephone lines and the LAN.

In Figure 5.1, leased circuits go to routers on two other LANs, and those LANs in turn have a connection to each other. You can describe this internetworking system as three internal remote routers connected in a ring. Many organizations have inter-LAN networks with dozens or even hundreds of routers and connecting circuits. Routers frequently can connect to several LAN segments and several inter-LAN circuits simultaneously. The ability to select from among different interconnecting paths and to limit the traffic flowing on certain paths is a unique advantage of routers over bridges.

HINT.   *Consultants use a rough rule of thumb saying that if you have more than 24 nodes on each LAN segment, you need a router rather than a bridge. But the type of applications you run, the speed of the inter-LAN circuits, and many other factors affect the bridge/router decision.*

The computers on each LAN segment address Ethernet or Token-Ring MAC-layer frames to the router when the frames contain packets destined for locations on a distant LAN segment. Note that I use the word *locations* instead of *computers*. Routing protocols can get so specific that they direct a packet of information to the attention of a program running on a computer instead of just addressing it to the computer itself. Routers can filter packets based on (among many other things) a specified list of originating addresses, so they can become a key component in providing network security. This specificity is very useful in mainframe computer systems, and it becomes increasingly useful in networks of PCs as more people use multitasking operating systems such as OS/2, Microsoft Windows, and Unix.

Figure 5.1

This simple diagram shows three routers interconnected by three circuits of different types. As the routers decide the paths the packets should take between LANs, they can consider the speed, cost, and congestion of the circuits along with the priority of the originating stations.

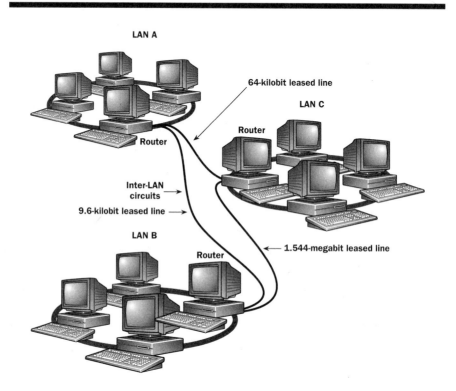

HINT.   *Make routers a part of your security scheme. The ability to route is also the ability to limit access.*

When the router receives a frame, it checks the data inside the frame, as shown in Figure 5.2, to see what type of protocol the data format follows. Note that the routing protocol is implemented as a special kind of packet contained and identified within the transport-layer packet. A packet formatted according to the IP standard of the TCP/IP protocol might hold any of the IP routing protocols described below.

A router might handle data formatted according to only one transport protocol, although multiprotocol routers are common. Devices that act as both bridges and routers are also increasingly important in complex networks. Some protocols, like the relatively old Local Area Transport (LAT) protocol used in Digital Equipment Corp.'s networks, don't contain enough information for routing, and so frames containing LAT packets must be either bridged or encapsulated into other packets that can hold more information. Newer protocols in the DECnet suite can be routed, so devices that can act as bridges for some protocols and as routers for other protocols are common on Digital's networks.

Figure 5.2

The IP protocol can encapsulate many different types of packets. The Routing Information Protocol and Open Shortest Path First protocol define two types of routing packets that might be inside an IP packet.

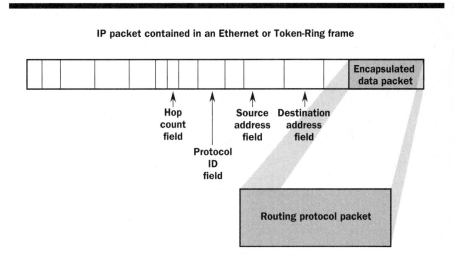

IP packet contained in an Ethernet or Token-Ring frame

Hop count field

Protocol ID field

Source address field

Destination address field

Encapsulated data packet

Routing protocol packet

The data in the routing-protocol packet can provide several different types of instructions and information for routers, but the various protocols used to route packets are very different. Even implementations of the same protocols can vary significantly among vendors.

Routing-Protocol Considerations

Routing protocols are designed as tools to accomplish several jobs. The data formatted according to a specific routing protocol can report on

- the throughput and quality of circuits between routers

- the operational status of specific routers

- the number of relay points or *hops* a packet goes through

- the alternative routes available during failures

The software in the router weighs this and other information using specific algorithms and then determines how to launch a packet on its trip between LAN segments. The software in the router considers such factors as transmission speed, propagation delay (how long a packet takes to travel from LAN to LAN), queuing delays, and cost. Queuing delays take place when routers or switches are backed up with traffic. You can input the cost of a link using any formula you like for monthly lease or dial-up phone-line charges. It's possible to tell the router's software to use a dial-up telephone line only as a last resort by giving that circuit option a higher cost than other circuits.

Modern routers use an adaptive and distributed architecture. The software can adapt to changes in the status of a circuit or another router in milliseconds, and each router keeps its own tables of information. Older systems were less responsive and relied on data stored in one central node.

Distance-Vector Routing

Routing protocols are divided into two different camps. The older protocols, called *distance-vector routing* protocols, send a packet off in the general direction of its destination. The newer protocols, called *link-state protocols*, maintain a complete table of paths in each router and can give specific routing instructions. Some companies refer to these as *first-generation* and *second-generation* routing protocols, respectively.

Distance-vector routing uses an algorithm called *Bellman-Ford* that divides the internetwork link into logical areas. When a router receives a frame, it reads the address of the packet within the frame and sends the packet on a path toward the destination's logical area based on using the least number of *hops* or relay points.

One of the first routing protocols, still found in many inter-LAN systems, uses distance-vector logic and is called the Routing Information Protocol (RIP). RIP, developed in the early 1980s, was originally defined as part of the Xerox Network Services (XNS) protocols; it is also defined as part of the TCP/IP suite of protocols as RFC 1058. You'll also find packets carrying RIP information as a part of the Novell IPX protocol suite.

RIP, like all distance-vector routing systems, uses distance-vector algorithms that report the shortest path between two points on a network in terms of the number of relay points or hops between those points. The lower the hop count, the more efficient the route. While this system works in smaller networks, RIP becomes less practical in complex internetwork systems. RIP does not allow for a hop count of more than 16, so a router can't pass a packet to another LAN segment that is more than 16 routers away.

RIP is not adaptive, and though it is distributed, routers using RIP pass whole address tables among themselves every 30 seconds, creating high overhead. These frequent updates can create their own network problems, because if one or more routers miss the update message, their routing tables can become different, resulting in poor efficiency. The poor efficiency creates more lost updates and even worse efficiency. The ability to resume the normal flow of network traffic quickly even after a major disruption of inter-LAN circuits is known as *convergence*. RIP is said to have poor convergence.

Because of all of these factors, RIP is on its way out, but it will hang on for many years in smaller networks where its inefficiencies don't show up.

Link-State Routing

The protocols falling into the category called *link-state routing* deliver more information than RIP. Link-state protocols require more power in the processor to analyze the variables and make decisions, but that's acceptable because today's microprocessors provide the needed data-sifting power at very reasonable prices.

Link-state protocols rely on a set of logical rules called the *Dijkstra algorithm* to find the shortest path between the origination and destination. The link-state protocol used most widely in TCP/IP networks—the one that replaces RIP in large networks—is known as Open Shortest Path First (OSPF) routing. OSPF, originally developed through the cooperation of Proteon and academic institutions, is defined by RFC 1131 as part of the TCP/IP protocol suite. Many companies offer routers with OSPF capabilities.

Routers using OSPF can make decisions based on traffic load, throughput, circuit cost, and the service priority assigned to packets originating from or going to a specific location. They exchange address tables only on an as-needed basis, and they do it more efficiently than routers that use RIP, so they have excellent convergence.

Dividing an inter-LAN system into smaller routing areas under the OSPF protocol not only reduces the amount of traffic on the backbone but provides another security enhancement. Since the topology of the entire network is not broadcast to every router, certain LAN segments can remain private unless specifically addressed. This makes them even more resistant to sophisticated attempts at intrusion or sabotage.

Partitioning large networks into routing areas also improves overall performance by reducing network-wide traffic. An OSPF feature called *type-of-service routing* defines eight types of service. Each type can have a separate routing path.

IS-IS

The OSPF routing protocol is part of the TCP/IP protocol suite. The suite of protocols designed specifically to the ISO's OSI model contains another link-state routing protocol called Intermediate-System-to-Intermediate System (IS-IS), which is defined under ISO document 10589. Dual IS-IS, a special version of IS-IS that can carry packets compliant with both TCP/IP and OSI standards, is defined by RFC 1195 and ISO document 9542.

IS-IS routers use the same kinds of criteria defined under OSPF to evaluate packets and send them on their way across the LAN-to-LAN circuits. IS-IS has the same benefits of OSPF, but (theoretically at least) it will permit greater interoperability between equipment from different manufacturers because it conforms to the international Open Systems Interconnection model.

Digital Equipment Corp. incorporates IS-IS into its DECnet Phase V network system to route OSI, IP, and DECnet packets in all routers. Other companies, including Cisco Systems and 3Com, have IS-IS routers with various capabilities and degrees of compatibility.

Spooning the Protocol Soup

Many other companies have created routing protocols or network protocols containing routing information. But these protocols are largely proprietary and only recommended if you are sure you will stay with one network architecture for years to come. If you are installing a new network system today, you should look at OSPF or IS-IS routing unless you are very sure that your organization will not grow in terms of the number or type of operating locations and interconnected LANs.

IBM was one of the first companies to introduce the concept of routing to computer networks. In the 1970s it developed its Network Control Program (called NCP, but not to be confused with Novell's NetWare Core Protocol or a couple of other NCP acronyms in common use). IBM's NCP is a part of its Systems Network Architecture (SNA), a plan for total networking on IBM equipment. IBM's latest routing plan is called Advanced Peer-to-Peer Networking (APPN). APPN has only limited backward compatibility with older portions of SNA.

The TCP/IP suite contains two protocols, the Serial Line Internet Protocol (SLIP) and the Point-to-Point Protocol (PPP), for communications over serial communications lines without intervening adapters such as modems or other types of terminating equipment. You will be interested in SLIP or PPP only if your network uses IP and you have direct connections. However, SLIP and PPP will become more important as ISDN grows in popularity in the mid-1990s.

As I described in the previous chapter, networks using the LocalTalk wiring scheme often require routers to keep the volume of network traffic to acceptable levels. The AppleTalk protocols include elements that address all seven layers of the ISO model and include routing capabilities.

Another entry in the protocol soup is the Interior Gateway Routing Protocol (IGRP), a TCP/IP protocol created by Cisco Systems and adopted by a number of vendors. Cisco's IGRP is an older distance-vector protocol.

Routing Under NetWare

Because of the popularity of NetWare, it's worth taking some time to understand how NetWare routers work. They are a little different from the TCP/IP, DECnet, and OSI models.

Under NetWare, every server has the ability to be a router. Additionally, you can set up a router in literally any node equipped with NetWare's Internet Packet Exchange (IPX). NetWare routing operates at the network layer, and the IPX packet holds the routing information. Novell has another protocol layer called Sequenced Packet Exchange (SPX), which provides the services associated with the ISO transport layer, but because it adds a lot of overhead, SPX is not commonly used.

NetWare servers and routers find each other by sending out messages in the Service Advertising Protocol (SAP) format. This short data field, contained within IPX, provides a way for NetWare servers and routers to identify their presence. Each NetWare server sends out a SAP message every 60 seconds.

Additionally, NetWare uses RIP packets to identify the network segments and inter-LAN circuits. Each server builds its routing table as it receives these packets.

As Figure 5.3 shows, the IPX packet contains a field called Transport Control. This field provides a hop count showing the number of routers the packet passed through to reach the destination. Each time a router handles the IPX packet, it increments the hop count field by 1.

Novell's release of NetWare 3.11 includes the ability to mix and route packets in the IPX, TCP/IP, and AppleTalk formats. This capability significantly improves the flexibility of network managers using NetWare. Before the release of NetWare 3.11 you might have needed an expensive multiprotocol router, but now, within certain traffic limits, NetWare can do the routing for you.

Protocol-Independent Routers

Companies such as CrossComm Corp. market products they call *protocol-independent routers*. These devices use some of the same techniques developed for learning bridges but apply them to all routed and some nonrouted protocols.

An independent router listens passively to all the traffic on its attached LANs. It builds an address table describing all the nodes it hears. Each router then exchanges information with the nearest attached routers. In this way, the routers eventually gather information about all nodes without intervention from the network administrator.

Figure 5.3

The Novell IPX packet contains fields providing information critical to inter-LAN routing. The **transport control** field provides 4 bytes for a hop count. The **packet type** field tells the receiving stations what type of packet is contained in the data field; the RIP and SAP packet types are used by routers. The **destination network address** field holds the network number of the destination station; if the destination is known to be on the local LAN segment, this field is set to 0. The **destination host** field contains the unique address of the Ethernet or Token-Ring adapter in the destination station. The **destination socket** field specifies a process within the destination station; the NetWare sockets include RIP and SAP.

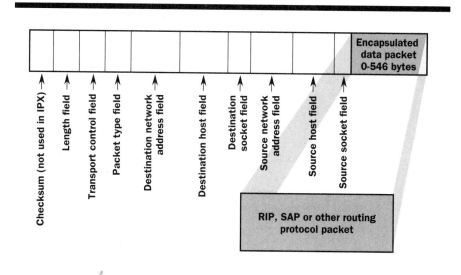

The major advantage of this type of router is that it can route packets that do not contain routing information such as DECnet LAT and NetBIOS. The disadvantage of these products is that you truly tie yourself to one vendor. Protocol-independent routers use powerful programs to read all the addressing information in all the nested packets and then to try to find the best path between source and destination stations. You are not likely to find interoperability between products from different companies.

■ Routers March On

Companies will continue to differentiate their routers in any way possible. There are many combinations of features they are likely to add and combine. While these combinations can complicate your buying tasks, they also offer you a great deal of flexibility to meet the needs of any collection of computers and operating systems.

CHAPTER

6

Electronic-Mail Links

- E-Mail, the Productivity Tool

- Not Messages Alone

- Two Types of E-Mail Gateways

- Finding People on the Network

- Linking LANs with E-Mail

Up to this point I've discussed LAN-to-LAN connection schemes that treat data on the level of frames or packets. But often each frame or packet moving across a LAN is not the complete thought of a person or the complete file from a program. The payload of each frame or packet might be only a tiny part of the entire message or file.

This chapter deals with LAN-to-LAN techniques that work with the whole message. I'll describe electronic-mail programs that either independently or combined with other programs can send complete messages across inter-LAN links. These programs operate at the application level of the OSI model and are called *gateways*.

■ E-Mail, the Productivity Tool

Most organizations don't install networks to gain the benefits of electronic mail. Managers typically decide to install networks because they want to share files, share printers, and connect to mainframe computers. However, some network operating systems like LANtastic come with electronic mail; if it does not come with the network, electronic mail is a logical feature to add to boost workgroup productivity. Within a few months, after upper management discovers the flexibility electronic mail provides, or simply after enough people use the system because of grass roots popularity, electronic mail becomes a completely new way of communicating within the organization.

Electronic mail breaks what I call the time tyranny of telecommunications. When you and I try to communicate by telephone, we both must be near an instrument and ready to talk at the same time. By design, voice telecommunications systems require us to be synchronized in time. But synchronization between the caller and the person being called is increasingly rare. People employ answering machines and voice-mail systems in vast numbers, either to shield themselves from the tyranny of the ringing telephone or in an honest effort to receive calls that come in while they are away from the phone.

Electronic mail is a nonsynchronous and nontyrannical communications medium. That doesn't mean it is not addictive. Personally, I get uncomfortable if I haven't checked my mailbox for 2 or 3 hours during the working day, but my mail system will hold the messages until I'm ready. Electronic-mail messages span time zones, wait for local holidays, and sit quietly during meetings. Then, when you are ready, they deliver their information or ask their questions with freshness and accuracy. Electronic mail soon becomes a new type of communications medium in many organizations. It overlaps with and to some degree replaces telephone calls, paper memos, and face-to-face

Electronic-mail systems:

👍 **Provide a flexible way of communicating within organizations**

👍 **Eliminate many phone calls and meetings**

👍 **Hold messages and files until you are ready to receive them**

👎 **Require management**

meetings, but e-mail also engenders its own fast and useful interaction between people in an organization.

■ Not Messages Alone

Electronic mail, or *electronic messaging* as it's formally called, is not simply the exchange of messages. E-mail programs allow you to attach data files— files containing data in binary, not ASCII format—to standard electronic-mail messages. In this way you can transmit spreadsheet, database, graphics, and other files in a format determined by an application program as attachments to an electronic-mail message. Some programs, like Ashton-Tate Corp.'s spreadsheet program Framework, have a built-in ability to send a file through an electronic-mail system. In early 1992 I counted more than 20 non-e-mail products with the ability to exchange special messages on a LAN.

Electronic-mail systems become the core for the growth of other work-group productivity programs such as scheduling packages and corporate telephone directories. Scheduling packages let people in workgroups plan their activities, set up meetings, and coordinate the use of resources such as conference rooms and projection equipment. On-line corporate telephone directories, updated and coordinated through electronic mail, reduce publication costs, provide current information, and make it easier to find names and addresses.

Finally, but for the purposes of this book most importantly, electronic-mail systems can link themselves across LANs. They can reach out either over dial-up telephone lines or over the links provided by bridges and routers to exchange messages and attached files with the electronic-mail systems running on different LAN segments. In many cases, using electronic-mail systems to link LANs and to transfer necessary files over dial-up telephone lines is so efficient and economical that organizations can avoid the cost of installing bridges, routers, and leased lines.

■ Two Types of E-Mail Gateways

Let's get the simple definitions out of the way first. As Figure 6.1 depicts, an electronic-mail gateway is simply a program running on a computer. The program knows either how to dial up a call through a modem or how to address transport-layer protocols such as NetBIOS, IP, or IPX to send messages between LANs and to exchange messages with people calling in from home or on the road. There are gateway programs that move messages in the form of facsimiles, and even some that convert messages to paper mail for transportation by the post office, but I will be focusing on e-mail gateways for LAN-to-LAN connectivity.

Figure 6.1

Electronic-mail gateway software runs in a PC on each LAN segment. The gateway-equipped PCs call each other using modems and dial-up telephone lines, then exchange any messages or attached files waiting in the queue.

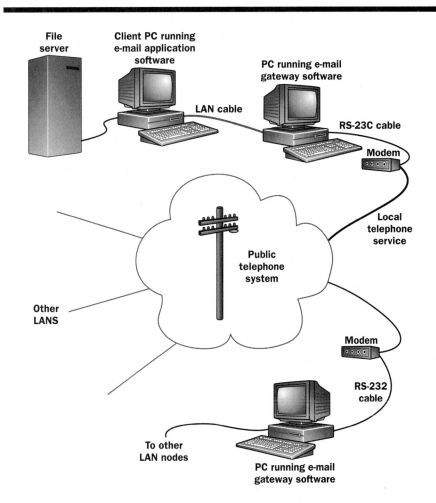

E-mail gateways fall into two general categories: *proprietary*—those that operate only within a certain group of products—and what the industry calls "open" or *nonproprietary*. Proprietary systems are the least complex, the easiest to set up, and often the most reliable, but you can typically use them only with products from a single vendor.

A proprietary electronic-mail gateway program—such as cc:Mail Gateway, WordPerfect Office Connections LAN Server EasyLink Gateway, or a gateway offered as part of Microsoft Mail—runs on a PC on each LAN segment. The PC can be any type of 80286- or 80386-based computer. Since you'll probably dedicate this PC to the gateway role, you should consider taking an older computer with a 286 processor from someone's desk for the gateway and giving that person a newer 386 PC.

The e-mail administrator can typically set up each gateway to originate telephone calls to the other gateways when there are a certain number of messages in the queue for a given destination, when priority messages arrive in the queue for that destination, or when any message for that destination reaches a certain age, specified in hours or minutes. The gateways will use any type of LAN-to-LAN link you provide, but in the real world, companies with thousands of nodes and dozens of LAN segments still find it practical to use dial-up telephone lines equipped with V.32 or V.32bis modems.

Just because an electronic-mail product has a proprietary gateway for LAN-to-LAN connectivity, don't assume that you cannot exchange messages with such very different electronic-mail systems as MCI Mail or IBM's PROFS. Companies like cc:Mail, Microsoft Corp., WordPerfect Corp., and others that market LAN-to-LAN products also market gateways for different electronic-mail systems. For example, you can buy a cc:Mail gateway to the MCI electronic-mail service, or a Microsoft Mail gateway to a PROFS mainframe electronic-mail system. But you must buy each gateway product separately and set it up separately.

Later in this chapter, I'll describe open gateway systems that let you move electronic mail among a wide variety of different electronic-mail products. These systems provide an alternative to the proprietary products. When you examine the features of electronic-mail packages, you must weigh the convenience, reliability, and security of proprietary products against the flexibility of products that can communicate with many different types of electronic-mail systems.

Another important consideration is the type of management software and reports provided by the gateway product you choose. Since the gateway is an important inter-LAN device, it should alert an administrator to problems such as uncompleted calls and lost messages, and it should provide reports on the number of calls made and received, the number of messages moved, the origination and destination of messages, and attachments.

Proprietary LAN gateways:

👍 Provide a custom-tailored solution for connections to dissimilar electronic-mail systems

👍 Use familiar names and routing information built into the electronic-mail application

👎 Require a separate purchase and installation for each gateway

👎 Might not be available for the combination of local and foreign e-mail systems you need

Open Electronic-Mail Gateways

In an ideal world, a network administrator would have a homogeneous mix of products that all use the same communications protocols and data formats. Unfortunately, few network administrators live in such luxury; mongrel networks are the rule. The typical network includes a wide variety of computers, operating systems, cabling, and protocols. The electronic-mail services typically aren't pure-blooded either. Often, individual workgroups and organizational divisions are using their own electronic-mail systems, and they have a considerable investment in terms of software, stored messages, training, and comfort level. They will strongly resist any change made for the sake of conformity.

Companies marketing mature and well-supported electronic-mail packages like cc:Mail and Microsoft Mail have their own products providing the format translation, addressing, and handling needed to link dissimilar electronic-mail products, but they do not have an answer for every case. Smaller companies with very fine electronic-mail products probably have even fewer ways of linking to "foreign" electronic-mail systems.

Three sets of standards exist to promote the interconnection of otherwise dissimilar electronic-mail systems: the Message Handling Service (MHS), the Open Messaging Interface (OMI), and X.400. These systems are not mutually exclusive. In very complex installations, you might find a proprietary gateway on the same LAN segment with an MHS gateway and an X.400 gateway. Each gateway computer would take the kind of traffic it handles best and move it to another mail system.

Message Handling Service (MHS)

The Message Handling Service (MHS) is a standard and a program first developed by Action Technologies, the people who developed The Coordinator (an electronic-mail package). Action Technologies sells MHS, companies like Mustang Software bundle it with their e-mail programs, and Novell makes it available at no additional charge to every purchaser of NetWare. In 1991 Novell bought the rights to the core MHS software from Action Technologies, and Novell is now developing its use within NetWare.

The MHS program runs on a dedicated networked PC called the MHS server—a type of communications server. It helps to think of MHS as a control program running a list of tasks. You load an MHS program called The Directory Manager with information about the people who use e-mail, their network e-mail applications, and the off-network electronic-mail services they use. The MHS server or communications server acts in the role of a network gateway. The word *gateway* becomes overused because separate software products, sold and marketed by different companies, are called gateways in the market. These gateway programs are incomplete without MHS.

Not all networked e-mail packages have MHS capabilities, but when products have the ability to send messages to MHS, they automatically gain the ability to exchange messages with each other, and also to exchange messages between geographically separated networks of PCs. For example, if some people in your organization use Microsoft Windows, they might want to use cc:Mail or Microsoft Mail, products with excellent Windows compatibility. Other people who don't use Windows might prefer the structured approach to mail handling provided by The Coordinator. The MHS server running on the network will automatically become aware of these programs and route messages between them. Each person with a networked PC could run a different MHS-compatible electronic-mail program and still stay in touch with everyone else, because MHS would move messages between the programs.

HINT. *Some e-mail programs, such as Da Vinci eMail and Right Hand Man, have a built-in interface to MHS. Others require a special software integration package. If you expect to use MHS, give strong consideration to programs with built-in MHS capabilities.*

MHS servers on geographically separate networks can communicate over modems and dial-up telephone lines. They exchange e-mail messages according to the schedule created by the mail administrator.

Other programs besides electronic-mail packages can take advantage of MHS. Ashton-Tate gives its Framework spreadsheet package MHS capabilities so that people can easily exchange spreadsheets even without a full e-mail system.

Moving messages between applications inside the network is one service MHS performs. Its other major function involves moving messages between e-mail systems on different LANs, or between its own LAN and completely different environments such as MCI Mail or mainframe-computer mail systems. To link MHS to the external environment, you need to add gateway programs, which run in the same PCs. MHS controls the operation of these gateways and runs them according to your script. You must program each gateway with the appropriate telephone numbers, communications parameters, account numbers, and access codes. Of course, you also must provide the modems or direct computer links between the MHS server and the external system.

The ability of MHS gateways to communicate with each other across LAN-to-LAN links is inherent in the MHS package. But if you want to link an MHS gateway to foreign electronic-mail services running on other LANS, then you need a special add-on gateway program. A variety of companies market MHS gateways for different mail and facsimile systems. REMS markets MCI Mail gateways for MHS, and Alcom sells an MHS product that links MHS to a wide variety of services including MCI Mail, Telex, and AT&T's EasyLink.

It's important to understand that MHS is only an engine for program-to-program communications. At both ends of the link you must have electronic-mail or application programs that can accept and submit files for MHS to handle. The link between the application programs and MHS is simple—they read and write files to the same shared subdirectory in the file server—but MHS can't present mail to users by itself.

Any application software package that addresses MHS can link to All-in-1, MCI Mail, PROFS, VMSMail, Wang Office, and other services via Soft-Switch, an on-line computer service. Subscribers use the MHS protocol to send mail to Soft-Switch, which then translates and resends the mail to the specified destination system.

On the bottom line, MHS isn't elegant, just sufficient. The application programs must provide all security and most of the administrative reporting for MHS, so you must judge the ability of your e-mail package to use MHS carefully.

Many gateway programs are available, and many electronic-mail programs can work with MHS, but different implementations of this open standard often create strange incompatibility problems. We use MHS for electronic mail at PC Magazine LAN Labs, and we've seen many problems. I've found cases where I couldn't read all the addressees of a multiple-address message I received, where I couldn't successfully receive an attached file, or where I was limited in the number of addresses I could put on a message. All of these problems were solved after conferring with different vendors, but troubleshooting isn't a task most network administrators enjoy. MHS-to-MHS links usually work well, but if you're using MHS to link very different electronic-mail systems, I suggest you get a good demonstration of the system's capabilities before you buy.

The New Entry: OMI

In the Fall of 1991, a consortium of companies including Apple computer, IBM, and Lotus Development Corporation announced a new standard for a messaging application interface. This standard, called the Open Messaging Interface (OMI), will be translated into software that Apple and IBM will incorporate into their operating systems. Lotus will include OMI capabilities in Lotus Notes, a distributed electronic information system that includes electronic mail, and in cc:Mail, their popular e-mail system.

The concept behind the OMI interface is more comprehensive than MHS. Using the OMI services, any OMI-conforming application can send messages—typically data files, but also information about the computer operating environment and about specific applications—to any other OMI application. Because the service will be a part of the operating system, it will be ubiquitous throughout a network of IBM and Apple computers, eliminating the need for a separate computer acting as a gateway.

The OMI specification provides ways for applications to look up a user's name, address a package of data, and send it across the LAN. Applications also have a way to receive alerts for new messages and to draw the messages from the OMI system.

Interestingly, Microsoft has not moved to support the OMI specification. Because OMI isn't supported by Novell and Microsoft, it's difficult to call OMI an industry-wide standard. It is more accurate to look at OMI as another standard for communications in addition to MHS and to whatever Microsoft will develop.

Of course, many companies will develop gateway software that links OMI-compliant systems with those having MHS services. OMI, MHS, and other evolving standards aren't an either/or thing. Because the development of links between existing LANs with established e-mail systems is inevitable and because people resist changing a system they know and trust, the concept of interoperability is critical to the future of electronic mail.

X.400

The CCITT developed a set of rules for e-mail communications described in the CCITT X.400 standards. First adopted in 1984 and updated every four years, the X.400 family of standards is now growing in popularity, and an increasing number of programs support it. The latest standards include the X.400 standard for electronic message-handling systems, the X.402 standard for X.400 architecture, the X.403 standard for testing compliance with the 1984 standards, and the X.420 standard for message-content specification.

The X.435 standard, called "Message Handling Systems: EDI Messaging Systems," provides a standard way to handle bills, invoices, contracts, and other business documents over electronic mail. The Electronic Data Interexchange (EDI) is an important tool for doing business because it provides a standardized way to move important business documents. ANSI standard X.21 describes the format of EDI documents.

In practice, the X.400 addressing scheme is burdensome and creates a great deal of processing overhead. Instead of seeing X.400 incorporated into every product, we've seen the evolution of specialized X.400 gateway services. The first gateways were provided by X.25 value-added networks such as Tymnet, Telenet, and AT&T's Accunet.

Several companies sell software that organizations can use to create their own X.400 gateway systems. AT&T, for example, sells a product called PMX/X.400 as a premises-based X.400 gateway. The software for an 80386-based computer is reasonably priced, but you must provide X.25 links to the distant systems. DEC offers X.400 gateway software to connect its VMSMail and All-in-1, and another gateway system that is built around its VAX 3100 minicomputer. Hewlett-Packard has an X.400 gateway on its proprietary systems that run the MPE and HP-UX operating systems.

A later evolution of the X.400 standard encourages building X.400 gateways over Ethernet instead of X.25. This option will allow the use of Ethernet routers and bridges, which are probably easier to set up than X.25 links.

The X.400 family of protocols uses a model called the Message Handling System (another MHS—not the same as the Message Handling Service). As Figure 6.2 shows, there are four major components of this model: the User Agent (UA), the Message Transfer Agent (MTA), the Access Unit, and the Message Store.

Figure 6.2

The CCITT X.400 model includes four functional layers of software. Many installations will only include the User Agent and Message Transfer Agent. The Access Unit and Message Store are used primarily for interim storage of messages.

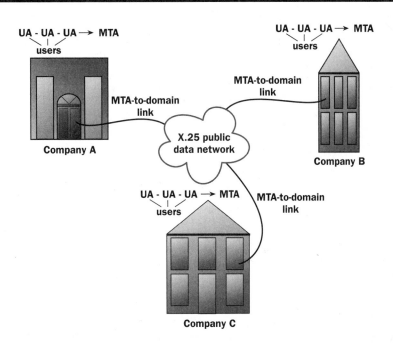

The User Agent function is performed by what end users typically think of as electronic-mail software. This is the software people use to create, read, reply to, and file messages.

The formal X.400 standard classifies User Agents according to the type of traffic they are capable of handling. A designation of P2 applies to practically all products in the market today; the mail format these products use consists of the header and the body. The header includes information on the originator, destination, data, and subject.

The software performing the function of the Message Transfer Agent routes messages to their final destination. This is specialized software, often running on a mainframe computer, minicomputer, or powerful PC. Together, MTA programs running on many LAN segments and large computers create a Message Transfer System. Each MTA collects traffic from its own UAs and from other MTAs, sorts the traffic, and forwards it to the final destination using a grouping of MTAs called *domains*.

HINT. *Consider moving to an X.400 electronic-mail system only if you have a lot of intracompany traffic. Otherwise, the complexity and cost will be hard to justify.*

A domain might be a major network service like Accunet or a single private LAN. An X.400 protocol called P1 establishes rules for the transfer of messages between MTAs. Another protocol called P3 defines the interaction between UAs and MTAs.

The X.400 Access Unit specification describes a way to link the electronic MHS system to paper-mail systems such as telex, fax, and postal delivery networks. It's correct to call this a gateway, although it might have a more electromechanical component (like a printer) than we normally associate with a gateway.

The Message Store is typically implemented as a piece of software running on a PC that holds messages from an MTA and makes them available to a UA. It often acts as a LAN gateway, moving traffic between the LAN and larger electronic-mail services.

Together, all of these pieces and parts can move electronic mail, files, and documents between very different and widely separated electronic-mail systems. X.400 holds the promise of invisible international connections—if you know the address of the person you want to send a message to.

■ Finding People on the Network

When you build a complex system of linked LANs and minicomputer or mainframe computer systems and try to use it for electronic mail, you immediately run into a major problem best described as "Where are you?" Finding the correct address for someone on a distant LAN segment, or for someone using an electronic-mail system on a larger time-shared computer, can be a frustrating exercise. This problem falls under the general category of naming and directory services, and it challenges every administrator of a network with more than two or three major segments.

Under VINES and NetWare

The problem of naming and directory services isn't confined to the arena of electronic mail, but it shows up here painfully. All interconnected LANs need a logical way to name their resources that will work across all LAN segments. While all network operating systems have a way of naming resources, only Banyan's VINES has a directory service that provides a discrete name for each resource (printers, disk drives, and so on) and for people on the network. VINES file servers interact and pass a constantly updated list of user and resource names. VINES uses a system called StreetTalk to name people and resources.

Electronic-mail systems designed for VINES networks make good use of this naming system to establish directories of users. Under StreetTalk, each person is identified by a name (with a maximum of 32 characters), a group name, and an organization name. This three-level model is typical of naming schemes for interconnected networks. Banyan makes the StreetTalk system easier for people to use by providing aliases or nicknames. These nicknames are held locally and not distributed across servers, but they make it easier for people to address other people and to use resources across the network.

There is no need to get into all the complexities of the StreetTalk system here. It includes lists of resources and different specifications for various classes of resources. Other major companies like Microsoft and Novell have plans and specifications for a global naming and directory service. They are already years behind Banyan in fielding this capability, but modern technology and the evolution of standards will let them catch up quickly.

Novell's network operating systems name resources in relationship to specific servers. NetWare servers keep the names of resources and users in a special database file called the Bindery on each file server. Under this system, NetWare administrators must carefully control arcane details such as the name assigned to every server on every LAN segment in the interconnected network. Worse, they must manually establish a user's profile on every server the person might access, wherever it might be. This management takes a great deal of time and often requires the personal involvement of people in many different locations.

Because of the limitations of the original naming scheme, designed for small networks with few servers, Novell has released an interim piece of software called the NetWare Naming Service. This first effort provides a means of moving the user information between servers. More extensive directory services will become a part of NetWare products.

HINT. *Novell has published an application interface specification for a new and more powerful naming service. Expect to see new programs and capabilities on NetWare systems in the mid-1990s.*

Novell will be upgrading NetWare to include a directory model in line with CCITT specifications. A database of users and resources will be shared among servers, and the database will include enough information to aid in routing messages to their final destinations.

Many electronic-mail systems can read and use a network naming scheme like Banyan's StreetTalk or Novell's Bindery. If you have a string of LANs using the same network operating system, you avoid a heavy administrative burden by using e-mail software that is compatible with the LAN operating system. But open systems, like the MHS and X.400 gateways, must have nonproprietary ways to identify users and their locations.

Under MHS

MHS uses a Standard Message Format (SMF) that includes a header section with addressing information, the ASCII message, and attachments. The header includes fields such as Date, From, In Reply, Subject, Signature, and To. The most important part is an address segment that can accept addresses in the form "user.application@workgroup." Each field is limited to eight characters, and in common practice people leave off the optional application field and send messages to a name at a workgroup. This eight-character-plus-eight-character address format works well for many installations, but it requires careful management and can fall apart in larger networks.

MHS works on a "next hop" basis. Each MHS gateway has information on how to send a message addressed to a specific workgroup on to its next hop. This is not a complete or elegant system; it can be particularly difficult to use if the e-mail application program does not have a good directory of users, but relies on something perhaps created manually by the network administrator.

If you can't find or make a good guess at the full MHS address of someone to whom you want to send electronic mail, you will probably have to call that person on the phone to ask for the electronic-mail address. Fortunately you only have to go through that exercise once, and then you can use the address until it changes. But it's evident that there must be a better way to deliver the mail!

HINT. *One of the most important jobs of an electronic-mail administrator is building a directory of commonly addressed people and organizations. Carefully evaluate the ability of an electronic-mail program to allow the creation and easy update of organization-wide and personal directories.*

Under X.400 and X.500

The gurus of electronic-mail theory are people who live in a real world driven by practical considerations. Some of the most important considerations faced by administrators of networks with many different links are how to identify electronic-mail destinations and how to route mail to the identified destinations. The CCITT developed a standard called X.500, reaffirmed in ISO standard 9594, for directory services. But it's important to understand that products which implement X.500 will primarily tackle international and intercompany addressing. Addressing within a company will rely on addressing schemes provided in network operating systems or electronic-mail gateways.

X.500 defines a naming model with interactive elements. It doesn't call for strict conformity, but it uses computer power to answer queries about names, routes, and resources. These queries are exchanged between electronic-mail programs in ways that the specification only generally defines.

In many ways X.500 is still evolving. The model calls for addresses that include a root (perhaps a large geographical area such as Europe), a country, an organization, an organizational unit, and a common name. But in many cases the common name isn't specific enough, and there will have to be further definition. Obviously, people writing X.500 software will have to add more flexibility to their products.

The specification further describes methods of updating and duplicating the database of addresses. It also describes how applications can look up and browse for names, and how applications can find specific types of addresses in a section called the Yellow Pages.

Although the standard discusses security, privacy and security remain an issue for any organization considering publishing an X.500 directory information tree (DIT). While you want to make it easy for people sending messages to find their addressees, certain privacy issues are also important. You don't want competitors, stock analysts, or intelligence agencies scanning directories to find employment data, special project groups, or other information. You also want to protect the privacy of individuals. These factors threaten to slow the acceptance of large electronic-mail directory systems.

Many developers will be tackling the problems of large-scale electronic-mail services, guided by standards like X.400 and X.500. Products supporting these standards will evolve over the next few years to provide powerful services for large and widely spread network systems.

■ Linking LANs with E-Mail

You can look at electronic mail as a way to link LANs, or you can look at it as something to do over linked LANs. In many cases, an e-mail system with active inter-LAN links can provide all the LAN-to-LAN connectivity your organization needs. The up-front costs for such systems are moderate, and they have very high efficiency. Don't overlook electronic mail as a primary way to link your local area networks.

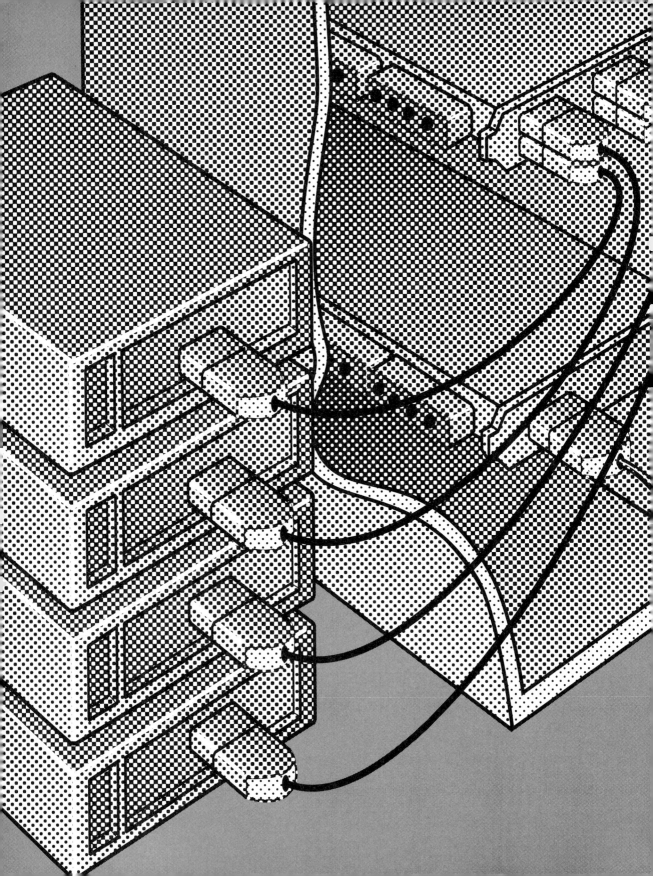

CHAPTER

7

Bulletin Boards, WAITS, and Access Servers

- Electronic Bulletin Board Systems

- WAITS

- Asynchronous Access Servers

- New Connections

The last chapter described one type of part-time access device for LANs, the electronic-mail gateway. There are other related types of products for LAN-to-LAN connections that you should know about. Bulletin board systems, wide-area information transfer systems, and access servers, like e-mail gateways, are part-time connections that can often eliminate the need for more expensive full-time connection alternatives such as bridges, routers, and their connecting links. The decision matrix guide at the end of Chapter 3 can help you decide among different full-time and part-time connection schemes.

■ Electronic Bulletin Board Systems

An electronic bulletin board system takes its name from the bulletin board in local stores and clubs where people post notices of mutual interest. The first Computer Bulletin Board System (a trademarked name) was put on-line in Chicago as the result of the creative talents of Ward Christensen and Randy Suess in 1978. The BBS movement grew with the power of PCs, and in many organizations a modern BBS is an electronic storage point for messages, notices, questions, offers of help, and files containing utilities and useful programs.

Modern programs such as PCBoard, RBBS-PC, and Wildcat! are effective and economical. The software typically costs less than $200 per simultaneous user. The number of simultaneous users you should pay for depends on the size of your organization and how heavily the bulletin board is used, but even if everyone in the organization checks in for 20 minutes a day, you only need to buy simultaneous user licenses for 3 to 5 percent of the number of people in the organization.

If you only want to accommodate one user at a time, these programs will run on low-cost 80286-based PC hardware. Packages that can support three or more simultaneous users require a PC with an 80386 processor and 4 or more megabytes of RAM.

Typically, the electronic messages and files available on a BBS are arranged according to topic in what are termed *forums*. People can call into the BBS using modems, but we will concentrate on using a BBS across a LAN or between LANs.

In many ways, the capabilities of a BBS overlap with those of an electronic-mail system, but the focus of each type of product is different. An electronic-mail system focuses on one-to-one communications, with some capabilities for sending messages to a group of people on a mailing list. The emphasis is on privacy of communications.

In a BBS, the emphasis is on open and public communications in the form of one person addressing many, often unidentified readers. A BBS serves as a place for all members of an organization to find and post the latest news. The ability to divide the BBS into semiprivate forums allows task groups and special-interest groups to hold discussions and exchange information among themselves. A BBS typically has some capability for person-to-person electronic-mail, just as an electronic-mail system might include a public bulletin board capability, but the e-mail system in a BBS is primitive compared with the specialized mail products.

HINT. *In addition to holding internal company information, a BBS system can serve as the interface point between the public and your organization. The BBS provides controlled interaction and public forums.*

A BBS that serves its users over a LAN provides the same public and file-distribution capabilities as one with only modem dial-in capabilities. BBS programs don't know whether the data they move resides on networked or local disk drives. They link LANs—and remote segments of your organization—invisibly. People calling in through modems and people using the BBS over the LAN can simultaneously access the same forums and file libraries. As Figure 7.1 illustrates, the person managing the BBS has control over a wide range of security and communications parameters.

Figure 7.1

This screen from the Wildcat! BBS depicts the status of the system and management options.

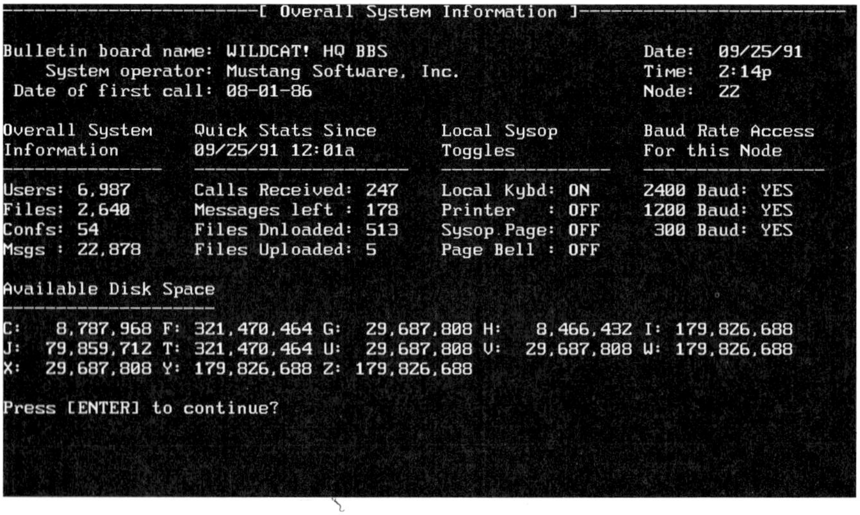

```
---------------------[ Overall System Information ]---------------------
Bulletin board name: WILDCAT! HQ BBS                    Date:   09/25/91
    System operator: Mustang Software, Inc.             Time:   2:14p
 Date of first call: 08-01-86                           Node:   ZZ

Overall System     Quick Stats Since     Local Sysop        Baud Rate Access
Information        09/25/91 12:01a        Toggles            For this Node
--------------     -----------------      -----------        ---------------
Users: 6,987       Calls Received: 247    Local Kybd: ON     2400 Baud: YES
Files: 2,640       Messages left : 178    Printer   : OFF    1200 Baud: YES
Confs: 54          Files Dnloaded: 513    Sysop Page: OFF     300 Baud: YES
Msgs : 22,878      Files Uploaded: 5      Page Bell : OFF

Available Disk Space
--------------------
C:   8,787,968 F: 321,470,464 G:  29,687,808 H:   8,466,432 I: 179,826,688
J:  79,859,712 T: 321,470,464 U:  29,687,808 V:  29,687,808 W: 179,826,688
X:  29,687,808 Y: 179,826,688 Z: 179,826,688

Press [ENTER] to continue?
```

The LAN-to-LAN capability of a BBS is similar to the LAN-to-LAN capability of an electronic-mail system. Computers running BBS software can call other computers running compatible software, typically using modems and public telephone lines, and transfer files and messages between specific forums and libraries.

Interestingly, it isn't even necessary to have the same software running on the communicating BBS PCs (although it's still a good idea). Many BBS products support standards for communications derived from within the industry—specifically FidoNet or PCRelay, or both—and they can typically interoperate.

A BBS system that supports the FidoNet or PCRelay standard periodically shuts off access from outside users and does nothing but transfer messages and files to other systems. You can program this message exchange so that it takes place at certain times or when a traffic queue reaches a specific level.

Electronic bulletin board systems provide an economical way to link networks for specific types of inter-LAN traffic. Some organizations will use BBS LAN-to-LAN connectivity as an important adjunct to bridges and routers, or even as a way of avoiding the cost of these full-time connection portals.

■ WAITS

BBS software is oriented primarily toward human interaction. But another type of automated communications software is aimed strictly at making efficient automated file transfers between computers. If you only need to transfer files—and you need to do it regularly, several times a day—then *wide-area information transfer systems* (WAITS) offer an alternative. WAITS are less concerned with the human element than e-mail or BBS systems; the only way they can send mail and messages is in the form of files. If handling individual mail messages is not important to you (and you'd rather not go through the complexity of setting up a BBS and a BBS network), the benefits of using unattended and fully automated WAITS can grow rapidly as your business expands and employees have less time to collect and distribute information.

A WAITS network consists of PCs running software that lets them communicate and exchange files with each other automatically. WAITS programs are single-purpose products that incorporate special management tools and, in some cases, support multitasking.

HINT. *Any application can benefit from WAITS. The application simply writes a file to a shared subdirectory on a LAN. You program the WAITS software to take specific actions with specifically named files. After the initial setup, everything happens automatically and repetitively.*

Large businesses usually have central offices housing their inventory, sales, and other data. Through the use of a WAITS system, the outlying offices, operations, or stores can exchange information with the corporate office at any time without monitoring the transfer. WAITS require only the use of a modem and a PC capable of running the software at each end. The solution usually proves more cost-effective than hardware-intensive linking devices like bridges and routers.

Retail operations best exemplify how valuable a WAITS product can be. Take, for instance, a company with a chain of retail clothing stores spread throughout a large metropolitan area or across the nation. The managers in each location typically spend several hours a day—during and after business hours—compiling sales, inventory, and payroll reports. Instead of managing by walking around and ensuring good service for their customers, they're spending a lot of time acting as desk clerks!

Organizations equipped with WAITS give managers more time to manage by using a central clerical staff—the centralized software—to compile raw data and message it into the next day's balance sheets, inventory orders, and withholding-tax deposits. WAITS products contact automated point-of-sale terminals in each retail operation by telephone or by some other electronic means; they withdraw the appropriate information, compile it, and then provide the store manager and central operations staff with finished reports.

You can also use WAITS to link electronic-mail systems on LANS, to update databases for businesses and organizations, and to print out messages in distant locations. Any organization with operations in more than one location can probably find a practical and profitable use for a WAITS system.

HINT. *WAITS use their own data-compression and error-handling protocols to ensure efficient and accurate delivery of data. Dial-up telephone lines can economically serve a WAITS installation with hundreds of nodes.*

The WAITS concept predates personal computers. In the 1960s, IBM marketed a point-of-sale and inventory system that could exchange information through modems. Crosstalk Communications/DCA's Transporter, a program written by my sometime coauthor Les Freed, was an early MS-DOS WAITS application, but the idea grew slowly. Now, developments like lower-priced long-distance telephone calls and private satellite networks, as well as the promise of the Integrated Services Digital Network (ISDN), have laid a firmer foundation upon which WAITS installations can rest. Just-in-time delivery of inventory and increased accounting controls drive the need for the fast reports that WAITS provide. OS/2 provides the multitasking capabilities that the most powerful WAITS products will need.

In the WAITS market, two products, XcelleNet's XcelleNet and SofNet's XChange Plus, lead the market and typify the levels of product available. They resemble one another in offering fully automated, unattended, wide-area information transfers. They differ in flexibility, price, and features.

XcelleNet

XcelleNet is best suited to large corporations with many operating locations. The XcelleNet software package costs several hundred dollars per remote node, plus several thousand dollars for a multinode host package. The central controlling computer, usually located in the corporate headquarters, runs a program called Network Manager over the OS/2 Presentation Manager graphical user interface. XcelleNet is specifically designed for network operations, and in very busy systems more than one controlling computer can intercommunicate and coordinate over a LAN while simultaneously moving information over the long-distance links.

A single central computer can manage up to 18 serial ports and communicate with the various local and remote nodes sending and receiving data. The Network Manager software, shown in Figure 7.2, provides automatic session scheduling in addition to data compression, error detection and correction, and a host of other features that allow for automatic and reliable data transfers. You need the dedicated resources of an 80386- or 80486-powered PC to handle these multiple communications sessions.

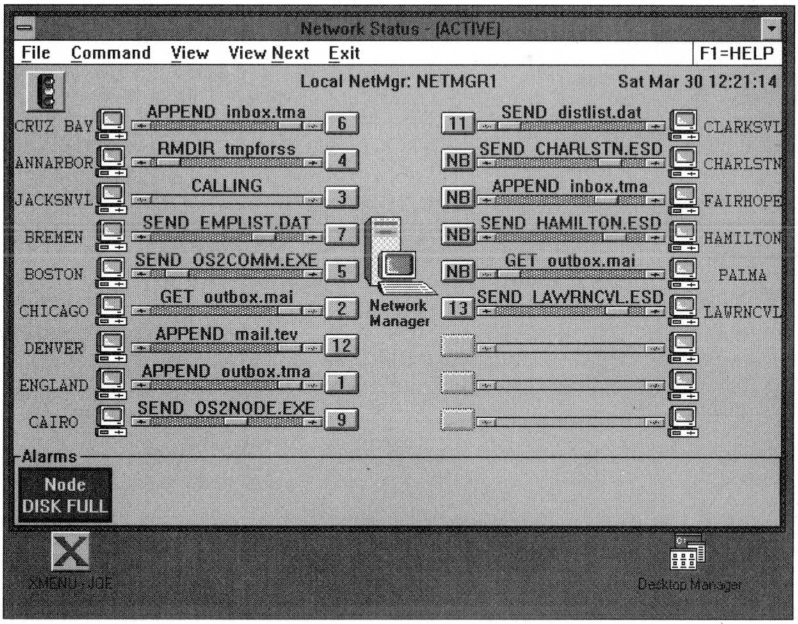

Figure 7.2

This XcelleNet screen shows many of the management and reporting options.

On the remote side of the WAITS connection, you install XcelleNet's X/Node program on any PC running DOS, OS/2, Unix, or Xenix. Operating as a terminate-and-stay-resident program (TSR) using 64K of RAM in a DOS PC, X/Node transparently and automatically performs its communications functions while the PC runs other applications. The system administrator at the central computer can use Network Manager to connect to a remote PC at any time without disturbing the remote computer's current operations.

XcelleNet works with any telecommunications carrier and supports different connections methods, including 800/WAITS, X.25 packet networks, and VSAT satellite terminals.

XChange Plus

SofNet's XChange Plus is designed for smaller organizations needing WAITS service. Priced at $199 per node, the XChange Plus package comes complete with the software needed to perform automated communications among remote PCs, facsimile machines, and internal fax boards.

XChange Plus is a DOS-based product compatible with NetWare or NetBIOS networks. Unlike XcelleNet, the XChange Plus package does not include different remote and central programs to enable automatic communications; a single program performs all functions. By using the same software at both ends of the WAITS link, XChange Plus can use a distributed topology instead of a centralized star. But note that XChange Plus runs in the foreground and requires a dedicated PC at each node.

At least two other products, BackMail and PC-tPost, are in the same market and offer features similar to those of XChange Plus.

Useful WAITS

Consider wide-area information transfer systems as economical alternatives to local area network bridges. They work within private-line voice-and-data communications networks, but installing a WAITS system using dial-up lines could actually eliminate the need for a private-line network in some organizations. If you need to move information just across the street or all the way across an ocean, it's worth the WAITS.

■ Asynchronous Access Servers

Networks are for sharing. But people often want to share a network's resources from wherever they might be, not just from within an office with a LAN installation. Devices called *access servers* provide a way for people to share the resources of the network from any place with a telephone line, while working around the speed limitations telephone lines normally impose.

There are two ways you can access a network from outside of the "fat" high-speed cable through a modem. In the first technique, called *remote client,* the remote PC uses redirection software just like a client PC on a LAN. The remote client PC treats the modem like a (very slow) network interface adapter and routes all of the networking activity through the serial port. The only advantage of this technique is that it gives the remote PC a full set of redirected drives, so application programs can use their standard paths for program and data files. The tremendous drawback of this technique is slow response time. Pushing and pulling all of the small low-level messages designed for network communications across the slow modem link is a very inefficient process. As I'll discuss just ahead, some companies have taken innovative steps to improve the efficiency of remote-client operation.

The second method of network access is called *modem remote control.* In this technique, the remote PC uses special software to control a PC on the LAN remotely through a modem connection. The remote-control software is the only software the remote PC runs; there is no LAN redirector. In effect, the keyboards and screens of the remote and LAN-connected PCs operate in parallel so that keystrokes from the remote PC control the LAN-connected machine, and the screen displays of the LAN-connected machine appear on the screen of the remote-control PC. The application programs run on the networked PC, where they have full access to the high-speed network connections and resources.

Up until the Microsoft Windows graphical user interface caught fire in 1990, the modem remote-control method of remote connection to a LAN was always much more efficient than the remote-client method. However, two things have happened to challenge that superiority. First, the multifaceted changes that take place in a Windows graphics screen every time you click a mouse take several seconds to traverse even a fast modem. This reduced the efficiency of the remote-control approach to something like that of the remote-client method. Second, companies like Shiva Corp. developed methods of reducing the amount of network traffic moving over the modems and the telephone line. This change in technique significantly reduced the time needed to move data under the remote-client arrangement. In the upcoming sections, we'll look at both remote-client and remote-control operations.

HINT. *The authors of modern remote-control programs have learned tricks for improving the slow transmission of graphics screens. But remote-client and remote-control techniques are relatively equal competitors in installations supporting modern organizations.*

Remote Control

The concept of remotely controlling a networked PC through a modem isn't new. Many people leave their office PCs running at night and continue working on the LAN from home by remotely controlling the office PC through modem remote-control software.

But this approach is susceptible to many human problems, like forgetting to load the software before bolting out the door at 5:00 p.m., and also to outside problems such as power failures. Additionally, using personal PCs for remote control on an ad hoc basis does not provide a standardized method of network access for people who normally work out of the office or in other offices.

With the prices for high-speed modems dropping, remote-control software has become more useful, and it now plays a bigger role in the connectivity picture in organizations where people still use character-based applications instead of the graphical applications of Windows or OS/2. People can work at home during times of temporary absence, and the popular telecommuting option is more viable.

Remote printing is another cost-effective use of remote LAN access. Instead of printing a document in your office and then using an expensive overnight carrier to get it to the company headquarters, you can call the headquarters' LAN and print your document there. Not only does this technique save you money, but the text arrives immediately and with better quality than a facsimile.

Access servers are devices dedicated to providing callers (including communications servers on other networks) with remote access to the facilities of the LAN. It is possible to set up any spare PC and use it as an access server on a one-at-a-time first-come-first-served basis. But it is more economical to set up an access-server system that can service several callers at the same time. In modern networks, access servers can typically handle four or more simultaneous incoming sessions. Many of these devices also have the capability to handle outgoing calls from the LAN. I'll discuss those capabilities later.

Many companies sell the bits and pieces, such as multiport serial boards and multitasking software for an access server, but wickering those parts together is a task for a highly skilled masochist. My advice is to buy an integrated package.

Setting up one computer to handle one call is easy. But large networks need to allow many people to call in simultaneously, and managers do not want to dedicate one computer per phone line because this technique uses too much space and money.

Most of the access-server solutions on the market use remote-control software. Such programs run on the computer acting as an incoming gateway on the LAN and provide access to all network resources. When you dial in to the network, these programs greet you with a log-on prompt. Once you log on, your PC acts as if it were on the network, although the processing actually takes place at the other end of the phone line. Until you hang up, the remote-control program controls what you do.

The access-server products use two significantly different techniques to handle multiple simultaneous calls. The first technique, used by Alloy Computer Products and Novell and depicted in Figure 7.3, uses a multitasking operating system to slice the power of a single 80286 or 80386 processor into several simultaneous sessions. Calling PCs control one session on the multitasking operating system.

Figure 7.3

Sharing the power of a single 80386 or 80486 CPU among several callers makes economic sense, but the shared CPU and shared LAN adapters both become potential bottlenecks and points of failure.

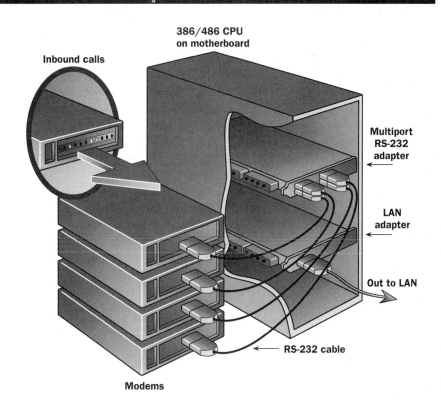

You can't just run out and buy DESQview 386 and create this kind of system yourself, because the transport-layer software used in NetWare and in other LAN operating systems expects to service only one user ID per LAN adapter card. If you tried to service more than one caller through a multitasking operating system using a standard version of Novell's IPX, for example, when the second caller logged on while the first caller was still connected, NetWare would log the first user on as the second user. The first user would no longer have the correct privileges and drive mappings. Novell has developed a special multiplexing version of its IPX software for the Novell Access Server, and Alloy reuses it in another product.

As a rule, the advantage of the multitasking architecture is cost; a single 386/20 PC can readily handle five simultaneous callers. The disadvantages are reliability and throughput. Some ill-behaved programs will bring down the session or the whole server in any multitasking operating system, and there is no way to control what applications the callers will try to run on the access server. If the system crashes, a live body must reset the session or the server. If a crash occurs in the middle of the weekend, your system might not be fully operational until Monday morning unless someone makes a special trip into the office. Also, when several serial ports share one CPU, its inability to cope efficiently with the frequent interrupts that occur in high-speed communications limits the available capacity to no more than four or five stations.

The other technology, used by Cubix, J&L, and a second Alloy product, uses multiple processor cards mounted in a single chassis. Calling PCs control one of several separate V20, 80286, or 80386 processors in a card cage or a host PC. While this technique—shown in Figure 7.4—is generally more expensive than using a multitasking operating system, it provides the best performance and reliability.

The card cage cabinets range from the small Alloy RedBox through several styles of the J&L Chatterbox (which looks like a cross between a PC AT and a high-performance stereo amplifier), and on to the Cubix ComBridge, a heavy-duty customized rack for modems and CPU cards that looks right at home nestled among the cabinets of an IBM mainframe.

These card-mounted processors might share a single network adapter card, as in the Alloy and Cubix products, or each CPU can get the full attention of its own LAN adapter card, as in the J&L product. As PC Magazine LAN Labs' benchmark tests show, when callers control a single CPU that has its own LAN adapter card, they get fast network performance. But this approach can cost $500 to $1,000 more per available call-in port than the architecture that uses a multitasking host on the LAN.

The costs of all of these products depend on what equipment you have already and how you want to account for it. An Alloy or Cubix CPU card can run in an old AT-style computer with sufficient slots for your needs, so you don't have to mount them in separate cabinets. The J&L CPU card does need its own special cabinet.

Figure 7.4

The technique of mounting multiple CPUs in a single specialized card cage is more expensive than sharing a single CPU, but each caller gets the use of a separate CPU and LAN adapter, improving reliability and performance. The shared cabinet contains control circuitry to monitor the performance and status of each CPU.

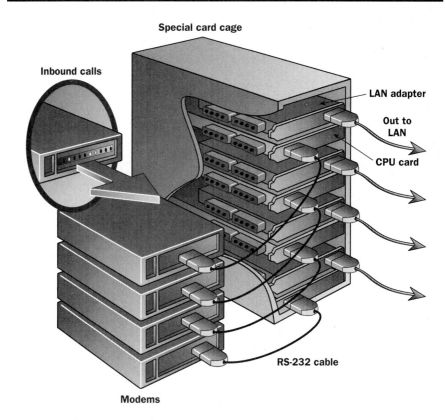

Dialing Out Through the LAN

Almost any access server product can also act as a modem server or, as it is also called, an *asynchronous communications server* (ACS). A network modem server is a specific subcategory of communications server. A modem server makes a group of modems (as many as 16, in the Cubix product) available to the client workstations on a first-come-first-served basis. People at the client stations use software that can communicate across the network, such as Crosstalk Mk.4, to establish a dedicated connection to a modem in the modem pool. The modem server gives its full attention to the PC that wins its services for as long as the call lasts—a condition called a *virtual circuit.*

At first glance, sharing modems may not seem to make sense, since even 9,600-bps modems are rapidly decreasing in price. But each business telephone line can cost $70 to $100 per month, and besides the cost of the modems and phone lines, there are other barriers to putting a modem on every PC. Many office telephone systems are not designed to accept modems. In some buildings, running the phone wires themselves presents a problem.

If you already have an installed LAN, you can add a modem server to avoid other costs. There is a catch, however. In order for the attached PCs to be able to use the modem server, each workstation needing access to the ACS must be provided with a *redirector*, which redirects the serial communications traffic to the modem server.

As Figure 7.5 shows, some redirectors are software-based, and some are a combination of hardware and software. The hardware-based approach employed by J&L allows you to use unmodified off-the-shelf communications software. The trade-off is that you must use one of the workstation PC's expansion slots for the redirector card. The other disadvantage of this approach is that only redirector-equipped PCs have access to the modem server, but this restriction can also be considered a security feature.

It is also possible to use software redirection. Software interrupt 14 hexadecimal, or INT 14H, is the way Microsoft's designers originally intended for communications software to access the serial ports. But because using INT 14H is so slow, the designers of communications software address the serial port hardware directly.

When IBM introduced the IBM Asynchronous Communications Server, the company also announced a new specification that defines the method a communications program should use to talk to the server, but this has seen little acceptance. When Novell introduced the Novell Asynchronous Communications Server, this company came out with yet another interface specification, using interrupt 6BH.

Access-server products are available with a variety of architectures, costs, cabinets, and capabilities. You'll see a clear trade-off between cost and performance. If the users in your organization will only need to use word processing programs and check their electronic mail, then the multitasking approach will meet your needs. But if your remote users want to run CPU-intensive tasks involving calculations, or to do jobs like sorting database records, then the separate-CPU approach offers them more power. In either case, turnkey access servers can provide an excellent portal for PC-to-LAN and LAN-to-LAN connectivity.

Remote-Client Systems

Many companies such as Banyan and Novell have marketed remote-client access systems for their networks. But these products suffer from poor throughput, because they try to shove all of the packets-within-packets, requiring multiple acknowledgments conforming to the various network layers, through the relatively slow telephone line.

Figure 7.5

A networked PC that can use the services of an asynchronous communications server (ACS) must either use communications software that can address a network protocol such as INT 14, use a hardware redirector that emulates the serial port, or use a software redirector that moves the data to the LAN driver. The LAN adapter and cabling carry the data to a PC running asynchronous communications software and equipped with multiple serial ports and modems. This system allows people to use high-speed modems without buying a modem and telephone line for every desktop.

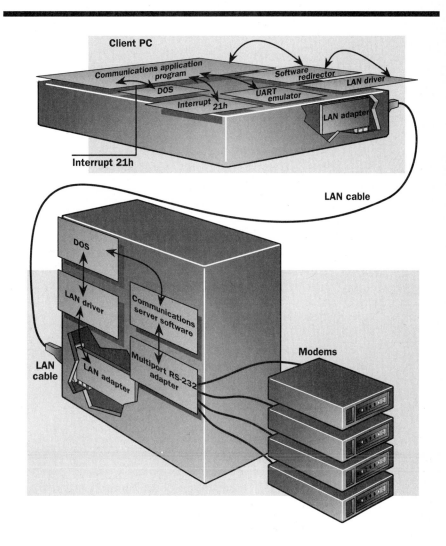

In mid-1991, companies like Shiva Corp. led the way in the development of a new category of products that are perfect for PC-to-LAN or LAN-to-LAN connectivity. These new products, typically designed for widespread networking protocols like NetWare, use software techniques to reduce the amount of data moving over the telephone line, while using the latest modem hardware techniques to move that data at the highest possible speed.

NetModem/E

The Shiva NetModem/E is literally a modem with an Ethernet connector attached. It becomes a node on the LAN instead of an attachment to a PC.

Its relatively small case includes a BNC connector for thin Ethernet, an RJ-11 telephone cable jack, and a power connection.

On the modem side, the NetModem/E uses 14400-bps V.32bis signaling and V.42bis data compression. Of course, it is downward-compatible with the more prolific V.32 9,600-bps modems. With some types of data and under the best line conditions, the V.32bis and V.42bis combination can move data as fast as 57.6 megabits per second. The Shiva dial-in software ships in DOS, Microsoft Windows, and Macintosh versions. The Shiva NetModem provides fast and flexible LAN dial-in, dial-out, and LAN-to-LAN connections.

The most practical use of this product is in its dial-in capabilities. Anyone using a modem-equipped PC or Macintosh computer can use the Shiva dial-in software and turn the computer into a remote node on the network. You run a special version of IPX and the NetWare shell on the remote PC, and as you sit with your notebook computer in a hotel room, you can access the same network drives you use on your desktop computer in the office.

The Shiva dial-in technique has two operational advantages over remote-control LAN-entry products: transparency and the ability to overcome LAN dial-in problems for people using GUI applications. When your PC becomes a node on the network, all of your drives and searches are mapped out, and you have access to all of the network's shared peripherals. When you want to copy a file from the LAN to your laptop, you type

```
COPY F:filename C:filename
```

instead of using special file-transfer menus or commands.

In contrast to systems using modem remote-control communication packages that let you take over a networked PC, you don't need a CPU on the network, either dedicated or shared, for remote control. The NetModem/E is the only hardware you add to the network.

The disadvantage of the NetModem/E's dial-in technology comes in slower throughput than with the modem remote-control systems. Modem remote-control systems pass only keystrokes and screen images over the telephone line. This used to be the fastest way to interact, because moving all the network protocols like Novell's IPX through modems creates a lot of overhead and slows throughput. But modern applications create such complex screen images in graphics mode that the old technique of remote control is no longer a good answer. The modem remote-control software companies are moving to change their programs to make them more responsive for graphics applications, but Shiva has attacked the problem from a different angle.

Shiva's programmers tokenize certain repetitive elements of the NetWare Core Protocol packet within the IPX packet, significantly reducing the overhead and improving throughput rate. This technique gives you the advantage of using your remote computer as a part of the LAN while still maintaining a useful throughput rate. However, there are two techniques you must follow to get the maximum benefit from the NetModem/E.

First, don't try to draw applications over the telephone line to run them; instead, load them from a local drive and point them toward the networked drives to read and write their data. This applies even in the case of the Net-Ware login and logout executable files. Because each NetModem/E has its own unique Ethernet identifier, it's easy to set up login scripts that will recognize a caller using a NetModem/E and direct searches for utility programs like Novell's MAP or SYSCON to a local drive.

Second, if you must run networked applications that move a lot of data—for instance, using a shared CD-ROM—then you can use a LAN remote-control program to run a networked PC or CD-ROM server. You enter the network through the Shiva modem and then, since your remote PC is a node on the LAN, run LAN remote-control software to use a PC with an attached CD-ROM drive, or to do database work.

The NetModem/E's dial-out capabilities give people in an organization the use of a high-speed V.32bis/V.42bis modem without making them buy a modem for every desktop. People can dial out using NetModem/E on a first-come-first-served basis from any networked PC that has the Shivacom communication driver installed, as long as it is running a communications program that can address the interrupt 14 or Novell NASI protocol.

The Shiva NetModem/E is a true network router for LAN-to-LAN connections. You can set up a NetModem/E as a router on each LAN and use these units to move appropriate packets across the dial-up telephone line. The throughput is adequate for many LAN-to-LAN tasks, and the price of the hardware is a fraction of what you would pay for more typical routers, which admittedly would have more features and speed.

ICC's Remote LAN Node

Another product that provides efficient remote-client operation is Remote LAN Node (RLN) from Intercomputer Communications Corp. (ICC). Unlike the Shiva NetModem/E, the RLN system will work with any network operating system that has drivers for either The Clarkson Packet Driver Collection or NDIS.

RLN is a software product that runs on any networked PC. The PC acts in the role of an access server. The software can theoretically handle as many as 16 remote connections, so you'll want to run it on a PC with at least an 80386SX processor running at 20 MHz. ICC sells its own multiport RS-232 adapter board with microprocessor augmentation to relieve the PC's CPU of many I/O tasks.

Each client PC calling into the LAN runs all of the LAN software it needs, such as IPX.COM and NETX.COM for NetWare. In the case of Net-Ware, you configure the IPX module for NDIS. RLN software in the client PC redirects the network communications out a serial port.

The client software and server software communicate using a relatively new industry standard called Point-to-Point Protocol (PPP). PPP provides specific tokenizing and compression techniques that work very well on net-work packets. These include Tinygram Compression (which strips the trail-ing 0's from any minimum-size packet), Header Compression (which reduces the redundant and unneeded data from a header), and Protocol Length Com-pression (which handles the problems of packets broken up for transmis-sion). PPP does not offer error handling, so you still need to use a modem with V.42 services to insure the integrity of the data going over the line.

Remote client products like the Shiva NetModem/E and ICC's Remote LAN Node make it easy to extend the LAN into many different locations and to link LANs. The NetModem/E can act as a router for LAN-to-LAN links. ICC's Remote LAN Node doesn't know or care whether it is moving data for laptops calling from an airport or for networked PCs moving data from server to server.

■ New Connections

In the last few chapters, I've described the details of several different kinds of LAN portal devices. You can use some or all of these devices to give rich interconnection capabilities to any group of LANs.

In the following chapters I'll turn to the inter-LAN connections. I'll describe everything from the ports, cables, and connectors you can use for attaching inter-LAN equipment to the many choices you have for inter-LAN circuits.

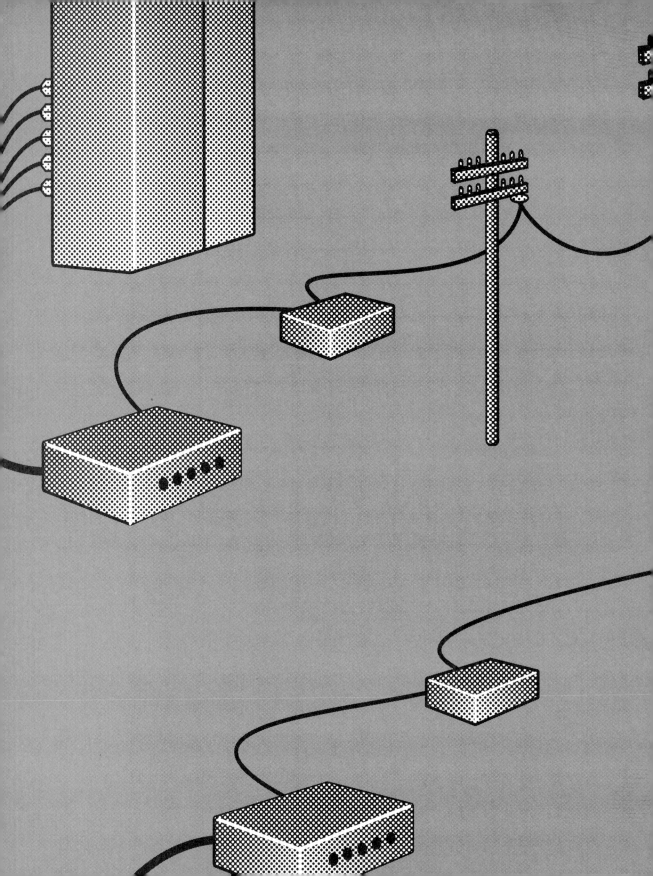

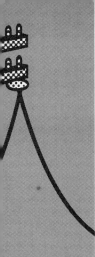

Serial Ports, Modems, and Multiplexers

- From Fat Cables to Spaghetti Links

- Modems and "Muxes"

- Digital Circuit Connections

- Making the Links

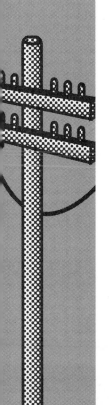

In previous chapters, I took you on a tour of the devices that act as portals on a LAN. The different types of bridges, routers, and communications servers control the flow of data between LANs. These devices can make local connections over fast LAN cables, or they can channel data between LANs that are remote from each other (and hence the name "remote" bridge or router); for this purpose, they use slower circuits covering longer distances.

Linking LAN segments within 1,000 feet or so of each other is a relatively easy task. You'll typically use a repeater or MAC-layer bridge that uses the same network architecture on both sides (for instance, Ethernet to Ethernet or Token-Ring to Token-Ring)—although specialized bridges that can link different media-access-control architectures are also available. Routers, used less frequently in local installations, can move packets or frames across different MAC-layer architectures, but they require a common routing protocol (such as IP, IPX, or NetBIOS) within the packets or frames. But whether you bridge, or route, or use a communications server of some type, the links will be made with relatively familiar LAN cabling and with systems using the same LAN adapters you have in all the other networked nodes.

■ From Fat Cables to Spaghetti Links

The various LAN cabling systems, such as ARCnet, Ethernet, and Token-Ring, move data at 10 megabits per second or more at distances out to about 1,000 feet. I refer to these connections as "fat cables" because they carry lots of data and move it quickly. Data moves so fast on the typical LAN cable that people using the shared network resources do not perceive a difference in response time whether an application program draws a file from a server across the room or from the internal hard disk in the desktop PC. In fact, because of the sophisticated data-retrieval techniques used by network servers, the response from the server is often faster than from a local drive.

By contrast, as the connection becomes longer than a local network link, it becomes increasingly difficult and expensive to keep the data moving at a high speed. The laws of physics and the principles of electronics combine to distort and overwhelm the data signals. As circuits get longer, we typically have to reduce the speed of the data going through them to retain accuracy. I call the long-distance circuits "spaghetti links" because they are long and thin.

I'll use the analogy of fat cables and spaghetti links to explain many of the problems and techniques of making connections between networks.

Signaling on the Fat Cable

Let's start with the LAN cable, examine some of the principles of electrical data transmission across the cable, and then see how those principles apply to the long-distance connections. The various types of local area network architectures, such as ARCnet, Ethernet, and Token-Ring, use different types of signaling on the cable running between the network adapter cards. Each type of network system packages data in different ways, uses different electrical connections, and sends different voltages to signal the presence of the 0s and 1s that make up the data alphabet. Yet there are also many similarities among the networking systems.

The data traveling over networks—of whatever type—moves in the form of 0s and 1s. These simple digits create characters in a data alphabet. The typical data alphabet is the American Standard Code for Information Interexchange (ASCII). According to ASCII convention, if we send the bit-stream series 101000 across a circuit, it represents the character P; the string 1000011 represents the character C. A similar data alphabet with a different encoding scheme, the Extended Binary Coded Decimal Interchange Code (EBCDIC), is used in IBM mainframe systems.

The large majority of local area networks installed today send data by imposing a direct-current voltage, exactly like that from a flashlight battery, over copper wire. This type of direct-current signaling defines what is known as a *baseband* LAN system. Typically, changing the voltage level on the wire by at least 1.5 volts is enough to signal the difference between a 0 and a 1 in a baseband system.

Another type of LAN signaling scheme, called *broadband*, uses radio waves over the coaxial cable. In the mid-1980s, baseband and broadband systems competed equally in the LAN market, but broadband systems have lost popularity because they are difficult to maintain.

As Figure 8.1 shows, the rise and fall of the direct-current voltages create square waves. This signaling scheme is called *biphase* or *Manchester II* encoding. In this scheme, the transition from one voltage level to another indicates the start of a new data bit, and the direction and timing of the voltage change indicates whether the bit is a binary 1 or 0.

Unfortunately, many factors conspire to reduce the sharpness of those square waves. The LAN cable itself has a variety of electrical characteristics, including the resistance, the accumulated capacitance (resistance to voltage change), and the lumped inductance (resistance to current change) of the wiring. These electrical characteristics have a cumulative effect on the signals riding on the cable. Some high-quality cable has less resistance, less distributed capacitance, and fewer inductive lumps than other cables. The differences come primarily from the size and spacing of the conductors, the quality of the insulation, and the quality of the connectors.

Figure 8.1

The most common method of encoding signals on an electrical cable is called *biphase*. The direction and timing of the voltage change are recognized by electronic components and recorded as digital 1s or 0s in the data stream.

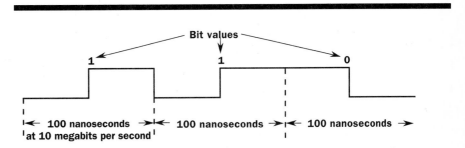

The factors of resistance, capacitance, and inductance work to reduce the amount of the voltage change and to round off the sharp corners of the square waves. As they travel across the wire, the crisp square waves gradually become rounded lumps that are much harder for electronic components to detect.

In addition, as the signals travel across the cable, they often encounter large induced voltages from nearby power lines and devices with strong electrical fields such as motors, fluorescent lights, and even standard electrical wiring. These induced voltages can bury the signals and prevent the network adapters from detecting them.

The degradation and interference problems are not too severe if there is a relatively big time gap between the voltage transitions. If the voltage stays at a high or low level for a long period (measured in milliseconds, but comparatively long to an electronic device), the circuits have time to detect the voltage change even through noise and despite rounding of the square waves. But if the data is transmitted at high speed where the changes are close together, as in Ethernet's 10-megabit-per-second signals with their 100-nanosecond spacing, bits can go undetected and the usefulness of the communications circuit will be compromised. When this happens, we say the *bit error rate* has gone up. The signaling speed and the bit error rate are two factors you must trade off as communications paths become longer.

For all of these reasons, as the distance goes up we typically must reduce the signaling speed on any type of data transmission circuit—local or remote. In modern network systems, the square waves can be regenerated and sophisticated processors can reduce the noise on the circuits to allow faster throughput. But these techniques increase the cost of the service. In LAN cabling systems, we specify both the signaling speed and the maximum permissible cable length to ensure an acceptably low bit error rate with economical equipment.

HINT. *As the distance covered by a communications circuit goes up, the speed goes down, or else the cost goes through the roof!*

Fiber-optic cables do not absorb electrical noise the way copper cables do, and that noise immunity is their biggest advantage. Though the glass or plastic fibers don't absorb electrical noise, they do offer resistance to the passage of the light signals, so distance is still a limiting factor when you use fiber-optic cables for network connections. However, because signals on fiber-optic cables do not accumulate electrical noise, the signals are easier to regenerate, so fiber-optic cable is the medium of choice for long-distance services and for LAN installations in areas of high electrical noise. Equipment for fiber-optic interconnection costs more than equipment that connects to copper cable, so copper is likely to compete with fiber in general use for decades to come.

HINT. *Fiber-optic cables don't absorb electrical noise from power lines, motors, and other sources, so they carry signals farther, particularly in noisy electrical environments. However, fiber-optic interconnection equipment can cost many times the price of equipment used on copper cable.*

Inside the Network Device

Inside the bridge, router, or communications gateway, the 0's and 1's arriving in a series from the fat LAN cable are converted to a parallel stream of data by the LAN adapter inside the device. The internal data bus (a set of parallel lines on a printed circuit board) carries the data into random access memory, where it is examined by programs running in the device's processor. The architecture is the same whether the device is internal (inside a PC) or external (with its own cabinet and processing system).

As Figure 8.2 illustrates, in a *local* device connected to another LAN segment, a second LAN adapter receives data that the programs decide to forward and moves it to the other LAN segment. In a device that moves data to a *remote* LAN, a communications adapter must interface with the long-distance circuit. This adapter must have the appropriate electrical signaling characteristics, connector, and data-handling abilities for the long-distance equipment.

Remote bridges, routers, and gateways offer communications combinations such as

- support for X.25 packets over circuits of 64 kilobits per second and faster

- support for the interesting new frame-relay protocols at the same speeds

- data compression for efficient use of the linking circuits

- alternatives for using data connections at more than 2 megabits per second

The communications adapter cards contain their own processors of the Intel 80186, Intel 80286, or Motorola 68000 class.

Figure 8.2

A local bridge, router, or communications server has two LAN adapter cards to move the data to and from each LAN segment. A remote device has one LAN adapter and a communications adapter configured for the long-distance circuit. Note that there is one remote device at each end of the long-distance circuit, but typically only one device on a local connection.

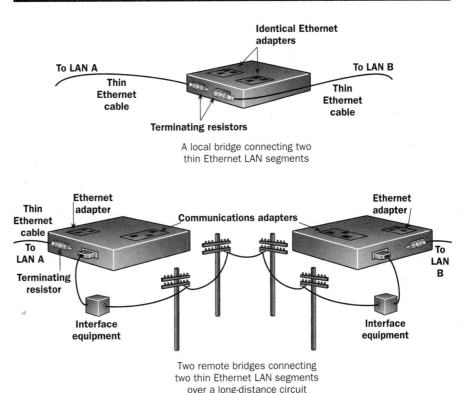

A local bridge connecting two thin Ethernet LAN segments

Two remote bridges connecting two thin Ethernet LAN segments over a long-distance circuit

Signals on the Spaghetti Link

On the long-distance side of the bridge, router, or other communications device, we find other types of connections with their own unique specifications, but these connections are still governed by the same rules of physics and electronics. The internetwork media available to link LAN segments include telephone lines, satellite networks, microwave radio, fiber-optic networks, and perhaps cable television coaxial systems. You are faced with many options, and each option has its own unique capabilities, complications, and costs. I'll discuss these options and more in this chapter and in Chapter 9.

Figure 8.3 shows the type of equipment that typically resides on the spaghetti-link side of a bridge, router, or communications server. The communications adapter might interface with a modem, a multiplexer, or specialized termination equipment for high-speed circuits. In each case, the designers of this equipment typically choose from among three commonly used specifications for serial interconnections, plus a couple of uncommon specifications with special applications. When you string together the devices you need for your circuits, you must make sure that they all conform to the same signaling and connection standard. This seems like a simple concept, but interface problems are easily the most common cause of delay and added cost during the installation of LAN-to-LAN systems.

Figure 8.3

The bridge, router, or communications server might make any of several different serial connections to equipment that will interface to long-distance circuits. These include a simple connection to a modem, connections to a multiplexer, and connections to specialized high-speed circuits.

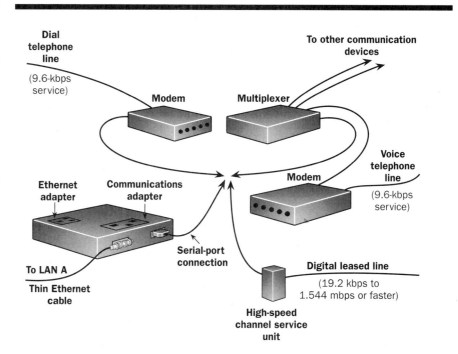

You typically must choose products configured to the EIA RS-232C interface standard, the CCITT V.35 interface standard, or the EIA RS-449 interface standard. These standards describe the types of connectors, the cables, and the electrical signals used on the interconnecting links.

RS-232 Forever

Many have tried to replace it. Organizations ranging from IBM to one-person basement hobby shops have tried exotic implementations. But no one has found a truly universal substitute for the RS-232 standard serial interface.

The Electronic Industries Association (EIA) is a body of U.S. electronics manufacturers that works closely with international organizations like The International Telegraph and Telephone Consultative Committee (CCITT) to establish standards for the interconnection of equipment. In

1969, the EIA established Recommended Standard number 232 in version C, or RS-232C. This interface was adopted by the CCITT as the nearly identical CCITT V.24 standard, supplemented by the V.28 standard for electrical characteristics. The U.S. Department of Defense adopted nearly identical specifications as Mil-Std-188C. The details provided here for RS-232C apply to V.24 and Mil-Std-188C as well. Figure 8.4 shows the pin connections and functions of an RS-232 cable.

Figure 8.4

The RS-232C signaling scheme includes a 25-pin connector with wires specified for certain functions. Few schemes use all of the wires in the full specification. The 9-pin connector saves space on many personal computers and provides full functionality.

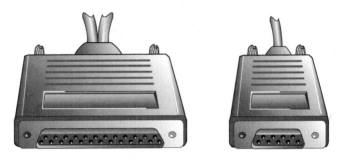

In the 1970s, this standard saw some use as a way to configure the wires linking terminals to minicomputers, and then as a way to link terminals to communications modems (more on modems later). The standard is complex, and the electrical characteristics of the cable it describes restrict the distance and speed to about 50 feet of cable signaling at 19.2 kilobits per second. In the 1970s, the EIA tried to replace RS-232C with a series of specifications for more robust connections called RS-449, RS-422, and RS-423. These three standards define the electrical and mechanical characteristics that are usually known collectively as RS-449. We'll see later how specific types of communications devices use RS-449.

Many companies (even IBM) implement RS-232C in ways that go around, under, and through the original specification. For example, the RS-232C standard—and the RS-232D revision of 1987—describe a 25-pin D-shaped connector between the cable and the chassis of any equipment. For many years, that 25-pin connector was the absolute standard for RS-232C wiring. But when IBM released the IBM PC AT, the developers needed room on the back panel, so they implemented RS-232C through a 9-pin connector, thus creating a huge overnight opportunity for garage-shop operations turning out 9-pin-to-25-pin adapters and cables. Today, it is common to see RS-232C cables with 9-pin connectors, and even with the modular RJ-11 or RJ-45 connectors used for telephone instruments. Getting the right types of RS-232C connectors and cables is only the first interface problem you'll have to overcome.

When you consider the RS-232C standard, you run into two terms that appear whenever you examine communications systems. DTE is an acronym for *data terminal equipment,* and DCE stands for *data circuit-terminating equipment.* The term *data terminal equipment* typically refers to terminals and PCs, while the *data circuit-terminating equipment* encompasses modems, printers, and certain computer ports.

So if you just examine the connection between a communications server and a modem, the connector on the communications server should be wired according to the rules for DTE, while the modem will be wired as DCE. The main difference between DTE and DCE has to do with the wiring of pins 2 and 3 on the connectors. DCE transmits on pin 3 and receives on pin 2, while DTE devices do just the opposite. But various companies designate their products in different ways. It isn't unusual to find a communications card or a PC's serial port wired as DCE.

If you want to connect a device configured as DCE to a modem, you need a cable designed to connect DCE to DCE. The wires on this cable would have to swap or cross over so that pin 2 on one DCE connector connects to pin 3 on the other, with an identical transposition in the other direction. This is often known as a *crossover cable.*

Certain types of network portal devices, like access servers, bulletin board systems, and electronic-mail servers, use RS-232C in an asynchronous mode. This means that each ASCII character travels with special start bits that mark its beginning. These start bits create some overhead on the circuit, but this technique for the synchronization of characters does not require sophisticated circuitry.

A technique that uses the circuit more efficiently but requires relatively sophisticated electronic equipment is called *synchronous* transmission. In a synchronous system, the bits of each data character are sent as a string without a space or break. Each group of bits constituting an ASCII character within the unbroken bit stream is designated or synchronized according to a clock pulse sent on a separate line. The clock pulse, in effect, says "Now!", and the equipment looks for a new character within the data stream. When you connect bridges or routers to leased lines, you typically use synchronous communications circuits. Synchronous connections require a 10-wire cable for an RS-232C connection.

HINT. *Don't pay for more cable than you need. Asynchronous RS-232C links need only an 8-wire cable, and synchronous links typically need only a 10-wire cable.*

The ubiquitous RS-232 interface

👍 **Is available on practically every type of equipment**

👍 **Uses widely available cables and connectors**

👎 **Is often implemented in nonstandard ways**

👎 **Limits signaling (in practical terms) to 38.4 kilobits per second**

V.35 Lingers On

Like RS-232C, an EIA serial standard called V.35 (whose CCITT counterpart is X.27, or V.11) is another example of how standards linger on because they are well known and comfortable. The V.35 standard describes serial connections recommended for a maximum signaling speed of 48 kilobits per second, but it is also used on faster circuits with specially formatted data. In the U.S., V.35 is typically used to connect LAN portal devices to the termination equipment for leased lines that can move data at 56 or 64 kilobits per second.

The V.35 interface uses a 34-pin rectangular connector that is standard throughout the industry (Figure 8.5). Only 16 wires are used in the V.35 cable. In the next chapter, we'll examine a circuit-connection alternative called Switched 56. V.35 is the interface standard for Switched 56 equipment.

Figure 8.5

The V.35 connector is a 34-pin rectangular connector, typically with a sturdy metal hood. Unlike the case with RS-232C, the implementations of V.35 are consistent, and you are not likely to need customized cables.

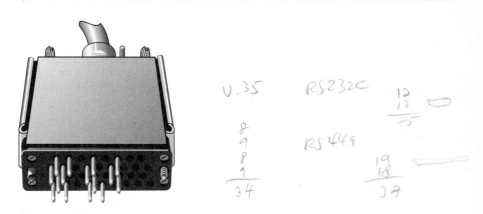

RS-449 Picks Up the Pace

The RS-449 standard describes a robust signaling scheme, with many internal control functions that help in automatic testing and diagnosis. The standard calls for a 37-pin connector, shown in Figure 8.6, that looks like a wide RS-232C connector, but there are major differences between the standards.

The RS-232C system uses a single ground wire, and all signals appear to have a voltage relative to that wire. In RS-449 and its associated RS-422 and RS-423 standards, each signal lead carries its own return wire. The system does not use a common ground. The associated wire pairs in the cable are twisted, just as in the popular unshielded twisted-pair network cable, so they benefit from the electrical shielding effect of twisting.

RS-449 is typically used to connect devices like bridges and routers to the interface equipment for circuits conforming to the popular 1.544-megabit-per-second T1 circuit configuration. The specifications require a system conforming to the RS-449 standard to be able to transmit data at speeds of up to 10 megabits per second at distances up to 40 feet. The specification also allows transmission at 2 megabits per second at up to 200 feet, but depending on the electrical environment surrounding the cable, people often exceed this guideline in their installations.

Figure 8.6

The RS-449 interface specification calls for a DB-37 connection. Because the specification uses matched wire pairs for signaling instead of referencing off a common ground wire as in other systems, all 37 wires are needed in practical cables.

■ Modems and "Muxes"

A variety of equipment can be interposed between the LAN portal devices and the long-distance circuit used to link LANs. The two most typical pieces of equipment are the modem and the multiplexer. *Modems* translate between digital signals and analog signals for transmission over long-distance circuits designed for voice service. *Multiplexers* provide a way for many devices to share a single long-distance connection economically.

There are two types of long-distance circuits you can use to link between LANs: voice (analog) or digital. Voice circuits are designed to carry audible sounds in the form of alternating current. Because of the design of analog systems, the direct-current signals used by network cables and interfaces like RS-232C, V.32, and RS-422 will not pass over the voice lines. So if you want to carry data on circuits designed for voice, you need a device that can turn the digital signals received over the interface into analog signals for the long-distance service. This device is the modem (the name is short for "MOdulator/DEModulator"). A modem translates between the direct-current square waves of the interface (usually RS-232C) and the alternating current representing analog sound on the long-distance circuit.

Modems for dial-up telephone lines typically carry data at signaling speeds up to 14.4 kilobits per second. There are some modems available with a signaling speed of 19.2 kbps, but they have limited application. After you reach the limit of a modem's data-handling capability over analog lines, your next step is typically to use an all-digital service.

As previously stated, you can get long-distance digital transmission service in many ways, including the use of your own cable, microwave, or even satellite links. But typically you will lease digital services from your local telephone company, or from a combination of local and long-distance telephone companies that cooperate to provide service between their various regions. Through the rest of this chapter I'll refer to digital leased-line services, but the information holds true whether you lease the service or install it yourself.

Digital leased-line services take data as direct-current voltages. These lines require special installation to counter the effects of resistance, distortion, and noise, but digital leased lines are readily available in industrialized areas around the world. Instead of a modem, the interface between the LAN communications device and digital leased line is a two-part piece of equipment called a *channel service unit* (CSU) and a *digital service unit* (DSU). I will describe CSUs and DSUs later in this chapter.

Modem Facts

You'll find catalogs full of modems that follow several different signaling standards. Some standards—particularly those labeled as Bell standards, like Bell 103 and Bell 212—date back to the 1970s and have no place in modern LAN-to-LAN connection systems. The CCITT V.32 standard describes how modems should talk to each other, using two-way signaling at 4,800 and 9,600 bps over dial-up telephone lines. A newer version, V.32bis, adds 7,200-, 12,000-, and 14,400-bps transfer rates. (*Bis* is a term meaning *again* or *new version*; it denotes a related standard, not necessarily an extension of the previous version.)

Unfortunately, the V.32 standard did not provide a method for controlling errors during transmission. Since high-speed V.32 signaling is more sensitive to noise and echoes on the telephone line than lower-speed protocols are, you need a hardware- or software-driven error-control scheme to retain accuracy.

Microcom took an early lead in providing error control for modem products by developing its own standard for asynchronous data error control, Microcom Network Protocol (MNP). Versions of MNP Classes 2, 3, and 4 are available in a variety of modems and communications software packages. The software implements the error-control protocols either in an application or in a modem's ROM, and the error checking operates independently of the signaling scheme the modem uses.

In 1989, the CCITT issued a hardware-implemented asynchronous error-control standard called V.42, which describes two error-control schemes. The primary protocol is named Link Access Procedure for Modems (LAPM). The secondary or support protocol is functionally the same as MNP Class 4. If you want to communicate between two modems claiming to be V.42-compliant, you should connect them using the LAPM protocol. If you use one V.42-compliant modem and another compliant with MNP 4, you should employ the MNP 4 protocol. The LAPM method offers slightly better error recovery and reliability than MNP 4.

On synchronous communications links, several synchronous protocols help format and transmit data. These include synchronous data link control (SDLC), High-level Data Link Control (HDLC), and Binary Synchronous Control (bisync). These protocols format the data into blocks, add control information, and check this information to provide error control.

Although the V.42 and MNP 4 protocols help maintain reliability, they do not improve throughput. After you increase the electrical signaling rate as much as possible and improve reliability, the next step in getting the most from the inter-LAN circuit involves data compression. When you compress data to remove redundant elements or empty sections, the time required to send them across the telephone line decreases.

Microcom again led the industry by introducing the MNP Class 5 data-compression protocol. It soon became a feature in many modems and some application programs. Modems supporting the MNP 5 protocol offer the ability to double the effective throughput rate over a communications circuit—provided that both ends of the circuit have the software or hardware to use the protocol.

By the way, there is always a difference between the *signaling speed*, sometimes called the *channel speed*, and the *throughput* in any communications system. The signaling speed describes how fast the bits are encoded onto the communications channel, while throughput describes the amount of useful information going across the channel. If you make the transmitted bits do double or triple duty by compressing the data characters into a kind of shorthand where 2 bits take the place of 6, you can double the throughput without paying for a faster channel speed.

HINT. *Don't confuse signaling speed (channel speed) with throughput. Data compression makes it possible for a modem with a 14.4-kilobit-per-second signaling speed to provide a throughput of nearly 50 kbps.*

In late 1989, the CCITT issued the V.42bis standard, describing a standard method of implementing data compression on the fly in hardware. The V.42bis protocol offers 35 percent greater data compression than MNP 5. For a 9,600-bps modem, this means a potential throughput of 38,400 bps for streams of data with repeating patterns. Fortunately, the most compressible data comes from ASCII files like those created by word-processing and electronic-mail programs, spreadsheet files, and some database files. For most file transfers, you can expect throughput of around 19,200 bps for files not previously compressed by other means.

Understand that the V.32 standard primarily describes the electrical signaling scheme used over the telephone wire. Other standards, such as MNP, V.42, and V.42bis, describe actions taking place above the level of electrical signaling. So you can have modems using different combinations of signaling and error-correction protocols. I strongly recommend that you use modems with V.32bis signaling, V.42 error control, and V.42bis compression for asynchronous links like access servers, bulletin board systems, and asynchronous communications servers. These modems will also offer MNP error detection and file compression as a fallback mode. On certain types of data, this combination will offer error-free throughput at up to 50 kilobits per second over standard dial-up telephone lines or any circuit rated for voice use.

HINT. *If you need a set of modems for an asynchronous LAN-to-LAN link over analog circuits, don't consider anything but modems with V.32bis signaling, V.42 error control, and V.42bis compression.*

The competition in the modem industry created a high degree of interoperability between modems made by different companies. It is always a good idea to use identical modems from the same manufacturer on both ends of a circuit, but it isn't necessary. You can shop for a good price or for good support from among the many competitive products available in the modem industry, confident that modems from different manufacturers will interoperate—as long as they meet the same international standards for signaling, error control, and data compression.

Multiplexers

Communications circuits always have been and always will be expensive. They are often the most expensive part of any LAN-to-LAN link. Because they are costly, it is desirable to have these circuits serve multiple purposes. Up to certain limits, you can share one inter-LAN circuit among several network communications devices by using a device called a *multiplexer* ("mux" for short).

A multiplexer takes the data traffic from several devices—which can be as diverse as a network router and digitized voice telephone—and interleaves them onto one circuit. The designers of multiplexers have developed several different and complex techniques to interleave data in a shared line.

In very simple terms, the multiplexing device can divide the circuit either by using a spectrum of radio frequencies—particularly over a coaxial

cable or fiber-optic cable—or by allocating each station sharing the cable specific time slots for transmission and reception. These techniques are known
as *frequency-division multiplexing* and *time-division multiplexing*. The sophis-
tication of the products using these techniques has led to many elaborations
and refinements. You might hear about synchronous time-division multiplexing, statistical time-division multiplexing, and character-interleaved time-division multiplexing. Each of these techniques has its own advantages and
drawbacks, but statistical time-division multiplexing is the most widely used
in commercial service.

A multiplexer cannot jam more data down the line than it is capable of
carrying, but since a great deal of data traffic comes in bursts, the multiplexer can achieve a high average throughput rate by taking data from several sources, buffering the data, and feeding it into the single connecting
circuit. This ability to have an aggregate speed higher than the composite
speed is typical of the technique called *statistical time-division multiplexing*.

Figure 8.7 depicts a PBX that can make serial connections to many terminals and PCs installed in the building. The PBX can make as many as six
9.6-kilobit-per-second RS-232C connections to an access server on a distant
LAN available through a multiplexer and the circuit termination equipment,
here labeled "DSU/CSU." The access server on the distant LAN makes six
CPUs available for remote control. The connecting long-distance circuit
operates at 56 kbps. While six devices with 9.6-kbps signaling connected to a
single 56-kbps leased telephone circuit could potentially exceed the capacity
of the leased telephone line, in practice each modem circuit is not transmitting at maximum capacity all of the time, so there is plenty of data-handling
capacity left in the circuit.

Unlike the case with modems, which are not terribly sensitive to the
nameplate on the front of the box, you should have a multiplexer from the
same company, and preferably the identical make and model, at both ends of
the circuit. Don't assume that multiplexers from different companies can
interoperate, even if they claim to follow the same multiplexing techniques.

Multiplexers are highly specialized and work only with specific types of
cabling on both the multiple-port side and the high-capacity-circuit side.
Equipment catalogs typically show commercial multiplexers that can link 4,
10, or 16 devices connected by RS-232C cables on one side of the multiplexer with a single communications circuit running at speeds ranging from
19.2 to 56 kilobits per second on the other side. Prices range from about
$1,500 to $2,000 for each device, and you need two for each circuit.

HINT. *Buy your multiplexers, bridges, and routers in pairs, and try to buy
from a company that can provide continued support.*

Figure 8.7

In this diagram, a LAN access server makes its six incoming lines available to a private branch exchange (PBX) in another city. People with PCs connected to the PBX can have direct access to the remotely controlled CPUs on the network on a first-come-first-served basis by dialing a local telephone number on the PBX.

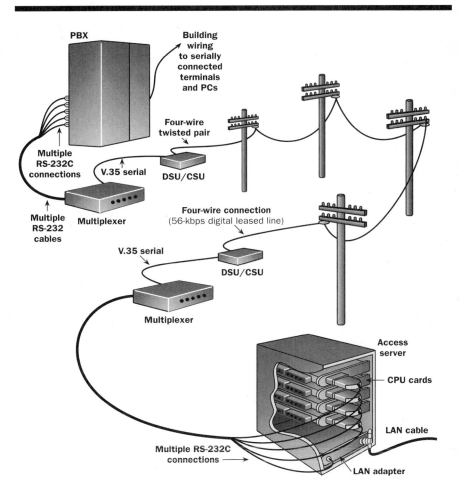

Local multiplexers—those that carry signals over twisted-pair wire out to distances of up to about 5,000 feet—carry price tags in the $400-to-$700 range for each unit. Other slightly more expensive local multiplexers connect to fiber-optic cable with a range of several miles.

■ Digital Circuit Connections

When your needs for data throughput exceed the limit of what you can get from analog lines (approximately 9.6 to 50 kilobits per second, depending on the type of data), you'll need to move up to some type of all-digital service. The next chapter describes the cost and benefit trade-offs of leasing data lines from the local telephone companies and from long-distance telephone companies called *interexchange carriers* (IXCs). This section will focus on the devices and signaling used to connect routers, bridges, and other LAN communications portals to digital circuits.

Speed Versus Cost

A few years ago, the typical leased digital telephone line was used to connect a cluster of terminals to a central mainframe or minicomputer. Using a line conditioned to accept digital signals at a rate of 19.2 kilobits per second made sense in this application. But today, three pressures invalidate that logic.

First, signaling at 14.4 kilobits per second over voice-grade lines with V.32bis modems is very economical. To justify a greater expenditure, the step up from 14.4 kbps must be a big one—bigger than the step to 19.2 kbps.

Second, because of the way modern telephone systems are configured, less equipment is actually required when the telephone companies deliver service in increments of 56 or 64 kilobits per second. For this reason, telephone companies, particularly in the U.S., put a high price on 19.2-kbps leased digital service and charge no more (or little more) for 56- or 64-kbps service.

Finally, while multiplexers are useful on lines with signaling as slow as 19.2 kilobits per second, they prove their value on faster circuits that can service more individual devices through a multiplexer. In the U.S., high-speed data circuits are epitomized by a 1.544-megabit-per-second service called *T1*. While T1 was developed for the telephone industry, and the local and long-distance telephone companies deliver the majority of T1 and higher-speed circuits, you can install your own T1 links across a campus or throughout a building using twisted-pair wire, fiber-optic cable, infrared-light links, and microwave systems.

It's common practice to break down T1 links into subchannels of 64 kilobits per second through a multiplexer. Many organizations find it economical to lease T1 circuits between operating locations to carry both digitized voice and data traffic.

Because the T1 circuit is the basis for much digital leased-line service—both historically and in practice today—and because the connection schemes are practically the same for 56-kbps, 64-kbps, and T1 service, let's take a look at the history, equipment, and logic of T1 technology. The same terms and practices apply for slower services.

T1 Digital Service

The theory and technology of the T1 connection goes back to the late 1950s, when the standards for 1.544-megabit-per-second digital transmission were developed by Bell Labs in an effort to reduce the number of telephone lines installed in underground conduits; the phone companies needed faster service so they could multiplex telephone signals and avoid running separate wires under the street. In practice, however, the T1 connection was not put to use until 1962 in Illinois. There were an estimated 100,000 T1 circuits in use in 1991, and the number is growing at 30 percent per year.

At this point in the story, we have to stop to develop a correlation of terms. *T1* is a term and a standard developed by AT&T and widely used in the U.S. A more generic set of terms and standards, used in the telephone industry in the U.S. and in other parts of the world (but sometimes with somewhat different meanings), refers to a concept called *digital service level*. This is a series of classifications of circuits based on the digital signaling speed the circuits are configured to carry. For example, a *DS-0* line operating at 64 kilobits per second is the fundamental building block of higher-data-rate services. Under the common schemes used to translate analog voice into data signals, 64 kbps will provide one voice channel.

In North America, Japan, Korea, and a few other countries, a leased digital data line specified as *DS-1* carries 1.544 megabits per second (the same as a T1), or 24 multiplexed DS-0 circuits. In the U.K., Mexico, Europe, and other countries that follow the CCITT standard, the term *DS-1* refers to a service providing 2.048 kilobits per second, or 30 DS-0 channels. This DS-1 is also called the E-1 or CEPT (Conference on European Post and Telegraph) standard. Other DS designations and the CCITT designations are shown in Table 8.1.

HINT. *If you do the math, you will notice that 64 kilobits per second x 24 channels = 1.536 megabits per second, not 1.544. In the AT&T multiplexing scheme, every 193rd bit is used for synchronization, so 8 bits are lost to overhead on a T1 (or DS-1) channel. Similarly, on E1 lines, 64 kilobits per second x 30 channels = 1.920 megabits per second. But the E1 line has two additional DS-0 channels for signaling and synchronization; thus, 64 kilobits per second x 32 channels = 2.048 megabits per second.*

Note that there is little correlation between the Digital Signal Number code used predominantly in North America and the CCITT levels used in Europe and other parts of the world. The potential for confusion is high if you don't carefully specify your terms.

The term *T1* denotes a very specific system consisting of two pairs of twisted copper-wire cable, just as you have in your home or office (one pair for sending and one for receiving), and amplifiers or regenerators placed every 6,000 feet—or approximately 1-mile intervals—in order to boost the signal and reduce noise.

Table 8.1

DS and CCITT Designations		
Digital Signal Number	Number of voice channels	Data rate (mbps)
DS-1	24	1.544
DS-1C	48	3.152
DS-2	96	6.312
DS-3	672	44.736
DS-4	4,032	274.176
CCITT level number	Number of voice channels	Data rate (mbps)
1	30	2.048
2	120	8.448
3	480	34.368
4	1,920	139.264
5	7,680	565.148

With the passage of time and the advancement of T1 technology, the distinction between the specific hardware of T1 and the signaling rate of DS-1 becomes even more hidden, and the result is the use of both terms *T1* and *DS-1* to denote the T1 signal, circuits, and services.

T1 Signaling

The technical aspects of how a T1 circuit arrives at your office are identical to those of slower digital leased-line services. On the customer's end, the T1 channel appears as two pairs of twisted wires. Today, the standard hardware connector for the twisted cables is the RJ-48C, which replaced the 15-pin DB-15 physical connector.

The digital signal itself is made up of a stream of 0s and 1s representing the presence or absence of electronic pulses, with a pulse translating into a

1 and the absence of a pulse representing a 0. The pulses are sent at a constant rate of 1.544 megabits per second, which is the basic characteristic of T1 connectivity.

The data stream in a T1 signal consists of a block of 192 bits organized into 24 8-bit words. The 193rd bit is a framing bit used for synchronization. The T1 signal stream also carries a clock, which is used to look at the pulses at a predetermined time in order to make sense out of the seemingly random stream of 0s and 1s and to keep the T1 terminal synchronized with the network. The data communications equipment at both ends of the link and the repeaters that are placed at 6,000-foot intervals track on the clock signal, but a pulse must appear at regular intervals to keep the data synchronized. There is a limit of 15 0s in a row, and at least one pulse must be present at every 8-bit interval; this is called the *1's density* requirement. If the signal carries more than 15 0s in a row, the chances of staying synchronized become increasingly uncertain.

CSU

As Figure 8.8 shows, at the service location, you must provide a device called the *channel service unit* (CSU). This is usually the first piece of hardware the T1 line comes in contact with. The basic job of the CSU is to terminate the digitized T1 signal and perform certain tests and diagnostics to allow the signal to be read by the attached data-communication equipment and the network. You can buy or lease a CSU from many equipment suppliers or the local telephone company. Increasingly, you'll find CSUs integrated into the multiplexers offered by many companies.

The CSU has several main functions with arcane names like loopback, "keep-alive," ESF monitoring, and 1's density. The *loopback* function of the CSU is a type of diagnostic where the transmitted signal is "looped back" to the sending device after passing through the data communications interface or network. The looped-back signal is then compared with the original signal in order to diagnose problems.

The *"keep-alive"* function of the CSU does just what its name implies: It keeps the signal alive when the connected terminal equipment malfunctions or is somehow disconnected. Although there are several ways to do this, the most common is to have the CSU send a constant flow of unframed 1's to the network to keep the T1 circuit functioning.

The *ESF (Extended Superframe Format)* is an AT&T-developed standard for frame synchronization, redundancy checking, and other diagnostic tests of the T1 signal. Some CSUs offer the option of *1's density* monitoring and control. By monitoring the stream of incoming and outgoing pulses, the CSU can insert a 1 if needed to offset a disruptive string of 15 or more 0s.

Figure 8.8

This diagram shows two widely separated locations connected by a dedicated T1 circuit. The well-connected organization represented here moves digitized voice, fax, data for a graphics terminal, and traffic between two LAN bridges over the T1 circuit by dividing the channel through a multiplexer.

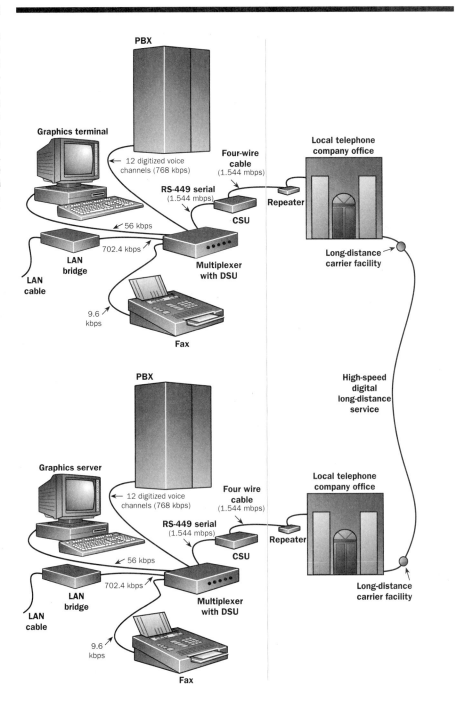

HINT. *The channel service unit (CSU) provides the termination for a T1 line in your office. You'll find CSUs combined with DSUs and with multiplexers in many products.*

DSX-1

The Digital Signal Cross-connect Level 1 (DSX-1) is a set of standards and parameters for cross-connecting DS-1 signals. In the past it was known as the point at which the long-distance carrier's responsibility for the T1 line stopped and the customer's responsibility started, but today that line is drawn at the CSU connection.

The DSX-1 interface defines the voltage limits, pulse width, and size and shape of the connectors. It is located on the customer side of the CSU, while the T1 line interface is located on the network side.

DSU

The *digital service unit (DSU),* or *data service unit* as it is labeled by some companies, is the hardware device that actually transmits the digitized data over the DS-1 signal or line. It connects the customer's data terminal equipment (DTE) to the line carrying the T1 signal.

A DSU converts the signals coming over the synchronous RS-422, RS-232C, V.35, or other interface to a bipolar DSX-1 signal, to be sent out across the T1 connection without the use of a modem. You use a DSU in conjunction with a CSU when your communications equipment lacks the proper digital data interface. If your equipment is intelligent enough to interface directly with the incoming DS-1 line, a DSU is really all you need to connect your equipment with the T1 network. The DSU and CSU functions are often merged into a single device, called either a DSU/CSU or just a DSU or CSU by different manufacturers.

Fractional T1

The idea of a being able to use a full DS-1 leased-line circuit sounds appealing to the organization with the traffic and the bucks to pay for it, but what if you don't need 1.544 mbps worth of channeling capabilities? Local and long-distance telephone companies sell individual DS-0 (64-kbps) circuits. They call this *fractional T1 service,* and it is the logical step for any organization that needs to pass more data than a voice-telephone circuit can handle.

Faster than T1

The ambitious organization looking for faster and bigger data communications links can order T1C and T2 service. The *T1C* link is capable of handling

48 DS-0 basic voice signals, and doubles the bandwidth of the ordinary T1 link. *T2* in turn doubles T1C, and is equivalent to four T1 links. At the top of the pile is *DS-3*, which is equivalent to 28 T1 links. In the next chapter, I'll describe the future of high-speed service and the economies of special services like Switched Multimegabit Data Service and the Integrated Services Digital Network.

■ Making the Links

You must pay attention to detail when you set up the links from a bridge, router, or communications server to long-distance communications circuits. A variety of standards, practices, and options appear at every connection. Keep in mind that money spent on high-quality connection devices usually pays for itself in reduced circuit costs and improved throughput. Now, in the next chapter, we'll look at long-distance circuit alternatives and their costs.

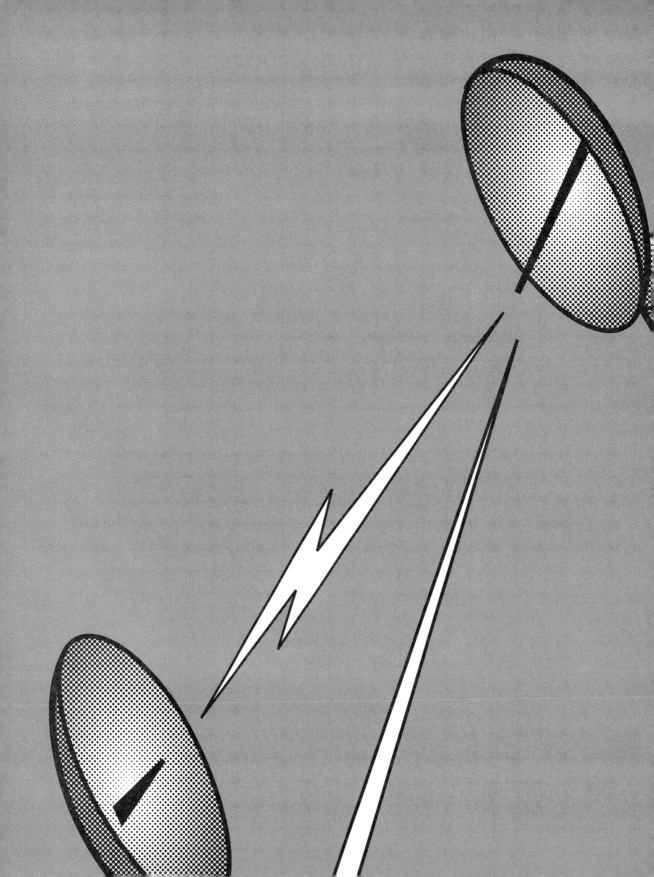

CHAPTER

9

The Medium Carries the Message

- Telephone-Line Systems

- Be Your Own Telco: Bypass

- LEC MANs and WANs

- Options Within Options

Nobody ever said LAN-to-LAN connectivity is easy or cheap. Other chapters in this book describe devices that control the flow of data between LANs, such as bridges, routers, and gateways. But finding, selecting, buying, and installing communications links between the LAN segments is a separate, often challenging, and always costly proposition. When you tackle this job you'll be faced with many options, and each option comes with its own list of capabilities, complications, and costs.

The internetwork circuits available for linking LAN segments run the gamut. They can include everything from telephone lines and satellite networks to microwave radio, fiber-optic networks, and even cable television coaxial systems. The purpose of this chapter is to help you understand your long-distance connection options and evaluate the differences among them in terms of effectiveness, ease of installation, and cost.

You might ask: Why do we need special links between LAN segments? Why can't we just plug in a couple of modems, dial up one LAN segment's modem from the other, and let them talk? The answer is, you can dial up an internetwork connection. In some cases you should. But when the data load is heavy and the duration of the call is long, the cost of this kind of service will be high and the efficiency low. That's why there are special services to meet special needs.

Typically, communications links of over a mile or so move data more slowly than shorter links because of induced noise and degraded signals. As the pulses of electricity or light representing data bits travel long distances through copper or fiber-optic cables, they lose their sharpness and degrade in strength. And as the copper cables travel over longer distances, they accumulate electrical noise. Unfortunately, because the signals needed to represent the 0's and 1's on a fast communications circuit are closely spaced, the equipment cannot tolerate signal degradation or noise in the data stream.

Despite these problems, modern techniques allow the transmission of data at high speed over long distances if you have the physical right-of-way, or path, to make the link. Multiplexers, repeaters, and other special equipment help offset the technical problems. But this equipment is expensive, so the combination of signaling speed and distance works together to increase costs. You can buy and install your own cable for less than $1 a foot to run data at 10 megabits per second for distances of several thousand feet. But you'll have to pay about $15,000 per year to lease a 1.5-megabit-per-second telephone-line link from New York to San Francisco. And you may need to spend several thousand dollars more up front for the equipment to interface your computers to the leased line.

In all of the decisions you make regarding linked LANs, you will have to balance throughput against distance and cost. Because the cost of the internetwork segment is typically the driving factor in the equation, you're usually better off putting a significant investment into network hardware that makes the best use of the long-distance media.

HINT. *Money spent on equipment like routers with compression, which can reduce the costs of communications links, is a good investment.*

■ Telephone-Line Systems

Telephone systems in every country offer the public two general types of connection services: dial-up lines and leased lines. When you *dial* a number, you actually program a computerized telephone switch that creates a temporary circuit between two points. This temporary connection lasts until either party hangs up; then the circuits can be reused for the next call. The second type of service uses a permanently connected line—a *leased line*—offering the user a full-time dedicated connection between two points. The connection is there whether or not you are using it to pass data at any particular moment. This dedicated circuit offers fast access (no dialing or call-setup time) and warranted quality.

Dial Versus Lease

Dial-up telephone lines:

👍 Standard dial-up lines can pass some types of files at 50 kilobits per second

👍 Dial-up lines do not require special installation, and you can control the costs

👍 The long-distance companies have many attractive pricing plans for frequently called numbers

👎 If you call for more than a few hours per day, other services are less expensive

It is important not to overlook the value of ordinary dial-up lines for basic LAN-to-LAN connectivity. Through the use of a modem complying with the CCITT V.32bis standard for signaling and the V.42bis data-compression and error-control standard, the user can effectively transfer e-mail messages and similar compressible files with an effective throughput of 50 kilobits per second or more over dial-up telephone lines.

The deciding factor between dial-up service and leased lines typically is cost. You pay for the dial-up circuit according to how long you use it—usually in 6- to 30-second intervals. The pricing of dial-up lines is said to be *time- and distance-sensitive:* The companies charge according to how long you hold up the circuit and how far apart the connected points are. Each U.S. carrier offers special pricing plans for frequently called numbers, so you might make some very favorable arrangements for dialed LAN-to-LAN calls.

Leased lines have only *distance-sensitive* pricing, so direct cost comparisons with dial-up lines are difficult. The general formula for determining the cost of a leased line is "Cost = base monthly rate + (monthly charge per mile x number of miles)." A good rule of thumb says that if your organization makes daily dial-up connections lasting 3 hours or more, you should consider a leased-line alternative.

HINT. *Consider using dial-up lines for LAN-to-LAN connections, particularly if you connect for less than 3 hours a day.*

Virtualized Service

In a technical market like telecommunications, the companies providing telephone-line services strive to differentiate their products and make maximum use of their resources. Long-distance carriers such as AT&T, MCI, U.S. Sprint, and others resell their switched-line services in ways that make them appear to be full-time dedicated lines. These virtual private data networks (VPDNs) offer the subscriber services equivalent to full-time leased lines at a lower cost, while allowing the various long-distance carriers optimal use of their switched-line systems.

When you subscribe to a VPDN service, the computerized telephone switch is programmed with information about the connection you want to make. When your modem goes "off-hook" on the telephone line, the switch makes the connection to the destination automatically. The appeal of this service comes from the special rates that make it cheaper than using traditional dial-up lines or leased lines over a wide range of connection times and traffic loads.

Switched 56

Switched 56 service:

👍 **Economical**

👍 **Flexible**

🤔 **Probably requires a special communications board in your PC**

A very important service for LAN-to-LAN connectivity is called Switched 56. This service, offered by local and long-distance telephone companies alike, provides signaling at 56 kilobits per second over dial-up telephone lines. The lines going to the customer's location and the local switch serving that location must have specific configurations, and you need special termination equipment, but this service is quickly becoming available throughout the U.S. In the early 1990s, many companies dropped the rates for their Switched 56 service to nearly the same rate they charge for regular long-distance voice calls.

When you order Switched 56 service, the local telephone company terminates a specified telephone line from your building in a special device called a *data line card*, which is installed in the phone company's switching equipment. As Figure 9.1 illustrates, you must buy an interface device for the end of the circuit in your office to communicate with the data line card. Telephone companies sell this device under several different names. They might call it a Digital Data Service (DDS) hub or an Accunet Interface if it comes from AT&T, or a Datapath Meridian Data Unit if it is manufactured by Northern Telecom. Prices vary, but the device costs less than many high-speed modems: $600 to $800.

The major drawback of using Switched 56 service comes from a limitation built into many PCs: an inability to provide a sustained throughput of over 38.4 kilobits per second from the serial port. Many PC systems, particularly some IBM PS/2s, cannot move serial data faster than 19.2 kilobits per second. If you want to use Switched 56 service from a PC acting as an electronic-mail gateway, you'll need a special communications adapter that can handle high-speed throughput using the V.35 connection standard. Such communications adapters are common in bridges and routers, so these devices easily connect to the Switched 56 termination equipment.

Once you have the Switched 56 service configured at all of the locations you want to connect, you create a LAN-to-LAN link that can pass high-speed data simply by dialing the destination number. Switched 56 offers tremendous potential for LAN-to-LAN connectivity, particularly when you don't need full-time connections between LANs.

Ordering Leased Lines

Leasing telephone lines in the U.S. became much more complicated after the 1980 Computer Inquiry II decision by the Federal Communications Commission (FCC) and the Federal Court's Modified Final Judgment (which continues to be modified and is never final). These broke the Bell System apart and imposed stringent guidelines on what services the fractured companies in the telephone industry could provide.

The companies providing local telephone service in the U.S. (the local exchange carriers, or LECs) remain monopolies; they provide all service within territories called their Local Access and Transport Areas, or LATAs. Most people think of the Regional Bell Operating Companies (Ameritech, Bell Atlantic, BellSouth, NYNEX, Pacific Telesis, Southwestern Bell, and U.S. West) and their subsidiaries as the only local exchange carriers. But actually there are hundreds of local telephone companies in the U.S. Some are very substantial, like Contel, and others (like Cincinnati Bell Telephone and Southern New England Telephone) are much smaller but still technically sophisticated. While each LEC has a defined monopoly area, there is hot competition among the long-distance companies (called interexchange carriers, or IXCs) that provide the links between the LECs.

Figure 9.1

A PC configured as a bridge or router—or a standalone bridge or router—connects to Switched 56 terminating equipment over a serial cable using V.35 signaling. This serial connection is typically made through a special communications adapter card, which you have to order as part of the bridge or router. The terminating equipment connects over a two- or four-wire circuit (depending on the manufacturer) to a special data line card installed in the telephone company's switching equipment. The switching equipment makes connections, typically over T1 links, to a similarly equipped switch at the call's destination.

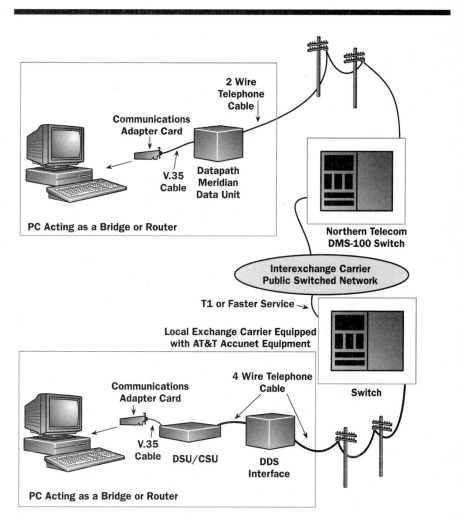

In the U.S., the price schedules the LECs use are regulated primarily by state public-utility commissions and the Federal Communications Commission. AT&T's schedules of prices (tariffs) are regulated by the FCC. Other competing long-distance carriers, like MCI and U.S. Sprint, are not obligated to file a schedule of public tariffs, but they do file tariff schedules to help stay in competition with AT&T's published tariff rates. There are at least eight interexchange carriers that can provide nationwide service, and many more that cover only specific geographical areas.

These different and tightly regulated roles confuse the ordering and circuit-management process. For example, if you want a leased line from Chicago to San Francisco, you can place the order with the local carrier in Chicago (Ameritech), with the local carrier in San Francisco (Pacific Telesis), or, more typically, with one of the long-distance carriers. In any case, the carrier receiving the order must coordinate with the two other carriers to install the service. This coordination sometimes goes smoothly, and sometimes poorly. You could also ask the company installing termination equipment to place the order, or trust a consultant, or place three separate orders yourself.

No matter how you order the circuit, be prepared for finger pointing when you have problems with the circuit, and prepare yourself for billing problems when you don't. The breakup of the Bell System in the U.S. brought with it a dilution of responsibility and a rat's nest of billing problems. The maze of LEC tariffs and IXC charges can result in companies providing widely different price quotes for the same service.

HINT. *Whenever you are ordering leased lines, it pays to shop around for service. Call several IXCs, your local telephone company, and perhaps a consultant for bids.*

Typically, when you need service between two points within the LATA, the ordering and billing process is simpler. Once your service leaves the LATA, however, it is subject to other schedules of tariffs, particularly if the service crosses state lines. There are people who spend their careers tracking the intra-LATA, intrastate inter-LATA, and interstate inter-LATA tariffs. Typically, you have little choice but to trust the price you get in a bid from a local exchange carrier. But later in this chapter I'll describe how you can be your own telephone company and bypass the services of the LEC and perhaps the IXC too.

Countries outside the the U.S. typically have a government-controlled monopoly telephone system that offers users a complete long-distance service package from one source. Unfortunately, it isn't unusual to have to pay thousands of dollars for the installation of a dial-up line, or to wait many months for leased-line service.

Within the U.S., over 6,000 communications consultants deal specifically in setting up the most reliable and efficient telephone service for companies. Clearly this is not a simple task. Typically, the consultants shop the different leased-line vendors to find the best price and best solution for their clients. If you're shopping on your own and want industry-standard performance statistics to help you make a decision, the major carriers can quote a variety of

Leased lines:

- 👍 Leased lines form the backbone of U.S. data communications circuits because they offer high quality with reasonable pricing and reliability

- 👎 The mix of regulated and competitive tariffs that apply to leased lines can result in a wide variety of costs for the same service

reliability measures. They can tell you about error-free seconds and uptime, or the availability of their leased, private-line services.

Digital Service Alternatives

Leased data lines are specially configured or conditioned for data transmission at several signaling rates, from 2.4 kilobits per second to 45 megabits per second. The standard measure of digital leased-line service is referred to as the *T1 channel*. The T1 channel is a circuit with a transmission rate of 1.544 mbps, meeting certain standards and characteristics for circuit termination and signaling. Although usually used for long-distance connections, a T1 channel can be set up between two or more buildings in a campus or between offices in one building, using only local wiring.

With prices of about $10,000 per month for a dedicated T1 connection across a 1,000-mile area and about $6,000 per month for the same line covering 500 miles, the T1 alternative is appropriate for organizations that need to move a lot of data. You'll have added costs for delivery of the service from local telephone companies and for terminating equipment.

For an organization looking for even faster connections, a *T3* link can transfer data at a rate of 45 mbps. This alternative is expensive; it can run the user approximately $100,000 per month for a 1,000-mile connection.

Not only does the subscriber have to pay for the T1 or T3 links, there are additional monthly fees for the LEC connection and for the termination equipment needed to interface the circuit to the computers at the end location. You must consider equipment cost, maintenance fees, and monthly charges when budgeting for T1 or T3 service.

T1 service provides excellent flexibility for managers in organizations with a variety of voice and data requirements. For example, one channel used solely for digitized voice typically requires approximately 64 kilobits per second, and with the proper equipment it can be compressed down to a channel of 32 or even 16 kilobits per second. Thus, you could use 768 kbps of the T1's 1.544-mbps capacity to provide 12 voice lines between your organization's PBXs and use the remaining capacity to carry data via routers, bridges, or other devices for LAN-to-LAN connections.

Interexchange carriers commonly sell fractional T1 service at rates of 384, 512, and 768 kbps. A 1,000-mile 512-kbps service costs about $7,000 per month, plus the fees for terminating circuits and equipment.

HINT. *You can vary the balance of digitized voice and computer data on a T1 circuit hourly, monthly, or as the nature of your business changes.*

Through years of testing at PC Magazine LAN Labs, we found that a typical PC (a 10-MHz 80286 processor) running on an average local area network—for example, Novell's NetWare 2.x—offers users a throughput rate of approximately 750 kilobits per second, so even a fractional T1 line can give a few users LAN-like response times over the long-distance link.

How and What to Order

The task of ordering telephone line services to link LANs can challenge and befuddle even highly competent PC and LAN experts. People in the telephone companies, a term that throws many different kinds of organizations in one generic pot, have a different vocabulary from the typical PC expert. Because of its checkered legal and legislative past, the telephone industry in the U.S. is fragmented along lines that often don't make good practical sense.

The first significant question someone faces when given the task of ordering circuits to link LANs, particularly in the U.S., is, "Whom should I call?" The answer to this question is another deceptively simple question: "Where are the ends of the circuits?"

If the ends of the circuits are in different states, then you clearly should call several of the interexchange carriers to discuss your requirements and get competitive bids. If the ends of the circuits are within the state, then you can try calling your local telephone company (the company that delivers your dial tone) to see if that company is allowed to provide leased-line service to both locations without an intermediary company.

Some local exchange carriers, Pacific Bell for example, offer a circuit integration service. They will provide the local access service, order the long-distance circuit segment, and coordinate the local access circuit on the other end. Because of legal limitations, the local carriers must act as your agent in these actions.

The interexchange carriers can arrange the installation of the connecting links at each end with the appropriate local exchange carriers. The local exchange carriers will bill you separately for the digital access service, and this local access service could be the most expensive part of the overall circuit.

Earlier in this chapter, I described the difference between full-period leased lines, regular voice dial-up lines, and switched dial-up lines like Switched 56 service. Switched 56 kilobits per second service was typically used to back up leased lines; when a leased line failed, the gateway device dialed a preprogrammed number on a Switched 56 circuit to reestablish the connection. However, modern pricing schemes make switched digital services economical and convenient for full-time LAN-to-LAN connections.

Interexchange carriers offer switched 56 kilobit per second, 64 kilobits per second, 384 kilobits per second, T1, and even T3 services under a variety of product names and marketing packages.

For example, AT&T offers Accunet Switched Digital Service at rates of 56 kilobits per second through 1.544 megabits per second. MCI Communications Corporation offers Virtual Private Data Service at speeds up to T3 rates, and U.S. Sprint offers a variety of services under three different names in 64k increments. You can call the interexchange carriers to order these switched digital services or full-period leased-line services.

Reliability

Experienced network administrators know that while computers, bridges, and routers seldom fail, internetwork communications lines fail frequently. When an interexchange carrier suffers a major outage, as such carriers historically have due to fire, high winds, and other types of physical damage, the service for an entire geographical region can go out. When an organization relies on leased lines for production and the conduct of business, any amount of downtime is a catastrophe.

One solution to this problem is the use of separate leased-line circuits from different carriers. With any luck, if the service from one carrier is interrupted, the other one will still be operational. This technique of buying redundant service allows your bridge or router to choose a line that is currently up and available. Some routers offer a backup service for your leased line through the use of a standard dial-up connection. But again, the question of cost comes into play when you are contemplating any remedies for possible downtime.

HINT. *Buying redundant or at least differently routed leased lines from different telephone carriers prevents the total loss of your communications service when one carrier suffers a major outage. You might pay higher fees because you split the service among different carriers, but think of it as good insurance.*

■ Be Your Own Telco: Bypass

In the U.S. there is a way to avoid the finger-pointing and billing problems between IXCs and LECs. As shown in Figure 9.2, you can use a technique called *bypass* to act as your own telephone company, go around the LEC, and set up your own private connection to the IXC's nearest service point (known as a point of presence, or PoP). Sometimes this is as simple as installing your own $20,000 microwave link over a path a few blocks long. In other situations, it is a very expensive alternative, especially when the IXC's PoP is far away from your facility and you need high-speed connections. Other metropolitan-area-network communications systems—such as FDDI, described below—also allow you to bypass the local exchange carrier.

Figure 9.2

You can act as your own telephone company, bypassing the services of the traditional telephone providers at several levels. You can bypass the local exchange carriers (LECs) by using your own microwave system, or by using FDDI or coaxial-cable services provided by some other company. You can bypass both the LECs and the interexchange carriers by using your own satellite system.

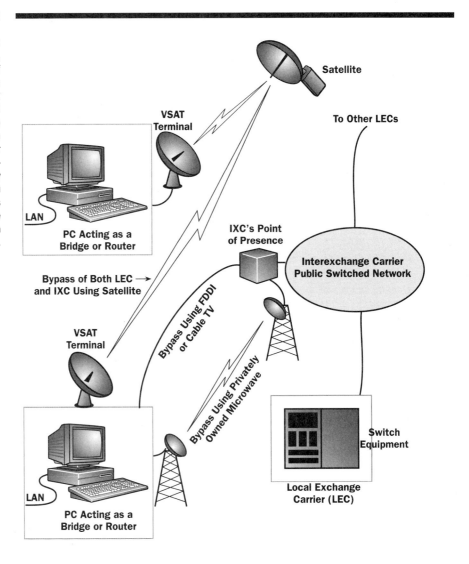

If you want to own your own communications service in a big way, many companies as diverse as Chrysler Corp. and Wal-Mart have found it practical to bypass both the LEC and the IXC and to establish their own private data networks using communications satellites and a small Earth terminal at each operating location. Let's look at both long-distance and local bypass.

Satellite Communications

Instead of leasing long-distance circuits from the telephone carriers, you can use your own private satellite radio system to carry data between widely separated enterprises. Offering services to the subscriber ranging from on-call emergency backup to full-time dedicated point-to-point service at data rates from 19.2 kbps to speeds comparable to multiple T1s, companies like Alascom, AT&T, Comsat World Systems, GTE Spacenet Corp., and others sell complete satellite communications solutions to private industry and government.

Communications satellites move in a geosynchronous orbit at the equator about 23,300 miles above the Earth. From this position, the individual satellites can receive data and relay it to large segments of the Earth. This orbital vantage point gives communication satellites a large advantage over the land-based leased-line systems. The satellite connection is safe from the problems that plague connections on terrestrial circuitry, such as physical disruption by accident or by natural disaster. The IXCs often use satellites to back up their copper-wire and fiber-optic-based systems.

Satellite circuits do not carry distance-sensitive pricing. The companies providing these services charge for the time of connection and the amount of information passing through their satellites' transponders. Another rough rule of thumb says that satellite communications are usually cost-effective only if used for connections over a distance of 500 miles or more, but large systems gain an economy of scale that makes it reasonable to use satellite communications for shorter links.

Important features of satellite communications systems include their ease of installation and their independence from the standard telephone-line cabling system. Satellite systems providing LAN-to-LAN links can use very small aperture terminals (VSATs) with antennas that measure approximately 1.2 to 2.8 meters in diameter (3.9 to 9.2 feet). Each VSAT antenna mounts on a rooftop, in a parking lot, or on a vehicle, allowing for excellent flexibility and easy installation. A simple cable runs from the satellite terminal to the office or building housing the LAN.

No communications system is perfect, and satellite links have their share of drawbacks. The first drawback is the need for bigger antennas if you want faster throughput. The second drawback of satellite communications is what is commonly called *satellite delay*.

The least expensive of the available VSATs normally provide a signaling speed of only 19.2 kbps. While this speed may be adequate for many applications, it is not very useful for transporting large amounts of data between LANs. To increase the signaling rate to T1 speeds, the user must install a larger and more expensive antenna—typically 3 to 4 meters—but the antenna size and circuit speed also depend on the geographical location of the station and the surrounding radio-frequency environment. If your antenna is in a noisy electrical environment, it will have to be bigger to capture more of the satellite's signal and block out the local electrical noise.

HINT. *You want to buy a satellite antenna only once, so make sure the antenna supports the service you'll need over the life of the contract.*

Satellite systems:

👍 **Offer easy installation**

👍 **Remain operational even when many other circuits are disrupted by disaster**

👎 **Can be costly for small organizations**

👎 **Introduce delay that is intolerable in some applications**

The problem of satellite delay is a problem of basic physics. Due to the great distances involved, even at the speed of light it takes 0.27 seconds for the signal to travel from the antenna to the orbiting satellite and back again. This delay is acceptable for intermittent updates for electronic mail, spreadsheets, and the like, but it provides a long delay to users expecting immediate replies to their individual keystrokes and commands.

A typical monthly charge using Scientific-Atlanta's SkyLinX.25 or SkyLinX Express ranges from $250 to $600 per site; another competitor, Hughes Network Systems, offers LAN connectivity solutions at between $380 and $450 per month per site, including installation and maintenance fees. Some VSAT systems are economical only for large systems with 200 ground terminals—certainly a solution limited to large organizations. But it is possible to share a satellite network with other companies to make networking economical even with only a few ground terminals.

HINT. *If you think you can't afford your own satellite-based network, ask about sharing the satellite service with other small organizations.*

Metropolitan-Area Networks (MANs)

Some LAN-to-LAN links don't have to traverse hundreds or thousands of miles. In many cases, organizations only need to link LANs across a campus or city. The limited distances of metropolitan-area networks (MANs) allow higher-speed communications. For planning purposes, you can think of a metropolitan area as a circle with a 100-kilometer (62-mile) circumference.

You can bypass the LEC with a MAN you set up yourself, share MAN services with other organizations in a private enterprise, or buy services from the MAN companies already operating in many cities.

A technology called Fiber Distributed Data Interface (FDDI) is the basis of wide-area fiber-optic service offered in several cities by private companies. You can set up your own FDDI network across a campus or a town, using it exclusively for the needs of your organization or sharing it with other organizations in the area that also need to move data.

The FDDI networks operate at speed of 100 megabits per second, although design constraints limit the maximum throughput to about 80 megabits per second. The FDDI networks are limited to approximately 100 km. of cable in each section, and the nodes must be within 2.5 km. of each other. Typically, the FDDI networks will serve as the backbone of communication services available in the area. FDDI networks will eventually serve as a gathering point for traffic that will in turn be fed to services offering more geographical coverage, like the Distributed Queue Dual Bus metropolitan-area networks described later.

The logical topology of the FDDI architecture is based on two rings of fiber-optic cable, the primary and the secondary rings, as shown in Figure 9.3. These rings are connected in a physical hub topology similar to the standard IEEE 802.5 Token-Ring architecture. All the nodes must be attached to the primary ring but, since the secondary ring typically serves as a backup for the primary ring, economics might dictate that some nodes do not get an attachment to the secondary node.

Products like BICC Data Networks' ISOLAN FDDI/802.3 bridge and the Raycom 5600 Series FDDI System use FDDI to link LAN segments. These bridges are attached to both the primary and secondary rings of the FDDI in order to move data between the Ethernet LANs while providing full FDDI fault-isolation capabilities to the LAN segments. Due to the large data-carrying capacity of the FDDI inter-LAN segment, routers are not necessary, and bridges can be used in their place with much the same effectiveness. Unfortunately, the FDDI bridges currently available are relatively expensive, thus making their independence from the expensive routers a catch-22 situation. For example, the ISOLAN FDDI/802.3 bridge is priced at over $22,000.

Even those companies known for their leased lines sell FDDI products. For example, AT&T's StarWAN products include everything from LAN hardware interfaces to multiport bridges specifically for FDDI networks.

FDDI:

👍 **FDDI provides fast and reliable data transfer**

👍 **While it is great for LAN-to-LAN connectivity in a campus or MAN environment, FDDI is also practical for desktop-to-desktop networking in heavy-data-load systems**

👎 **FDDI is not cheap; connectors, transceivers, and cable remain expensive**

FDDI technology should prove to be an excellent asset for connecting networks in a metropolitan area. Because they use fiber-optic cabling, FDDI systems are free of the normal electrical noise and interference gathered by copper cables. This independence from interference allows FDDI cables to be installed in ways and places impossible for copper wires. Because fiber cables are much thinner than copper, they are also a good choice for installation in the overcrowded conduits found in many cities and individual buildings.

Figure 9.3

The FDDI hub topology uses a primary ring for data and a secondary ring as a backup. In this simplified diagram, one node is not on the secondary ring and cannot benefit from its redundancy. On the other hand, a node with a single connection has a lower cost for installation and equipment.

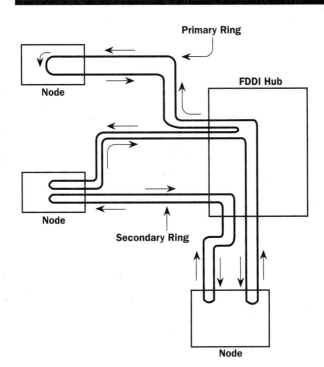

Other Metropolitan Bypass Solutions

In today's high-tech environment, you should not limit your search for efficient MAN connectivity to the major communications companies. You can buy services for LAN-to-LAN connectivity from some unlikely vendors. For instance, some cable television companies have installed two-way coaxial links that can handle data. Many railroads are equipped with fiber-optic cable installed along with the tracks; companies use gas pipelines for fiber installations, and some television companies offer their excess microwave capacity for use with LAN-to-LAN connections. Many specialized companies, such as Diginet Communications and Metropolitan Fiber Systems, offer solutions for connecting LANs in various cities throughout the nation.

For the independent-minded consumer, companies including M/A Com, Microwave Networks, and Motorola offer ways for you to set up your own microwave radio system, as shown in Figure 9.4, for connecting networks within a metropolitan area. If you can find a line-of-sight vantage point for a microwave antenna, you can aim and shoot data between two locations at throughput speeds of up to 1.544 mbps. Microwave radios generally operate at a frequency of 23 gigahertz and are limited to a distance of 3 to 5 miles between antennas. You can expect to pay about $20,000 for the hardware, but there are no other fees.

Figure 9.4

You can set up your own microwave radio system in a window or on a rooftop to carry data at T1 rates over distances of several miles.

Photonics has a product called Building-to-Building Photolink that can carry data over line-of-sight distances up to 600 feet by using light beams. The transceivers used in Building-to-Building Photolink are specially tuned to operate in the direct sunlight that could interfere with window-to-window operation. A pair of transceivers for Building-to-Building Photolink sells for $3,990.

HINT. *If you only need to link LANs a few hundred feet or a few thousand feet apart, then look at setting up your own optical or microwave systems. They are easily installed and very practical.*

■ LEC MANs and WANs

The local exchange carriers understand the threat of privately owned bypass facilities, and they have a confusing series of high-speed data offerings in the works for metropolitan-area services. These offerings, like the Integrated Services Digital Network (ISDN), start out as WANs and are planned for expansion to international coverage by the mid-1990s.

IEEE 802.6 Distributed Queue Dual Bus (DQDB)

In early 1990, the IEEE 802.6 committee approved a standard protocol for MANs. This standard is called the Distributed Queue Dual Bus (DQDB) and involves a physical topology based on the idea of two parallel cables linking each pair of nodes in the system. The standard specifies fiber-optic cables. The nodes on the cable will typically be routers that connect the LAN segments. The dual-cable topology offers its users a reassuring level of reliability while operating at high speeds over the MAN. The signaling is 100 mbps, a speed capable of handling almost any application or data transfer.

While some private companies will implement their own IEEE 802.6 MANs, the major service will be provided by the local exchange carriers. Bellcore, a research agency for the Regional Bell Operating Companies, has designed a system called Switched Multimegabit Data Service (SMDS) that follows the IEEE 802.6 standard.

SMDS (Switched Multimegabit Data Service)

SMDS will be offered to customers at T1 speeds and above; it is designed to be used in virtual private data networks and large public networks. With SMDS capabilities, you can dial any computer in the world if it has an SMDS address, even if it is not normally a part of your own network. In effect, this makes the dial tone for data universal.

Some of the Regional Bell Operating Companies suggest that SMDS tariffs will be similar to private lines. But until the tariffs are set, there is no way to pinpoint the costs. SMDS is a service very different from what the local exchange carriers typically offer. The whole technology of the telephone system has been based on service switched through a central office. SMDS is a nonswitched service, but one that the local exchange carriers must have to stay competitive. The emerging tariff structure of SMDS is critical for its commercial success.

The seven Bell companies plan a three-phase introduction of SMDS; the first phase started in 1991, and the final stage is proposed for 1995. Phase 1 defines the service that provides wide-area connectivity within LATAs. Phase 2 will include the specification of interfaces between local exchange and interexchange carriers. After implementation of this phase, SMDS will be able to operate both nationally and internationally. This phase will also introduce features allowing users to manage and monitor the operation of the SMDS network, within limits.

Phase 3 of the deployment of SMDS will rely on a technology called SONET, or Synchronous Optical Network. SONET is a family of standards calling for high-speed transmission rates, up to 13.22 gigabits per second.

SMDS has several advantages over other technologies—including FDDI. SMDS has no real distance limitation. In SMDS's full maturity, users will be able to communicate nationally and internationally. FDDI's use of Token-Ring media-access control limits the perimeter of the FDDI ring to just 60 miles, typically described as a campuswide environment.

SMDS is more adaptable to existing communications technology. It is a carrier-provided service and will require few changes to customer equipment. FDDI works more effectively in dedicated fiber-line environments, while SMDS is based on standard public-network speeds.

The prospects for the success of SMDS brightened in mid-1991 when a consortium of internetworking and WAN vendors announced nonproprietary interface specifications for SMDS termination equipment. The proposed interface standard would allow routers to connect directly to SMDS networks through standard DSU and CSU products. This approach will allow practically all existing products such as bridges and routers to connect to SMDS services as soon as they become available.

ISDN

Another inter-LAN connectivity alternative, available in a growing number of metropolitan areas, is the Integrated Services Digital Network (ISDN). ISDN is an international program designed to digitize the telephone systems and eliminate all analog voice lines. ISDN should have been in place in the U.S. in the mid-1980s. However, factors such as excessive marketing emphasis on the ability to identify incoming callers and an astronomical price for PC ISDN adapter cards have prevented the service from becoming popular in those metropolitan areas where it has been offered. Now, the future of ISDN ranges from cloudy to dim. Services such as virtual private data networks, Switched 56, and SMDS draw potential users away from ISDN or cause them to sit on the sidelines until the situation sorts itself out.

ISDN is a broader strategy than SMDS. Its goal is to provide digital service on all lines, while SMDS provides specialized subscription service at much faster speeds than the present ISDN. The proponents of ISDN claim that services such as Switched 56 and ISDN can interoperate. I've seen the diagrams and the technical specifications, but I can't suggest that you trust your corporate data to that kind of system anytime in the mid-1990s.

For local service, the ISDN architecture divides the available bandwidth into three data channels. Two of the channels move data at 64 kilobits per second. The third channel operates at 16 kbps and provides a path for telephones to send requests to the ISDN switch while moving data from applications at full speed on the data channels. In ISDN systems, the 64-kbps data channels are called B-channels, and the slower 16-kbps signaling channel is a D-channel. The typical type of desktop ISDN service is called 2B+D or *basic-rate* service. Figure 9.5 illustrates how ISDN service connects PCs in a typical office environment.

The typical connection between a PC and the ISDN system is through a serial port on a special ISDN telephone. This telephone converts voice into data (and vice versa) and provides a serial-port connection, typically at 19.2 kilobits per second. That connection speed is acceptable for remote terminals passing keystrokes to a mainframe, but it has little value for networked PCs. To make ISDN really useful for networked PCs you need an internal adapter card that can handle the two 64-kilobit-per-second ISDN B-channels.

Unfortunately, the few companies making the internal PC adapters for ISDN are faced with high-priced special chip sets and components. Because the components cost so much, the adapters cost well over $1,000 each through retail channels. This price level is unacceptable to most organizations; when a 10-megabit-per-second LAN adapter costs less than $200, it's difficult to justify buying $1,000 adapters. Thus the ISDN PC adapter business is stuck in a self-destructive pricing loop: The vendors are waiting for volume sales to reduce costs so they can cut prices, but at the present price levels the volume will not develop.

People who are used to reading about 10-mbps Ethernet and 16-mbps Token-Ring might assume that ISDN is slow by comparison, but LAN schemes like Ethernet and Token-Ring use sophisticated media-access protocols to control the access of each node to the cable. LAN nodes must wait, retry, repeat, and perform many overhead tasks to share the cable. ISDN provides dedicated channels for data transfer.

Because an ISDN telephone call is digital, the phones and switches can pass a lot of information about the call. The people who market ISDN services have focused on a feature called *incoming caller ID*, or ICLID. This feature has become controversial and is the subject of legislation in some states and Congressional hearings. The market would benefit if the ISDN community would refocus on moving data as a more lucrative and less flammable way to sell services.

Today, ISDN is available only in segments of major cities in the U.S., although it is becoming available more rapidly in Europe and parts of Asia. Some LECs in the U.S. have not even developed tariff schedules for ISDN services, so potential buyers have legitimate concerns about costs.

Microcom markets the MND/5500 ISDN LAN Bridge with a retail price under $10,000. If you can get ISDN service and want to use an interesting technology, this product is one of the few in the ISDN arena that makes good sense today.

ISDN:

👍 Offers flexible connections between PCs throughout a wide area at 64 kilobits per second

👍 Provides flexibility for the integration of digitized voice and data

👎 Requires overly expensive adapters for the PC

The future of ISDN might be in the development of a much faster service called *Broadband ISDN,* or BISDN, which will move data at a basic rate of 34 megabits per second over IEEE 802.6/SONET circuits. However, companies have had so many problems fielding economical PC communications adapters for 64 kilobits per second that the promises about BISDN seem hollow.

If you manage a group of PCs in one of the increasing number of geographic areas with ISDN service, you need to know how this alternative might serve you to link PCs, mainframes, and existing LANs across the miles, and eventually across thousands of miles, with fast digital service. Today ISDN is economical mainly for linking LANs, primarily on an experimental basis, but in the near future it may replace and displace today's traditional local area network in many installations. The key is in the intelligent pricing of PC adapter cards for ISDN and in strong marketing of the service. Your local exchange carrier is the best source of information about ISDN in your area.

■ Options Within Options

As you can see, your inter-LAN circuit choices are driven by interacting variables of distance, speed, flexibility, and cost. You have to factor *how much* data you have to move *how far* over *what increment of time*. For example, if you use mail gateways to move messages between LANs, they don't require high-speed links. Dial-up voice lines or leased lines running at 19.2 kilobits per second will support the e-mail needs of large organizations.

Figure 9.5

ISDN carries voice and data over standard telephone lines digitally. Several different rates of service, each combining 19.2- and 64-kilobit-per-second signaling, can link subscriber locations and the central telephone equipment. PCs with ISDN terminal adapters and special telephones with RS-232 connections can combine voice and data on the same desktop.

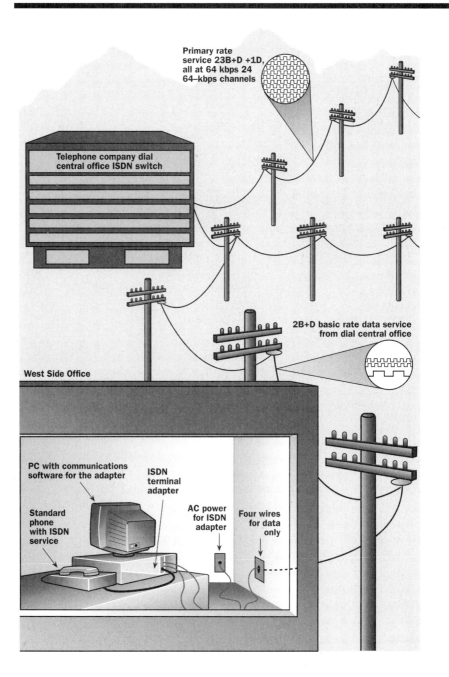

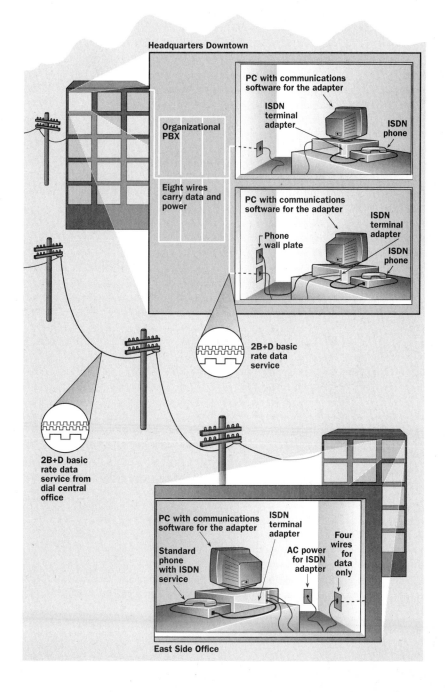

Headquarters Downtown

PC with communications software for the adapter

ISDN terminal adapter

ISDN phone

Organizational PBX

Eight wires carry data and power

PC with communications software for the adapter

Phone wall plate

ISDN terminal adapter

ISDN phone

2B+D basic rate data service

2B+D basic rate data service from dial central office

PC with communications software for the adapter

ISDN terminal adapter

AC power for ISDN adapter

Four wires for data only

Standard phone with ISDN service

East Side Office

If you are using bridges or routers to carry the traffic between LANs, the applications running on the network will determine the types of links you need. Even a few people transferring large graphics files, such as those used in medical imaging, can force the use of high-speed links operating at 1.544 megabits per second or better. By contrast, when many people on one LAN segment are updating a database on another LAN segment, they don't move much traffic, but they need to move it quickly to avoid long waits for data-entry screens.

Devices that typically use asynchronous modems and dial-up lines—such as access servers, wide-area information transfer systems, and bulletin board systems—can use fractional T1 channels through a PBX to carry data economically between two locations. But since these access servers and bulletin boards typically serve traveling members of the organization, it might be appropriate to equip them with toll-free 800 numbers from the public dial-up network for easy access.

Deciding on the best service for LAN-to-LAN connectivity is not an easy task. It requires careful collection of information and planning for both present and future requirements.

X.25 and Frame-Relay Inter-LAN Connections

- Gaining Flexibility and Reliability

- Packet-Switching Systems

- Make-or-Buy Decision

- Frame Relay

- Pick a Technology

You don't get very far into the subject of LAN-to-LAN connectivity without hearing the term *X.25*. In this chapter I will describe private and public inter-LAN connection schemes that use the X.25 protocol. We'll also look at a new and simpler technology called *frame relay* that augments and often displaces X.25.

From the previous chapters you know that you can create your own network of interlaced leased digital telephone lines, switched 56-kilobit services, microwave circuits, or even satellite links to join your LANs. You can also effectively use bridges or, more typically, routers with multiple ports so that a given device can send a packet or a frame over one of two routes to different destinations. It's possible to build a network with great redundancy by using multiport routers and either a star, branching, or ring physical topology.

Figure 10.1 illustrates the different classic circuit topologies. Assuming a corporate headquarters in New York with regional and branch offices in other cities, you could arrange all communications circuits in a star topology, a branching configuration, or a ring. The *star* topology offers centralized management, but its economics depend on how traffic typically flows; if most data does not flow directly to the New York headquarters, this topology requires too much repeating activity to move data between the outlying offices. The *branching* topology can be both expensive to install and difficult to administrate, but if the data flows from field offices to regional headquarters to national headquarters, then this arrangement makes sense. The *ring* topology offers flexibility and reliability because of its alternative routing capabilities. The *spoke-and-ring* topology, an augmentation of the classic ring, is used when reliability is paramount.

■ Gaining Flexibility and Reliability

Creating a network of fixed long-distance circuits provides a good way to link a few locations. But this type of system has three major drawbacks: rapidly increasing complexity, lack of flexibility, and less than optimal leveraging of alternative connection routes.

As the number of locations and the number of circuits in an inter-LAN system grow, the planning, administration, and management of the system increase geometrically. Managing the efforts of the companies providing the equipment and service, ordering the right circuits with the right capacity, and monitoring the minute-by-minute operation are all important actions that will occupy the time of employees or paid consultants.

Figure 10.1

The star, branching, and ring topologies are classic ways to arrange communications circuits, but they appear in real-life installations too. The spoke-and-ring topology, used in some specialized wide-area networks, provides very high reliability.

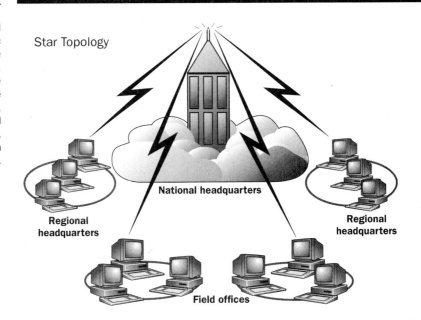

Star Topology

National headquarters

Regional headquarters

Regional headquarters

Field offices

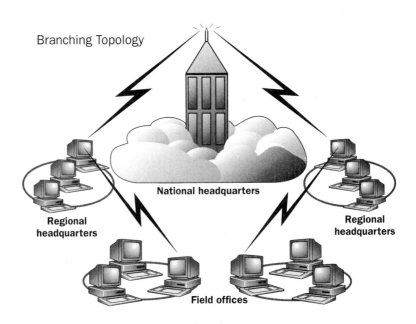

Branching Topology

National headquarters

Regional headquarters

Regional headquarters

Field offices

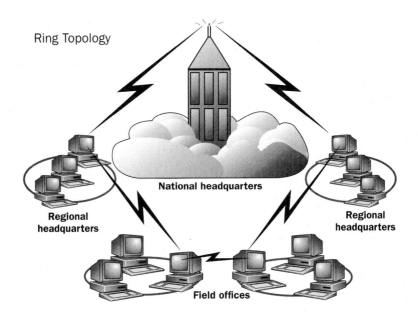

Ring Topology

National headquarters

Regional headquarters

Regional headquarters

Field offices

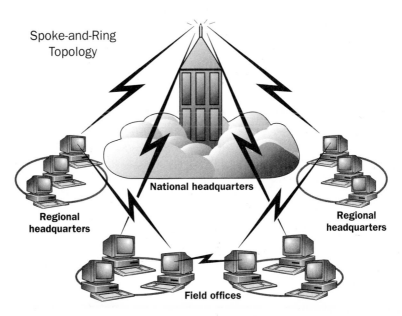

Spoke-and-Ring Topology

National headquarters

Regional headquarters

Regional headquarters

Field offices

When you are planning the circuits in an inter-LAN system, the shortest distance between two points, A and B, is always the most desirable path. But it's also reassuring to know that your data can travel from A to C and on to B if the primary route is out of operation or congested. Unfortunately, planning for that alternative path is often difficult. It isn't easy to set up a router as a relay point, and this kind of operation takes away from the router's primary job of acting as a network portal.

If you want the best flexibility and overall network reliability from your investment in inter-LAN circuits, you'd be wise to make them part of a network that dedicates computing power to network routing and management tasks. This type of system breaks the streams of data going between LANs into small groups called *packets* or *frames*. Each packet is routed on a millisecond-by-millisecond basis via the most economical or efficient route.

■ Packet-Switching Systems

Packet switching is one of three major switching techniques in communications systems. The other two techniques are *circuit switching* and *message switching,* also called *store-and-forward switching.*

You use circuit switching every time you make a telephone call. The lines the call traverses are dedicated between you and the person you called and remain fixed until you hang up. These lines are unavailable to anyone else, even when neither party is talking, until the call is completed.

In store-and-forward switching, the complete message, like a Western Union telegram, is sent from switch to switch. When the message reaches the destination switch, it is either printed out or stored until someone disposes of it. Your voice answering system is an example of the store-and-forward concept.

Each switching technique has its own advantages. Circuit switching makes the circuit's full throughput available throughout the duration of the connection. However, if the connection is broken, it can be difficult to reestablish contact in a timely manner. Store-and-forward switching works well for certain types of traffic, but it can't handle real-time interaction or messages with immediate time sensitivity. Packet switching offers an excellent combination of flexibility and reliability, thanks to immediately available redundant connections. The two drawbacks of packet switching are the high overhead in the channel, caused by all the routing and management information attached to each packet or frame, and the need for specialized computer systems to handle the network activity.

The most widely used internationally agreed-on protocol for packet switching is X.25. The CCITT X.25 standard was first adopted as an international standard in 1976 and has been revised and updated every four years since. The X.25 protocol describes how data communications devices like bridges and routers package data into specially addressed and configured packets, and how the computers acting as packet switches route these packets through a network.

You can use X.25 data packaging and routing over any of the terrestrial, satellite, or MAN communications circuits described in the previous chapter—even if you don't have an extensive network of circuits. Establishing your own point-to-point links using packets conforming to the X.25 protocol has several advantages: Equipment is readily available, the protocol includes error control, and if you start with X.25 point-to-point links, you can later install your own computers acting as X.25 switches for $5,000 to $25,000 each when you want a larger multipoint network with more features.

Packet switching breaks messages into small bundles or packets (for instance, 128 characters). These packets are sent out as they are built in a *packet assembler/disassembler* device or *PAD*. A PAD may be nothing more than a special kind of adapter board with its own processing capability and software. A PAD can reside in a PC, and Hayes Microcomputer Products even builds a PAD into the V-Series Smartmodems. The packets coming from a PAD are interleaved on a circuit with packets from other sources to make maximum use of the available bandwidth.

The X.25 protocol details a specific exchange of packets that has to precede the passing of information. This exchange establishes what is called a *virtual circuit* from the sender to the destination. Many virtual circuits can exist simultaneously on the network.

A *call request packet* is sent to the requested host, which can grant permission for the exchange by issuing a *call accepted packet*. The call is set up and information exchanged in the form of packets that contain addressing information. Of course, these packets also contain the actual data that the sender wishes to transmit.

The call is ended when a *call clear packet* is sent and a *clear confirmation packet* is received in acknowledgment. Each packet in this exchange has a specified structure, and each field is defined. Special *reset* and *restart* packets add to the robustness of X.25. These, along with other prescribed packets such as the *diagnostic packet,* make X.25 extremely versatile and easy to use.

X.25 networks:

- Offer high reliability

- Provide multipoint flexibility

- Meet the need for temporary and permanent virtual-circuit connections

- Carry heavy overhead in the form of setup and control information, slowing useful throughput

- Require powerful computers running complex software to act as switches

Because networks based on the X.25 protocol insure the accuracy of the data they carry and because they can offer other associated services, they are called *value-added networks* or VANs. As Figure 10.2 shows, X.25 packet-switched VANs route each packet to any destination on the fly, creating the ability to link thousands of locations simultaneously. You see this best in networks like CompuServe, where people calling in from locations around the world simultaneously communicate with and through the central database computers.

■ Make-or-Buy Decision

People who must transport goods or material in the course of business have the option of acquiring their own trucks and hiring their own drivers or contracting the services of another company to move their goods. The choice between owning and contracting for a transportation capability depends on many factors, including the volume of traffic, the distances and territories involved, the funds available, and the managers' attitude toward long-term investment. Exactly the same factors apply to data transportation.

You can choose to lease your own inter-LAN circuits, buy your own computers equipped with packet-switching software, and establish your own packet-switching network system. If you have more than a few nodes on the network, you will get better flexibility, better overall reliability, and more efficiency than you would get from a network of leased lines and routers. But if you don't want to be in the business of running your own packet-switching system, several companies will provide this kind of service for you on an economical shared basis.

The companies selling data-transportation services are known as *public data networks* or PDNs. They will accept your data at access points near you, route it to its destination, provide protection along the way, and guarantee its delivery. PDNs provide an economical way for many organizations to link their LAN segments, particularly when traffic flows between multiple locations.

PDNs consist of networks of computers interconnected over telephone lines that often span much of the globe. The computers within the PDN act as switches, routing packets on the fly between the various points where the customers access the network.

Some PDNs lease the connecting circuits between their switches from the long-distance telephone carriers, and some PDN companies—notably AT&T and U.S. Sprint—are major long-distance carriers in their own right. Other major PDNs include CompuServe, Datapac, General Electric,

Infonet, and Tymnet. These companies provide services that can carry your data throughout North America and Europe and, in some cases, to many other portions of the world.

Please note that this list does not include all the PDN vendors you might find in your area. Almost all of the local exchange carriers—the local telephone companies—have X.25 PDN offerings within their service areas, and private companies might also offer city-wide or regional data networks. In countries outside the United States, government monopolies often offer PDN services. In many countries, PDN service is much more readily available than digital leased-line service.

HINT. *In the United States, you can subscribe to X.25 services from many companies. Outside the U.S., you must often work with a monopoly, at least for local access.*

When we evaluated a selection of PDN companies at PC Magazine LAN Labs, we provided each company with a scenario for the connection of four LAN segments located throughout the United States and asked them how they would recommend connecting the segments together. Here is the scenario depicted in Figure 10.3:

New York (national headquarters)	A 24-hour-a-day operation with a high volume of data. This office transfers 10 million characters of data daily at a speed of either 56 or 64 kilobits per second.
San Francisco (regional office)	An 18-hour-a-day operation (no weekends) with a moderate data rate. San Francisco moves 2.5 million characters daily at either 9.6 or 19.2 kilobits per second.
Seattle (branch office)	A 10-hour-a-day operation with a low to moderate data rate. This office moves 1 million characters daily at 9.6 kilobits per second.
Dallas (branch office)	This office has a low-volume data rate and operates for merely 2 to 3 hours daily. It transfers 30,000 characters daily at 9.6 kilobits per second.

Figure 10.2

The software in each computer that acts as a packet switch tries to route packets over the most direct route to the destination. But if line outages or congestion block one route, the software will route through one or more switches to the destination. When LANs are connected through dial-up lines to a PAD within the network, the data is protected only by MNP4 or V.42 error checking, not by the X.25 protocol. When a PAD is at the customer location, the entire circuit has a full X.25-assured connection.

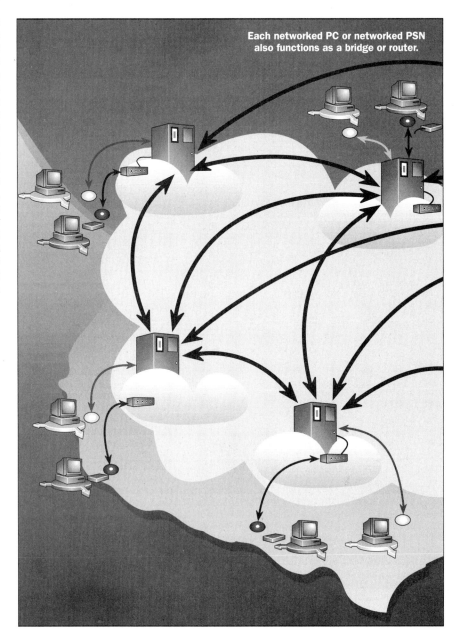

Each networked PC or networked PSN also functions as a bridge or router.

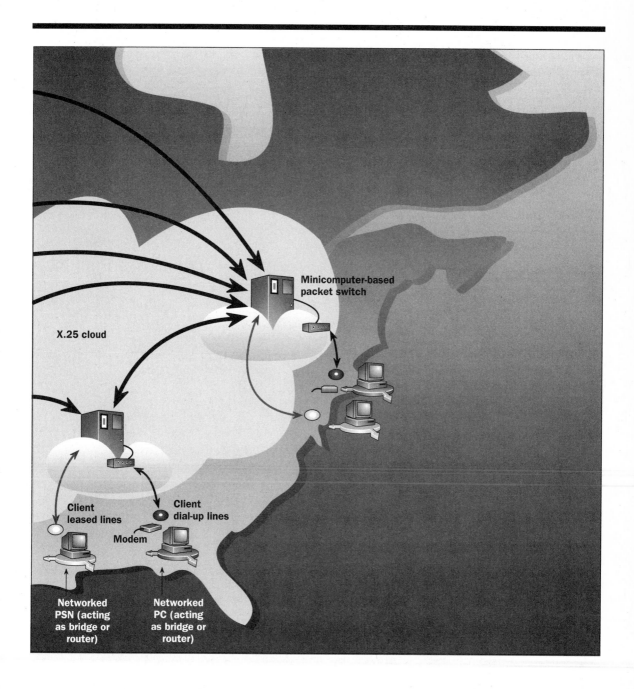

Minicomputer-based
packet switch

X.25 cloud

Client
leased lines

Client
dial-up lines

Modem

Networked
PSN (acting
as bridge or
router)

Networked
PC (acting
as bridge or
router)

Figure 10.3

Our scenario portrays an organization with four operating locations connected by an X.25 PDN. Each operating location has a LAN running NetWare over Ethernet and an X.25 bridge. Most of the communication takes place between the New York office and the individual offices, but the three branch offices do have some communication among themselves, particularly in the form of electronic mail.

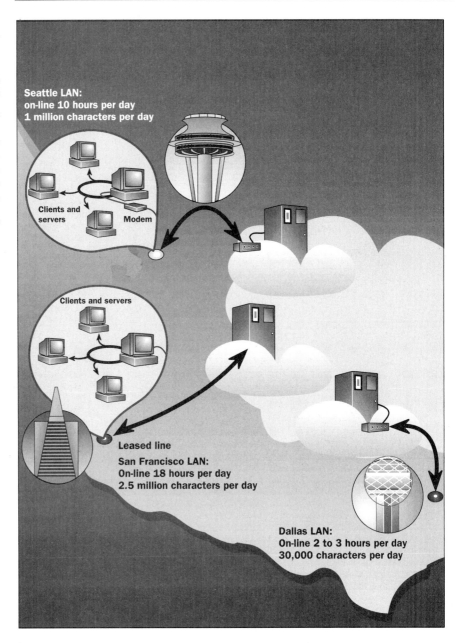

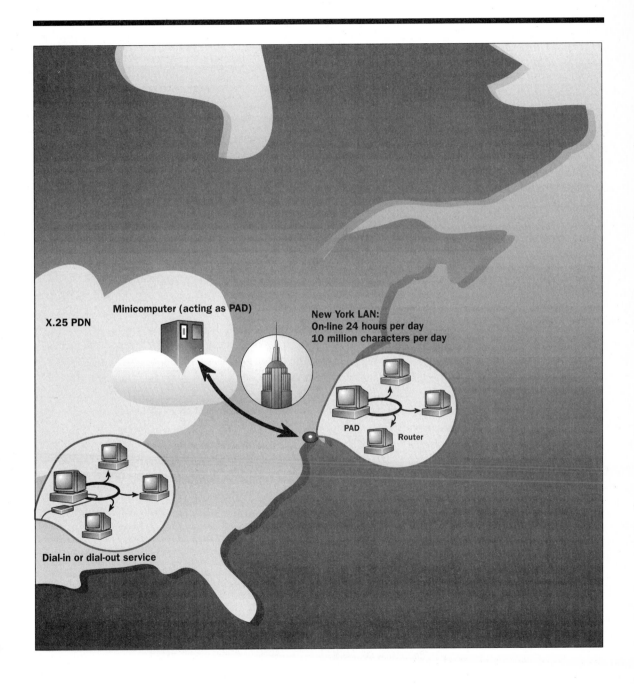

X.25 PDN

Minicomputer (acting as PAD)

New York LAN:
On-line 24 hours per day
10 million characters per day

PAD

Router

Dial-in or dial-out service

Public data networks:

👍 **Guarantee end-to-end service and delivery**

👍 **Offer complete services down to the installation of the LAN equipment and the leasing of access lines**

👎 **Charge you in many different ways**

👎 **Make it difficult to compare costs**

The companies gave us a variety of estimates for this scenario, proving that it pays to put your requirements out for competitive bid whenever possible. The typical monthly charges were in the ballpark of $800 per branch office and about $1,800 for the service to the headquarters. The total monthly charge for connecting these offices ranged from $3,200 to $4,700. In addition, the customer would have to provide the local loop service, plus circuit termination and network portal equipment.

Public data networks are generally more popular in Europe than in the U.S. This is primarily because digital leased lines in the U.S. are competitively priced and readily available. In France, X.25 PDN services are widely used because of a public policy that makes the services available at very attractive prices.

VANs and X.25

You can put the PDN access services into two categories: leased access and dial-up access. *Leased-access* lines can carry data at signaling speeds of 19.2, 56, or 64 kilobits per second, or in rare cases even 1.544 megabits per second, using the full X.25 protocol from the LAN to the switches of the PDN. Leased-access lines are expensive connections, usually reserved for the LAN segment in a busy headquarters that is the focal point for traffic with LAN segments in branch offices. The other type of connection is a *dialed-up* telephone line, which does not provide full X.25 data handling between the computer and the X.25 network.

X.25 packet-switching networks provide effective solutions for many applications. For example, X.25 works well where multiple protocols must be handled, interactive operations require a fast response, or users need to connect to multiple hosts for short periods of time. Users must decide whether to build a dedicated, private network or use the services available from a public network. This decision is largely an economic one.

Vendor Profiles

The best way to explain how you can order and use PDN services, and to help you get a sense of some of the alternatives they offer, is to survey some of the major international companies offering public data network services. The prices cited here may have changed before much time passes, and term and volume discounts are available, but this information should give you a good idea of the costs and pricing schemes involved.

CompuServe

CompuServe, a wholly owned subsidiary of H&R Block, has been operating since the early 1980s. Its packet-network offerings include high-speed X.25 connections for host computers, dial-up access service, and access service over digital leased lines. CompuServe has over 1,300 access nodes in the United States, and it offers worldwide connectivity through international services such as WORLD-Connect and EURO-Connect.

CompuServe offers a package called Fixed-LAN Services that includes the LAN equipment, termination equipment, and leased lines to the CompuServe network, complete with installation and maintenance. Fixed-LAN Services supports speeds from 9.6 to 56 kilobits per second and supports 8, 16, or 32 simultaneous users. Service is available at a fixed monthly charge, which depends on the terms of the agreement.

CompuServe's Dial-Up Access Services consist of FIXED-Dial, USAGE-Dial, PRIVATE-Dial, and an Open Port Arrangement. Each of the dial-up services is available at connection speeds ranging from 300 to 9,600 bps.

FIXED-Dial is an asynchronous dial-up access service that is not usage-sensitive. The prices for this service are based on a flat hourly rate. The pricing scheme works on a sliding scale. For example, for up to 750 hours a month, the hourly rate is $5.75; for 2,501 to 4,000 hours a month, the price drops to $4.40 per hour.

Rates for USAGE-Dial, another asynchronous dial-up access, are based on both connect time and the number of kilocharacters (sets of 1,024 characters) transmitted.

PRIVATE-Dial allows you to have dedicated asynchronous network access ports. The PRIVATE-Dial ports include a dial-up phone line and a modem at the CompuServe access node. The flat fee for this service is $350 per port per month, and an installation fee is added.

CompuServe's Dedicated Access service consists of FIXED-X.25 and PRIVATE-Async services. The pricing structure for these services varies. As the name implies, FIXED-X.25 provides a digital leased-line type of service; it is based on a fixed monthly rate depending on the speed you choose (from 1.2 to 19.2 kilobits per second) and the number of channels per location (up to 32). You are also billed $0.02 per kilocharacter for sessions that originate from any host network link or third-party FIXED-X.25 station and terminate at your FIXED-X.25 location.

GE Information Services

GE Information Services, founded in 1964, achieves worldwide connectivity through its Mark*Net Services. Mark*Net supports a number of asynchronous and synchronous devices. GE Information Services leans heavily toward offering an integrated data solution.

Asynchronous support is available through PADs that GE owns and operates within its networks, or via PADs located at the user's site. These dedicated PADs can be leased through GE Information Services. Asynchronous access is available in over 750 cities worldwide, through both asynchronous dial-up and leased lines at speeds ranging from 300 to 9,600 bps.

Synchronous support is available through *switched virtual circuit* (SVC) and *permanent virtual circuit* (PVC) services. Virtual-circuit service is available worldwide, with leased ports in 24 locations at speeds from 4,800 bps to 64 kbps.

GE Information Services offers a dial-up X.25 service, available at connect speeds of 2,400, 4,800, and 9,600 bps, and with two pricing options. The first option is priced according to a fixed port charge plus a kilocharacter charge. The second alternative is a flat monthly rate based on unlimited usage.

IBM

The IBM Information Network (IN) is an international public data network that offers services ranging from networking and messaging systems to database access, capacity-planning services, and e-mail. All of the services are compatible with the full line of IBM hardware and software as well as many non-IBM devices.

IBM IN services are available through leased-line connections in over 50 U.S. cities or via a toll-free 800 number for dial-up connectivity from virtually anywhere in the United States. International service is also available in more than 80 countries.

IBM's Information Network Support Services include X.25 support, with speeds from 9.6 kilobits per second to 56 kilobits per second. The service includes a dedicated leased line between the user's site and IBM's Information Network, modems for both locations, and an IBM IN communication controller port to enable access to the network.

IBM's rates for X.25 service include a monthly carrier charge that depends on the speed you choose, plus an hourly usage charge rate and an installation fee. The monthly rates range from $1,050 at 9,600 bps to $4,200 at 56,000 bps. These monthly charges include network traffic for communications sessions and the leased-line port. The charge also covers management of the communication line.

Infonet

Infonet Services Corp. was a division of Computer Sciences Corp. (CSC) until the late 1980s. As a part of CSC, its people worked on developing worldwide X.25 packet-switching networks for the U.S. federal government. Today, MCI holds 25 percent ownership in Infonet, and ten international PTTs (post, telegraph, and telephone companies) jointly own the remaining 75 percent. The PTTs involved in the joint ownership are the national telephone administrations of Australia, Belgium, France, Germany, Holland, Japan, Singapore, Spain, Sweden, and Switzerland.

Infonet is proud that most of its business is international. Its customers consist mainly of multinational corporations around the world. Infonet's philosophy is based on global networking solutions providing "one-stop shopping." Its network services are accessible in 111 countries.

A specialized service from Infonet, INFOLAN, provides LAN connectivity service. Released in June 1991, INFOLAN is a fully managed end-to-end service. INFOLAN offers speeds ranging from 9.6 kbps to 1.544 mbps in the U.S. LANs communicate using native LAN and WAN protocols (such as Source Route Bridging or TCP/IP). Infonet offers two solutions based on the existing equipment at the target sites. The first package includes a network port, an in-country circuit with modems or DSUs, and an unlimited volume of data. The second option is aimed at customers who will require a LAN router at the local site for LAN connection to the network. In the second case, Infonet leases the router along with the bundled package.

Pricing is based on a fixed monthly rate, with no additional charge for the data volume in either direction. The pricing depends on a number of factors specific to a customer, such as the number of locations, domestic versus international service, connection speed, the distance from the Infonet node, and regional versus global communications.

Datapac

Datapac, located primarily in Canada, is not an incorporated business, but rather an association of ten Canadian telecommunications companies called Telecom Canada. Three of the ten companies that are members of Telecom Canada are Bell Canada, Manitoba Telephone System, and Telesat Canada. Although Telecom Canada is not incorporated and earns no income for itself, it provides service to Canadians 24 hours a day, 7 days a week.

Datapac services are available in over 200 locations in Canada. The services interconnect with eight other packet-switched networks in the U.S. and achieve worldwide connectivity through Teleglobe, available in over 96 locations serving nearly that number of countries.

Telecom Canada's X.25 service, Datapac 3000, is an access service providing support for synchronous communications lines. X.25 dial-in is appropriate for users with low-volume applications.

Datapac's old rate structure is based on two factors: the city of origin in the Datapac service area and the distance between the originating and terminating points of data transmission. The access charge, or installation fee, is currently the same for all areas. An emerging new rate structure considers only the distance between the origin and destination of the data. The access charge will depend on whether a city is a high- or low-density area, with low-density areas being the more expensive of the two.

U.S. Sprint

U.S. Sprint gains its strength in the PDN arena through a variety of sources. Telenet Communications Corp. was founded in 1972 to develop packet-switching technology. Telenet was acquired by GTE Corp. in 1979. The path doesn't stop here; in 1986, through a joint venture, GTE Telenet merged with Uninet (U.S. Telecom Data Communications Company)—United Telecom's long-distance voice division—and GTE Sprint to become U.S. Sprint. Finally, in 1990, Telenet as a subsidiary was fully absorbed into U.S. Sprint; it no longer exists as the public data network Telenet but is now known as SprintNet.

U.S. Sprint markets an integrated LAN/WAN product line called LAN Reach in conjunction with Eicon Technology, a major vendor of bridges and routers. A major selling point for the various SprintNet LAN Reach services is U.S. Sprint's use of the Eicon adapter card, a LAN X.25 gateway product for LAN-to-LAN communications. The link between Sprint and Eicon provides for smooth integration and strong network-management and trouble-shooting capabilities.

SprintNet Data Network offers services that include both Dedicated Access Facilities and Dial Access Services, with options for each category. SprintNet has chosen a flat-rate pricing structure for these services. International service is available through U.S. Sprint nodes as well as individual local carriers.

LAN Reach X.25 Service, through the use of packet-switching technology, allows you to integrate geographically dispersed LANs into a single enterprise-wide corporate network. With a fixed monthly fee of $800 per site per month at 9.6 kilobits per second, and a monthly fee of $1,200 per month per site at 19.2 kilobits per second, LAN Reach allows users on a LAN to connect to and interact with computers on a remote LAN as if they were connected locally. All data is transparently routed while allowing multiple sessions across a single X.25 line.

SprintNet's Dedicated Access Facilities services include a leased line between the customer site and the access center, a leased channel port, and the required termination equipment. Asynchronous service ranges from 300 to 1,200 bps and involves a monthly charge of $600 plus an installation fee of $1,200. The X.25 DAF service also involves a monthly charge and a fixed installment charge depending on the chosen speed of service, with speeds ranging from 2,400 to 56,000 bps.

SprintNet's Dial Access Services also give you the option of asynchronous dial-up or X.25 service, with pricing based on an hourly charge. The pricing for DataCall Plus, either asynchronous or X.25, depends on the dialing location.

HINT. *It pays to shop around for X.25 service, even if you get your local lines from a monopoly carrier. Generate a scenario for your operation and request bids from all available vendors.*

Tymnet Global Network

With over 4,500 nodes worldwide, Tymnet is currently the largest value-added network in the world. McDonnell Douglas owned Tymnet until November 1989, then sold it to British Telecom. British Telecom established BT Tymnet, the parent company that owns and operates Tymnet Global Network. Providing value-added network services and fostering European expansion are high on the BT Tymnet list of priorities. BT Tymnet has offices throughout North America and Europe, and in many other locations throughout the world.

One of the ways that Tymnet provides LAN connectivity is through Xlink Express, Tymnet's X.25 service. Xlink is a package of nine services with different speeds and connection options. These services support anywhere from 8 to 64 simultaneous users, and support speeds ranging from 2,400 bits to 19.2 kilobits per second. Pricing for the Xlink services is based on a monthly fee of $650 at 2,400 bps or $1,600 at 19.2kbps. Included in the service is a leased line and modems for both the Tymnet site and the customer site.

TymDial X.25 service allows users to access X.25 and asynchronous applications through dial-up lines, as opposed to leased lines. Tymnet's new Out-Dial X.25 service provides a way for a customer to initiate a call out through the network to any location to establish a temporary link. This provides a cost-effective alternative to leased lines, besides serving other uses such as disaster recovery and communication with infrequently used locations.

BT Tymnet supports customers through local communications specialists, through a 24-hour toll-free telephone customer-support service, and through a technical support center.

■ Frame Relay

The X.25 protocols and products underlying the PDNs are proven, stable, and reliable. Because of these factors, it is particularly interesting to see the high level of interest shown in an alternative technology called *frame relay*. Frame relay has exploded from a concept in 1988 to become an evolving ANSI and CCITT standard that challenges the supremacy of X.25.

The X.25 protocol is a conservative design that numbers, acknowledges, and supervises every packet and even asks network switches to retransmit packets that don't make the trip across the network. This conservative design protects data, but it also requires placing a lot of expensive computing and communicating resources within the network to do all the work.

The concept of the frame-relay protocol is based on the realization that modern transmission systems are quiet and reliable and that reducing the protective overhead will allow more throughput at lower cost without unacceptable data loss.

The frame-relay concept takes away some responsibilities from the switches in the VAN and puts them on the terminal equipment at each end. If there is a problem with a packet—for example, if bits are lost, or if a node is so congested that it receives more packets than it can process—the frame-relay network discards the data and expects the terminal equipment to take corrective action. Typically, this involves retransmitting the data that failed to make it across the frame-relay network. Because LAN protocols like Novell's SPX/IPX have their own error control, which would be redundant with the error control in X.25, they fit nicely into the frame-relay architecture.

On the downside, the end-to-end recovery scheme can be costly because it builds traffic on the network. If the frame-relay packets are discarded because of congestion, retransmitting the data can merely aggravate the problem. So even though the terminal equipment can recover discarded blocks, it is still important to minimize frame discards.

Congestion Control

Since LAN traffic tends to occur in great bursts, by nature, the probability of occasional congestion is high unless the user overconfigures both the lines and the switches and pays unnecessarily high bills for network costs. For this reason, a frame-relay network should have excellent congestion-management features. The frame-relay standards make several suggestions about how the network can signal congestion and how the LAN portal devices could react. Because these suggestions are not mandatory, companies can market devices that conform to the frame-relay protocols but do not have congestion-control capabilities.

Two important frame-relay congestion-control systems involve using the *discard eligibility* (DE) bit in the frame-relay format and establishing an estimated rate of traffic called the *committed information rate* (CIR).

Setting the DE bit to a binary 1 marks the frame as eligible for early elimination in the event of congestion. The DE bit could be set by a LAN portal device on lower-priority traffic—perhaps traffic that can tolerate a few seconds of delay, like electronic mail. Marking frames for potential sacrifice with the DE bit offers a good way to allow other traffic to pass with a higher priority.

The committed information rate represents an estimate of the normal amount of traffic coming from a node in a busy period. On a commercial network, the higher the CIR the higher the monthly cost. On private networks, the CIR is still an important budgeting and network-management tool. The network measures the traffic coming from each node, and if the load is less than the CIR, the network passes the frames untouched if possible. But if the load passes the CIR, the network sets the DE bit on the excess frames. If the network experiences congestion, those frames exceeding their own CIR will be eliminated before those that don't have the DE bit set. Because of the importance of congestion control, I strongly suggest that you select products providing DE and CIR capabilities. Because this is new technology, it's wise to select products from the same vendor or from vendors with proven product compatibility.

HINT. *The actual throughput you enjoy from a frame-relay network depends on the raw signaling speed of the circuits and the ability to manage congestion.*

Frame Relay's Popularity

The remarkably fast evolution of the frame-relay standard demonstrates the need for this economical protocol. In 1988 the CCITT approved recommendation I.122—"Framework for Additional Packet Mode Bearer Services"—as part of a set of ISDN-related specifications. The frame-relay architecture follows the Link Access Protocol—D Channel (LAP-D) signaling standard developed for ISDN.

Frame relay:

👍 **More efficient and less costly than X.25**

👍 **Retains the multipoint and alternate-routing advantages of X.25**

👎 **Requires careful shopping for equipment and services to ensure compatibility**

The PDN companies—and companies that make termination equipment and devices like bridges and routers—are generally excited about frame relay. CompuServe's FRAME-NET, a 1992 release of frame-relay service, supplements CompuServe's present X.25 packet-switched network. GE Information Services is focusing more heavily on customized solutions, and is in a good position to offer frame-relay service to end users. Frame relay will complement SprintNet's existing X.25 data-network service, and will be targeted toward LAN communications.

Roll Your Own

If you don't want to buy frame-relay services from the PDN companies, you can buy a frame-relay switch from a company called Netrix Corp. and establish your own network. Because frame relay uses little processing power on the network switches, Netrix offers products that can pass both frame-relay and X.25 packets on the same network.

■ Pick a Technology

The public data networks provide a wide variety of alternatives for LAN connections. They offer a flexible, portable, expandable, pay-as-you-go method of moving data between LAN segments.

The choice between using a PDN and creating your own network of private or dialed lines involves more than monthly costs. The decision also involves making long-term economic and technical investments in the future of your organization. Some organizations don't consider data transportation a core part of their business, and they delegate it to a PDN. Others want to control their own data-transmission systems. Fortunately, there are alternatives designed to match your management style and financial needs.

☒ Fragments

☒ Short Frames

☒ Long Frames

☒ Alignment Errors

☒ Late Collisions

☒ Jabbers

☒ Out of Spec. Transmission Freq.

☒ Auto Partition History

☒ Start Frame Delimiter Errors

CHAPTER

11

Network Management Techniques and Tools

- Understanding Network-Management Systems

- Standards for Network Management

- Interoperability Answers

- Management Under NetWare

- Management Futures

In LAN-to-LAN connectivity, network management is like hurricane insurance: You don't think you need it until it's too late. A network administrator is usually responsible for internetworking devices (bridges, routers, and gateways), general equipment (cabling, workstations, and servers), and all other "connected" data-processing equipment. With all of these components making up the modern-day inter-LAN system, managers need some way to track and receive reports on every major device or subsystem operating in every location.

Unfortunately, the need for network management and the existence of high-quality network-management tools do not always go hand in hand. In particular, the problem of interoperability seems to rear its ugly head anew any time you try to interconnect disparate networks and devices.

For example, imagine a complex internetwork composed of Ethernet, Token-Ring, and AppleTalk cabling systems linked by Cisco Systems and Digital Equipment Corp. bridges and routers. An ideal network-management system would keep a central database of all network data, including statistics, alarms, and other significant events. In an ideal system, the network manager and other workgroup managers could access this information through the PCs sitting on their desks no matter where they were. A number of companies promise such a system, and you'll be able to buy it off the shelf in 1994 or 1995, but today it would be a coat of many colors held together with string and a prayer. This chapter is designed to help you find a practical network-management system that works well enough for today's needs and that will set the foundation for network management into the next decade.

■ Understanding Network-Management Systems

Network-management systems fall into two rough categories: *standards-based* and *proprietary*. The limitation on this categorizing scheme is that proprietary systems often undergo a metamorphosis and become standards —particularly when they have IBM as a parent. Standards-based systems follow the guidelines established by organizations like the ISO or the U.S. Department of Defense. The ISO calls its set of standards for management systems the Common Management Information Protocol, or CMIP. The management protocols described in the TCP/IP suite are collectively called the Simple Network Management Protocol, or SNMP. The designers of CMIP and SNMP tried to make their systems open to all vendors. Proprietary systems, like IBM's Net-View, typically claim to offer more features than standards-based systems, and they are typically more streamlined.

Management systems, whether standards-based or proprietary, are designed according to a basic framework that defines the components of the network system and how those components interoperate. In their most general form, management systems have seven elements:

- Managed elements

- Agents

- Information databases

- Managers

- Management-information protocols

- Application program interfaces

- User interfaces

Those terms are the buzzwords of network-management systems. I'll define them so you can build a basic working vocabulary.

Managed elements are the active components that make up the network to be managed. The most common managed elements are bridges, routers, and wiring centers. In today's implementations, the managed elements typically include their own microprocessors running under the control of programs contained in firmware.

Exactly what components of the network should be considered managed elements is being heavily debated by vendors and standards-making organizations. I come down on the side that says the more information you have, the more you can do with it. I believe that all segments of the network—down to and including network adapters—should be able to make some reports on their identity, workload, and status.

Agent is the term given to the firmware program running in a particular node or managed element on the network. As the name implies, agents are local representatives or monitors for the management system. Agents are categorized according to the types of information that they monitor. Agents typically use specialized processors or processors with the power of the Intel 80186.

Various systems give their agents the ability to perform different tasks, such as initiating reports in the face of specific problems or even shutting down a system or link in the event of a malfunction that damages the ability of the network to carry traffic. The descriptions of the managed events are referred to as the *management information base* or MIB in the SNMP frame of reference and simply as *object definitions* by the CMIP designers. In either case, this is an information database of status reports and alarms created by the agent and held in the managed equipment.

Information databases contain data retrieved by the agents concerning the managed nodes. Agents use this store of data to forward information to the management software.

The *manager* is a piece of software, typically running on a PC under Microsoft Windows or some computer running Unix, that communicates with the agents in the managed elements of the network. The manager software polls each agent for information concerning a particular managed object on the network. The agent replies to the queries and reports the contents of its management database directly to the software making the query.

As an example, Hewlett-Packard has developed a management system called OpenView Hub Manager that it markets with HP SmartHub 10BaseT networks as well as other systems. Other 10BaseT vendors such as Cabletron Systems use OpenView as the kernel for their 10BaseT network-management systems.

Management-information protocols define the way management programs and agents ask for and exchange information. These protocols describe the format of the queries, the information in the databases, the timing, and many other factors. Companies of all kinds design products to conform to the protocols.

Application program interfaces (APIs) are specifications describing how application programs can interact with the network-management system. The publication of clear APIs allows third-party developers to create programs that contribute to and take advantage of an interoperable network-management system. Developers use the APIs to create unique user interfaces, as described below.

User interfaces include Microsoft Windows for DOS-based PCs, OS/2 for IBM machines, and Motif and X/Windows in the Unix world.

The ideal solution would be a single user interface that could be used across disparate networks and operating systems. In the next few years we will certainly see operating environments such as OS/2 or Windows that run on a PC and act as both an agent and a management system. In other words, your operating system will report its health and activity to a central management point and will gather basic information about the health of the network to alert you to any problems.

Some application programs, like complex database, accounting, or publication systems, could also interact with the network-management system for the same purposes. It is always better to handle problems at the highest possible level. For example, it's much better to have an application program alert you with the message "The communications link to the database location is down" than to think you have completed a task and then see the message "Network error: server not responding" on your screen.

■ Standards for Network Management

In order to ensure interoperability between managed networks, there must be a standard that vendors can and will follow. Although much work is being done, a truly comprehensive network-management system is not available today—particularly for PC-based LANs. There are, however, three glimmers of hope on the horizon. The standards-based network management protocols SNMP and CMIP and the proprietary IBM network-management system NetView are the three fertile and growing sections of the network-management field. Each system has its own unique assets, drawbacks, attributes, and culture.

SNMP

The specification for the Simple Network Management Protocol (SNMP) was first released in 1988 by the Department of Defense and the commercial developers of TCP/IP (Transmission Control Protocol/Internet Protocol) in an attempt to develop a way of managing the different network topologies of complex internetwork systems. Since then, SNMP has grown into a widely accepted network-management protocol, not just for interconnected networks but also for smaller LANs using the same technology and topology. In May of 1990, SNMP became a TCP/IP standard, further increasing its acceptance.

SNMP has gained the lead in the race to become the de facto standard for network management. One reason SNMP is receiving so much recognition and support is the pragmatic approach taken to standards implementation and definition. While other standards-based network-management protocols (including CMIP) have developed slowly through the deliberations of committees, SNMP has already been implemented by a large number of vendors.

SNMP defines a set of network-management variables as well as the protocols or rules used to exchange network-management information. In other words, SNMP provides a common format for network devices and equipment such as bridges, concentrators, hubs, routers, and modems to use when sending management data via an agent to the network-management station. One or more manager programs can control the managed elements of the network through the agents located in the different pieces of network equipment.

The agent typically consists of firmware and a special-purpose processor located in each SNMP-compatible piece of equipment. The management host can be either a PC using Microsoft's MS-DOS (typically running the Windows environment) or a computer running Unix.

The manager software polls each agent over the network cable for pertinent information regarding the individual nodes on the network, any error messages, and other statistics. This control over the network is known as *in-band* signaling, a term carried over from telecommunications systems. Management control through a separate RS-232C port, usually done during setup and from a remote PC through a modem, is known as *out-of-band* signaling. The agent responds to the manager's request in a format designated by the particular vendor's implementation of the management protocol.

Many management programs take advantage of the graphical environments of Microsoft Windows, OS/2, and certain Unix-based computers to give a visual presentation of the network. As Figure 11.1 shows, various network elements like hubs and concentrators show up as specific elements on the screen and as menu selections for more specific management and display.

Figure 11.1

The DSI ExpressView software, marketed by David Systems, offers a graphical view of the devices containing management agent software. The layered menus allow you to select different agents for more detailed inspection or control.

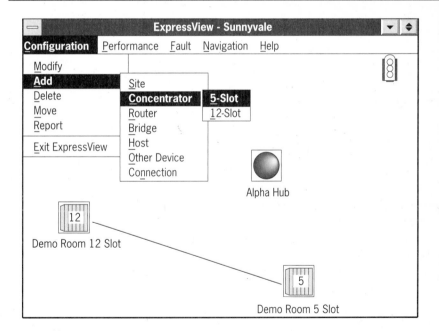

Each agent stores information concerning traffic, equipment, and error logs in a virtual database called the *management information base*, or MIB. A device like a router or a modem controller would typically hold its MIB in random access memory associated with its on-board processor. The RAM would have a battery backup and might hold as much as 30 days' worth of data to facilitate out-of-band inquiries into the MIB. The standards defining the contents of the MIB have evolved and improved to take more labor away from the network administrator and let the PCs do all the work. The agents can also send the management stations unsolicited information, such as indications of possible link failures or other alarms.

The TCP/IP community has developed standards describing two MIBs, MIB I and MIB II. Both sets of standards contain object definitions needed for a network-management system. While MIB I is in full implementation, MIB II is an extension of MIB I containing definitions for 171 standard object definitions. Each object definition is some specific type of occurrence—for example, some type of improperly sized frames—to be counted and reported to the management software.

The ExpressView screen in Figure 11.2 shows some of the elements reported by the agent software in a wiring hub. Managers can set specific alarm levels for certain types of events. When the number of events exceeds the alarm criteria, the software can do something as simple as changing the stoplight displayed in the upper right corner to red, or something as complex as dialing a telephone number for a pager and passing a special message.

Figure 11.2

In this Set Thresholds dialog box in DSI ExpressView, all of the event alarms are set to a level of 5. The network administrator can use a mouse or other pointing device to activate or deactivate an option or to raise or lower a threshold.

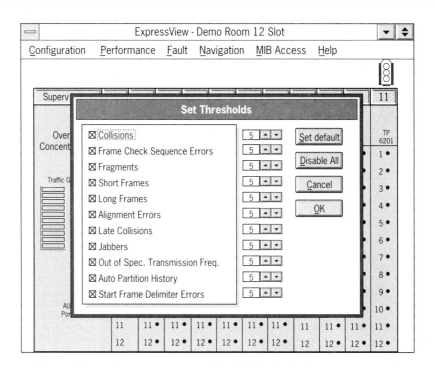

One problem that is inherent with SNMP (and with any protocol that is implemented by many different companies) is compliance versus compatibility. Products can comply with the standard, but slightly different implementations challenge interoperability. Some vendors put proprietary information called *extensions* into the MIB. Management software from other companies can't read these extensions, and errors result. Similarly, management software looking for proprietary extensions cannot effectively display the reports from another vendor's agent.

The definition for SNMP includes using the IP protocol for communications across the network—a carryover from the origins of SNMP as a management program used on the Internet. Since few local area networks use IP, network administrators using SNMP on a LAN must find a way to load IP simultaneously with typical LAN communications software such as Novell's IPX. Some SNMP products, such as DSI ExpressView, use the Clarkson Packet Driver Collection to multiplex IP with the other network protocol (typically IPX) on the same network adapter. This arrangement takes some of the flexibility away from the concept of controlling the SNMP agent from any networked computer. The multiplexing packet driver requires careful installation, and it doesn't work on all LAN adapter cards.

Unfortunately, the deliberately simple nature of SNMP is one of its drawbacks. In its current state, SNMP is only able to retrieve information one variable at a time, potentially creating a lot of network traffic. This technique is less effective than CMIP or some proprietary management systems that can retrieve the same information all at once.

Yet it appears that SNMP will be an early winner in the protocol race simply because so many companies support it. SNMP is, for all practical purposes, the only standards-based network-management protocol available today for PC-based LANs.

CMIP

Common Management Information Protocol is the International Standards Organization/Open Systems Interconnection (ISO/OSI) model for network management (ISO IS 9596, including IS Amendments 1 and 2; this is the same as CCITT X.711). The ISO's OSI network-management information is encoded in CMIP. The interface for defining the commands that are used to perform network-management tasks is CMIS, or Common Management Information Services (ISO IS 9595, including IS Amendments 1 and 2 and CD Amendment 4 [scheduled for incorporation into IS in 1992]; CCITT X.719).

CMIP is the network-management protocol that is generally accepted, even by SNMP advocates, as the ultimate goal. Implementation of CMIP, however, has been hampered by the ISO's bureaucratic approval process, which is designed to allow comment on the standard from all over the world. The process of promulgation, dissemination, comment, and final approval takes a considerable amount of time, and the final CMIP definition only became available in late 1990.

In fact, the ISO/IEC (ISO and International Electrotechnical Committee—the actual standardization body), unlike the TCP/IP community, does not require or even expect a working prototype for evaluation or testing until the actual standard has been defined. The Internet standardization process requires the existence of evaluation copies and a prototype before the draft of the standard ever gets approved.

The OSI specifications for CMIP divide network management into five functional areas:

- Configuration management

- Performance management

- Fault management

- Security management

- Accounting

Configuration management is commonly referred to as a "network map" because the model gives names to all the managed elements on the network or inter-LAN system. Some management applications represent these managed elements as graphs or icons that can change colors as their state of operation changes.

Performance management involves counting things such as disk access requests, packets, and access to certain programs. It determines the utilization of the network or LAN-to-LAN link, allowing the network managers to monitor network usage, throughput, and response time closely.

Fault management detects problems on the network and takes steps toward the isolation and correction of the errors.

Security-management functions control data access and protect important data from unauthorized access. The developers of CMIP are determined to implement strong security safeguards, a feature SNMP developers have yet to put into motion.

Accounting features keep track of what network resources authorized network users are accessing, and they log each person's time on-line. The log can be used simply for managerial purposes or in some instances to bill people for the time on the network.

The biggest problem inherent in CMIP, especially with PC-based LANs, is its dogmatic use of the entire ISO protocol stack. Any device using CMIP on the network is required to use the full seven-layer OSI protocol stack, which in turn can easily take up 300k of code. The size and complexity of the required code limit the ability of developers to include CMIP in application programs and operating systems.

Although the first products lack some polish, companies such as AT&T and Digital Equipment Corp. have complete implementations of ISO's network management protocol installed in such systems as the Unified Network Management Architecture (UNMA) and Enterprise Management Architecture, respectively. Unfortunately for the PC-based LAN user, these systems are designed as enterprise-wide "host" systems. The CMIP community has not made much progress in developing a system to run over PC LANs or LAN-to-LAN communication links.

CMIP needs refinement and reevaluation if it is going to work as a viable standard for LAN-based management systems. As skeptical as I may seem regarding CMIP's viability, the government mandate to use OSI protocols under the Government OSI Profile (GOSIP)—and the existence of equally strong mandates made by some businesses—ensure that CMIP implementations will appear and be used.

CMOL

In an effort to scale down the excessive use of RAM on PC-based LANs, IBM and 3Com Corp. have jointly proposed a new version of CMIP that would run over the logical-link layer of the OSI protocol stack, thus requiring less memory. The IEEE LAN standards committees are working on the proposed protocol, called CMOL (CMIP Over Logical-Link Layer). CMOL is designed to perform the same functions as SNMP and to collect information from all workstations, bridges, routers, printers, servers, and host processors attached to the network. Under CMOL, an agent in a certain LAN-attached device reports back to a central console.

CMOT

Another interesting development to cross CMIP's hurdle of multiprotocol requirements is called CMOT (CMIP Over TCP/IP). Neither SNMP nor CMIP is technically tied to or limited by a specific transport mechanism. While CMIP uses the OSI TP4 transport method, CMOT uses the same TCP/IP transport mechanism as SNMP.

Proprietary Vendor-Based Management Systems

Although seemingly the best choices for interoperable network-management systems, SNMP and CMIP may not be the best choices for some networks. Certainly CMIP in its current state is not even a choice for use on a PC-based LAN. Several vendors are working on vendor-based network-management systems. Currently IBM has a usable and available network-management system called NetView that is being supported by other vendors.

IBM's NetView was initially released in 1986, and its latest version — Version 2, Releases 1 and 2—became available in the last quarter of 1990.

NetView's architecture is based on PCs running software called NetView/PC on an intermediate level to gather data on the network and report to the NetView program, which runs on a mainframe. Unfortunately, IBM's earlier DOS version of NetView/PC did not fare well, primarily because it required a dedicated computer that did nothing but gather, store, and forward information. But IBM has hopes for its newer version of the program, running over the multitasking operating system OS/2.

NetView was originally designed for IBM Systems Network Architecture (SNA) networks, and it may prove to be a central organizing principle for networks of networks until such time as the OSI's CMIP takes off and dominates global communications.

■ Interoperability Answers

After examining the three major solutions to the problem of interoperable network-management systems, we see that there are really no absolute solutions available on the market today. The best a network administrator can hope for is finding a system that will work acceptably for the network or LAN-to-LAN connection. Today, smart managers split their bets and use SNMP while planning for either CMOT or a big, disruptive move to a network system that conforms to the full OSI model, including CMIP.

NetView has been around for a while, and it offers PC LANs connected to larger inter-LAN systems a reasonable solution to network management. On the other hand, IBM appears to be spending a lot of time and effort on new standards-based systems such as CMIP, and one wonders whether IBM will continue to help NetView grow and prosper.

■ Management Under NetWare

Because NetWare has such a large share of the LAN operating-system market, many readers will be interested in how Novell implements network management. In a nutshell, this company aims for compatibility with all three major network-management systems.

Internally, NetWare offers several management utilities (including FCONSOLE, SYSCON, and FILER) that have some capabilities as network-management tools. They allow you to implement excellent security measures and (after a few hours of setup work) to generate detailed reports on what people and equipment have used the resources of the network, and even to assign costs to that use. The server software in NetWare, particularly in the NetWare 3.*x* series of products, contains excellent monitoring capabilities that can alert a manager to situations where people are running out of resources such as disk file space, to abuse of the security system, or to malfunctions such as bad Ethernet cable connections.

NetWare 3.*x* also has the ability to operate as an SNMP management product. This Novell software can poll SNMP agents on the network one at a time and generate simple reports on the information it receives. The software is not as encompassing as products that run in graphical environments like Windows, or on powerful Unix computers—those products can draw network maps and create many clever displays—but it is a functional and practical management product.

Novell also sells optional products that add more management capabilities to the NetWare environment. The LANtern Network Monitor is an impressive SNMP management product that gathers information about network traffic as well as specific information from each device on the network.

LANtern Services Manager, a Microsoft Windows 3.0 application, allows users to communicate with LANtern devices on the network. It also allows users to display network resources on a graphical map and receive alerts from these resources. LANtern Services Manager is SNMP-based and can be used to communicate with multiple LANtern Network Monitors across the LAN or via asynchronous phone lines.

Novell has developed an entry-point implementation of NetView support in NetWare 3.11. This is the same implementation that IBM uses in its products. Using Novell's NetView interface, a NetView administrator at the host console can receive alerts and request statistical information from the NetWare 3.11 servers.

■ Management Futures

The pieces and parts of a network are expensive to buy and expensive to own. They are valuable resources that deserve high management visibility in any organization. Network-management tools are as important to the production capabilities of today's organizations as personnel policies and real-estate ownership policies. Network management is a critical tool of modern business.

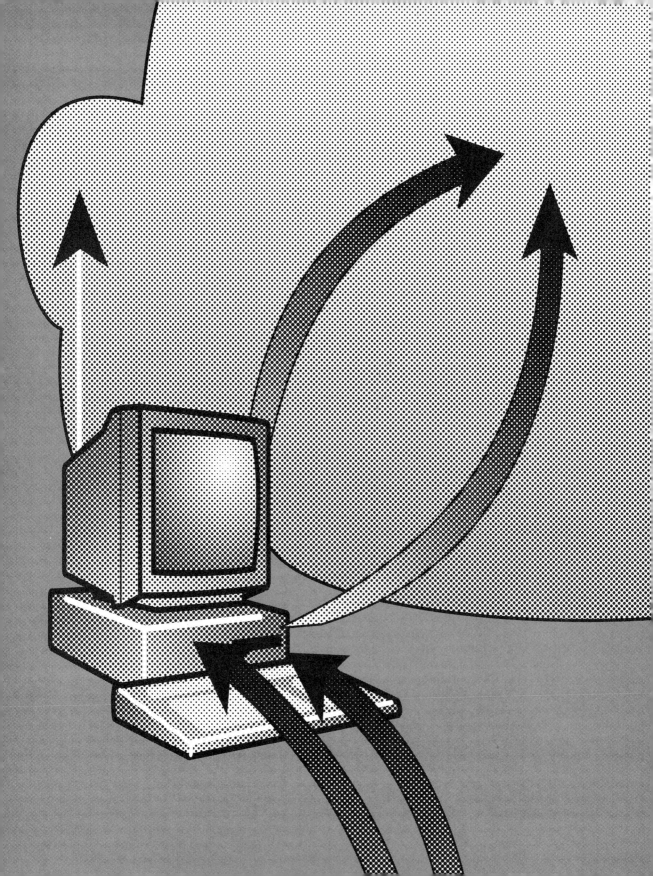

Interoperability

- Searching for Common Ground

- Real Versus Ideal

- Realism and Pragmatism

- Novell's NetWare Solution

- Links to Unix

- A Pragmatic Future

Mongrel networks of computers with mixed bloodlines are the rule in most organizations. Networks grow in small incompatible pieces and parts, and networks made of totally homogeneous elements are very rare. By definition, e-mail gateways and WAITS handle the differences between the various computer architectures, operating systems, LAN operating systems, and network communications protocols on the LANs they link. Companies design each version of a gateway or WAITS product to work in specific environments while interlinking and communicating in common ways. But bridges and routers are not as talented. They forward frames and packets with machinelike indifference to the ability of the computers at the destination to use the data once it gets there.

The art (and it is more art than science) of making data useful to computers with different internal architectures, disk operating systems, LAN operating systems, and communications protocols is called *interoperability.* In the broadest sense, interoperability involves a wide variety of elements, ranging from different file formats created by application programs to different packet envelopes created by communications programs. For the purposes of this book, I'll focus on a narrower definition of interoperability that deals with network communications protocols. I'll look at two different approaches to interoperability, one that moves toward common standards and a more pragmatic approach that uses multiple standards simultaneously.

■ Searching for Common Ground

An old computer joke reads, "Standards must be important, we have so many of them!" In the late 1960s and through the 1970s, the movement toward openly developed and published standards for network communications software was fueled by the need of many smaller companies to escape the technological grasp of the giant IBM Corporation. As IBM's share of the market waned in the '80s, the push for open standards continued as a way to find a common means for communications between otherwise incompatible computer systems.

Companies as different as IBM and Tiara Computer Systems (makers of a DOS-based LAN) have marketed network communications software products conforming more or less to the Open Systems Interconnection (OSI) model. Digital Equipment Corp. deserves credit for investing great energy and resources to deliver OSI-compliant products.

The U.S. government has given energy to the movement toward open systems by issuing the Government OSI Profile (GOSIP) standards, which establish conformance with OSI. U.S. public law requires that large systems purchased by the government conform to the GOSIP standards. Many state governments, institutions, and large businesses have adopted the same standards. Governments in England, France, Germany, Sweden, and Japan are developing their own open-system profiles.

Each element in the open-protocol architecture, typically a piece of software, must interoperate with those elements above and below it. For example, each piece of transport-layer software must always work with the session-layer software above it and the data-link-layer software below it, regardless of who wrote or what company marketed the upper and lower layers. The interfaces to the upper and lower software pieces should conform to a standard so they interlock and interoperate regardless of who designed, wrote, or marketed the code.

In the LAN-to-LAN arena, using open standards typically boils down to using routers that can recognize packets formatted according to the ISO's transport-protocol family. Even this criterion is not simple, since the ISO describes four classes of transport protocols with varying degrees of error detection and recovery. The class called TP4 provides the highest degree of functionality, but for reasons I will describe below, all TP4 products are not the same. Above the transport layer of products, implementation of the open protocols becomes especially complex. You'll probably have to write your own application programs to run on the open presentation-layer and session-layer software; only a few high-quality commercial applications are written to run on open systems.

■ Real Versus Ideal

In an ideal world, all vendors would create software that works together under the framework of the open standards. In theory, programmers write to the standards by giving people a common way to use software and by employing standard techniques to interface between applications and the layers of software that move the data for the applications. If they follow these rules, then the programs they create, the network communications software, and the network hardware from different manufacturers should all work together. But in fact, only the lowest layers of hardware—the Ethernet and Token-Ring connections, for example—are really standardized and interoperable all of the time. As soon as you try to string different pieces of software together into an operational system, you get tangled into the knots of incompatibility.

Vendors don't want to sell software that does not interoperate. But implementation of the standards is an art, and the standards are so broad that before they become really effective the people who implement them need years of practical experience. Even reading the documentation is a problem. The OSI documentation is issued by two standards bodies: The International Telegraph and Telephone Consultative Committee (CCITT) and the International Standards Organization. The 61 documents issued by the CCITT occupy a shelf about 2 feet wide and cost over $2,500 for a complete set. The ISO documents are not so neatly packaged, and a complete set could cost more than $3,000. Everything is protected under copyright, so companies trying for ISO compliance typically must purchase several copies of the expensive documentation.

In an effort to promote compatibility, members of the industry founded The Corporation for Open Systems International (COS), an independent group of organizations and vendors advocating the Open Systems Interconnection/Integrated Services Digital Network (OSI/ISDN) standards. COS offers compliance-testing services to its members and to the public, and issues a "COSmark" to products that pass the tests.

Unfortunately, no tests are perfect. Even when the string instruments in an orchestra use a common tuning fork, they still need to tune together before they play a symphony. Similarly, while different network communications products might perform according to a common standard, they often need fine-tuning and customization before they can play together in a real network.

My bottom-line advice about adopting open protocols is to proceed slowly. The engineers, programmers, and designers of products conforming to open protocols need years of experience before they can field products that interoperate the first time and every time. They have to refine procedures and products, and there is no way to hurry the process.

Unless you have the resources of the U.S. government or a major international corporation to back you, don't try to use the "open" tools to solve your interoperability problems yet. Instead, I suggest using gateways such as electronic mail and WAITS to link dissimilar LANs, or taking advantage of some of the pragmatic multiprotocol techniques I'll describe in the next section.

Open protocols:

👍 **Provide interoperability between very different computer systems**

👍 **Give users the freedom to choose products from more than one vendor**

👎 **Offer no guarantee of success**

■ Realism and Pragmatism

An interesting thing happened as the networking and computer companies shuffled along the road to the promised land of open systems. The people in the companies traveling the road each learned more about protocols and writing structured software. The promised land was still a long way off, but the people looked at each other and said, "Let's work together!" As a result, today you can link LANs of dissimilar computers and operating systems using a variety of products developed by pragmatic companies.

The building blocks you'll have to work with when you try to erect an integrated network can vary widely. In your organization you might find pockets of Macintosh computers using the AppleTalk protocols, large sections of PCs working over Novell's IPX/SPX protocols, some PCs in a network running NetBIOS, and computers using the Unix operating system and the TCP/IP protocols. While at first inspection this mix does not look promising, there are several ways to give PCs the ability to access and use the resources of each of these very different LANs.

The Building Blocks

Let's look first at the raw material you have to work with when you create a network out of dissimilar systems. The following paragraphs highlight the various architectures and protocols you might see when you try to link the separate LANs in any organization. The actions of routers using some of these protocols were described in Chapter 5.

The Apple Macintosh presents an interesting study in compatibility. On the one hand, it isn't as easy to write network communications software for Macintosh computers, so few network operating system companies tackled the job of putting their own software in the Mac. On the other hand, Apple supplied an excellent suite of its own networking software with each Macintosh, so networking companies elected simply to modify their operating systems to work with the Macintosh. As a result, you can add software to NetWare, LAN Manager, VINES, and some Unix-based LAN operating systems enabling them to recognize and respond to the requests and transport-layer packets generated by Macintosh computers. The Macs become full clients of the LAN while running their own native Apple networking software. In effect, no other computer architecture is as interoperable as the Macintosh because so many companies have extended their own products to include the Mac protocols.

The TCP/IP protocols were developed by the U.S. Department of Defense when DoD scientists faced the problem of linking thousands of dissimilar computers. The DoD paid companies like IBM, Honeywell, and Sperry (now Unisys) to develop TCP/IP software for specific combinations of computer architectures and operating systems used in the government. Many other companies used their own funds to get onto the TCP/IP bandwagon. Each machine's TCP/IP module must be customized for the computer and its operating system but standardized for the network—typically Ethernet. TCP/IP modules are available for hundreds of different mainframe and minicomputer systems and for many different PC networks, including NetWare.

The native transmission protocol for NetWare is IPX/SPX. As described in Chapter 5, Novell provides software that acts as a router for IPX/SPX. I'll delve into the integration capabilities built into NetWare 3.X later in this chapter.

NetBIOS is a network interface and LAN communications program originally developed in part by IBM. It is used in LAN operating systems like Artisoft's LANtastic, Microsoft's LAN Manager, and Performance Technology's POWERlan. As a transport-layer protocol, NetBIOS has limited addressing capability, but Performance Technology has some interesting products that can help move NetBIOS packets across inter-LAN links (more about them later).

The pieces of software that conform to the AppleTalk, TCP/IP, and IPX/SPX protocols are generally proven and stable. Different companies' implementations of NetBIOS vary in their interoperability, but there aren't many versions, and it's possible to make allowances for the major products like those from Artisoft, IBM, and Performance Technology. You can use these hunks of software as the raw building blocks for your interconnected network of different LANs, but fitting them together takes some skill.

Fitting the Pieces

You can buy multiprotocol remote external routers to link LANs, but using these devices introduces complexity and confusion. For the sake of interoperability, simplicity, effective management, and reliability, I suggest that you do as much routing as possible using the same single protocol across all the inter-LAN links. This is a worthy goal, but reaching that goal can require some creativity.

HINT. *Whenever possible, use the multiprotocol local internal routers that come with NetWare, LAN Manager, and VINES to translate between incompatible media and protocols. These products work well and immediately channel most of the traffic to its destination at the file server. Besides that, chances are that you've already paid for them!*

Using one routing protocol means establishing interoperability among different PCs and different LANs, translating between different LAN wiring and access schemes, and either encapsulating some packets within your routed protocol or translating some packets into the routed protocol. In PC-based networks, you'll typically route on IP, IPX, or perhaps the AppleTalk protocol.

HINT. *Because of the number of tried and tested Ethernet products and the wide support for this protocol scheme, interoperability is easier to establish over Ethernet than over Token-Ring. But whether you use Ethernet or Token-Ring, choose adapters that have the NDIS protocols available.*

In essence, there are three techniques you can use to gain interoperability. These approaches have different strengths, but each allows you to make LAN-to-LAN links using a single standard protocol:

- Use multiple protocol stacks in the client PCs.

- Use multiple protocol stacks inside a server, and connect each client PC to the appropriate adapter board and software in the server.

- Use a special product that translates between the protocols.

Loading Multiple Client Stacks

Figure 12.1 shows an organization with four typical local area networks. Since the corporation is growing, the management sees the advantage of being able to exchange accounting information and electronic mail between the LANs. But because they were acquired and installed independently, the LANs do not use the same networking software or LAN adapter cards. This appears to be a difficult problem, but today it has several relatively simple solutions.

Perhaps the easiest solution to this connectivity puzzle is to load multiple protocol stacks into each client PC. Each PC would have only one network adapter card, but by using special software to moderate the access to that card, you could allow two separate redirectors and two separate transport-layer network communications programs to access the adapter (Figure 12.2). At the headquarters locations, people using PCs could load one software stack containing the NetWare shell (Novell's name for a redirector) over IPX and the LANtastic redirector over NetBIOS. At the branch office, each PC would load the NetWare stack and a stack using the NFS redirector over IP over a single Ethernet adapter.

This solution doesn't provide 100 percent of the connectivity we need in this scenario; each PC can't use the resources of all four LANs simultaneously if we use remote routers. We could get that connectivity using remote bridges, which would pass all packets and the included protocols, but this configuration could put a heavy load on the communications link, and it is appropriate only if there isn't much traffic on any of the LANs. We'll solve the problem of providing full access with routers a little later.

Using multiple stacks is not confusing to the person sitting in front of the network client PC. The user of a PC loaded with multiple stacks sees only a lot of network resources represented by separate DOS drive letters and printer designations. The network administrator must use different commands and utility programs to configure each redirector with appropriate links to the server software, and will probably use some type of memory-management software to save as much RAM for application programs as possible. The downside of using multiple protocols is that the technique takes up a lot of RAM, and each individual machine requires a lot of attention from the LAN administrator.

HINT. *It takes a strong knowledge of batch files and login scripts to configure PCs running multiple protocol stacks. These topics are covered in more depth in* PC Magazine Guide to Using NetWare, *ISBN 1-56276-022-X, published by Ziff-Davis Press.*

Running multiple protocols on a single strand of LAN cabling isn't difficult because LAN hardware—particularly Ethernet LAN hardware—is

Figure 12.1

This figure shows four LANs in two separate geographical locations. At the headquarters, one LAN uses Novell's NetWare operating system running over Ethernet adapters, while the other LAN uses Artisoft's LANtastic over Ethernet adapters. At the branch office, one LAN uses NetWare over Ethernet, while the other uses the TCP/IP transmission protocols over Ethernet to connect PCs to a computer running Unix, TCP/IP, and Sun Microsystems' network file server software NFS. The goal is to connect all the LANs in and between the two locations.

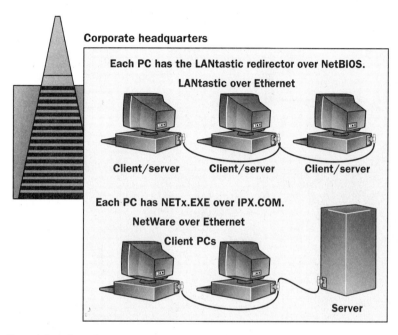

Corporate headquarters

Each PC has the LANtastic redirector over NetBIOS.

LANtastic over Ethernet

Client/server   Client/server   Client/server

Each PC has NETx.EXE over IPX.COM.

NetWare over Ethernet

Client PCs

Server

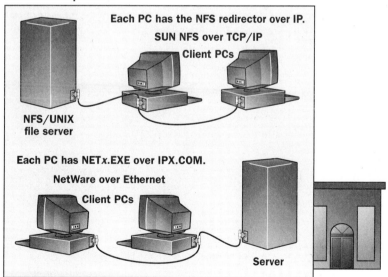

Branch headquarters

Each PC has the NFS redirector over IP.

SUN NFS over TCP/IP

Client PCs

NFS/UNIX file server

Each PC has NETx.EXE over IPX.COM.

NetWare over Ethernet

Client PCs

Server

designed to support multiple protocols. But in DOS-based PC systems, the real difficulty is running multiple protocols using a single network adapter. That's because most DOS networking software assumes that it "owns" the network adapter card. Today, with increasing emphasis on multiple protocols and connectivity to multiple hosts, DOS networking software is starting to adopt a new-age "adapter-sharing" consciousness.

Figure 12.2

This diagram shows how two separate stacks of redirectors and transport-layer programs can use the same LAN adapter card.

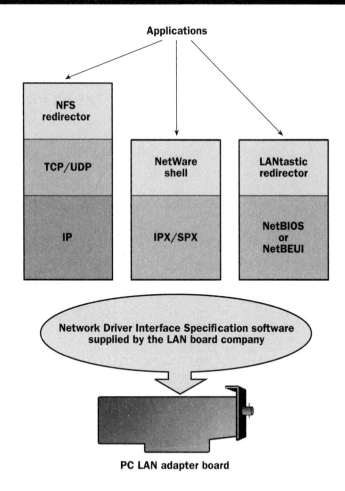

The ability to share adapters in PCs was greatly facilitated by FTP Software, which created and publicized a packet driver specification. A packet driver is a software interface between the transport-layer software and the network adapter. When a packet driver is used, the transport-layer software talks to the packet driver instead of talking directly to the network adapter hardware. When a network transport-layer program starts to operate, it registers

The Clarkson packet driver collection:

👍 **Offers many ways to use multiple protocol stacks on the same LAN adapter**

👍 **Low cost**

👍 **Relative simplicity**

👎 **No guarantee of support**

Loading multiple stacks of LAN software in a PC:

👍 **Provides great flexibility**

👍 **Delivers excellent throughput**

👎 **Requires a lot of RAM**

👎 **Requires separate setup and administration at each node**

itself with the packet driver and tells the packet driver what types of packets it wants to handle. When a relevant packet arrives, the packet driver passes it on to the registered transport-layer software. This relieves you of the technical challenge and cost of installing multiple adapters in a single PC.

An important force behind the development of the packet drivers has been a man named Russell Nelson and staff members at Clarkson University. Following FTP Software's specification, Nelson created a skeleton packet driver. Based on his framework, many people around the world have created packet drivers for nearly every networking board. These drivers can be acquired through the Internet and on many public bulletin board systems.

The only drawback of using the Clarkson packet-driver system is the lack of reliable support. Since the packet-driver programs and the transport-layer programs designed to go over them are donated for free and supported only by volunteers, you can't always call for help if your system doesn't work. Yet these drivers are used in hundreds of large networks around the world, and the drivers for the most popular LAN adapters have been refined and proven.

In 1989, Microsoft and 3Com delivered a product called Demand Protocol Architecture (DPA) that allows loading both IPX/SPX and a LAN Manager protocol stack over the same adapter. Hughes LAN Systems markets a product called ProLINC that runs over any LAN adapter with NDIS software and can multiplex IP, Digital Equipment Corp.'s Local Area Transport (LAT), IPX/SPX, VINES' InterProcess Communication (IPC), NetBIOS, and LAN Manager protocols over the adapter. Spry markets a program called Concurrent for NetWare, and Walker Richer and Quinn markets a similar program called 3000 Connection.

The technique of loading multiple protocol stacks into a client PC, illustrated in Figure 12.3, gives that PC the full capability of each LAN in each location in our scenario. Obviously, one of the protocols—in this case IPX—can be routed to services on other LAN segments. This approach gives great flexibility and performance with good security, but you'll need time to set up and configure each PC.

TCP/IP Connections

There are two ways networked PCs running DOS can use TCP/IP. The first has a TCP/IP software module loaded into every machine on the network. The second configuration uses one machine on the network as a gateway out to a TCP/IP network or device.

When your network has a great deal of interaction among different types of machines, giving every PC its own TCP/IP module makes sense. However, in doing so you pay the penalties of greater RAM use and more network overhead.

Figure 12.3

The two business locations are now linked by IPX/SPX routers, so the remote link takes place from NetWare LAN to NetWare LAN. As needed, each PC in each location can load one or both of the protocol stacks used at the location and access the resources of either LAN. This approach makes the resources of all NetWare LANs available to all PCs in both locations, but it doesn't provide all PCs access to all LANs.

From the standpoint of administration, usefulness, and security, this is a good configuration. Note that the branch office links the existing LAN cables with a local Ethernet bridge to isolate traffic, while the headquarters makes a simple physical cable connection.

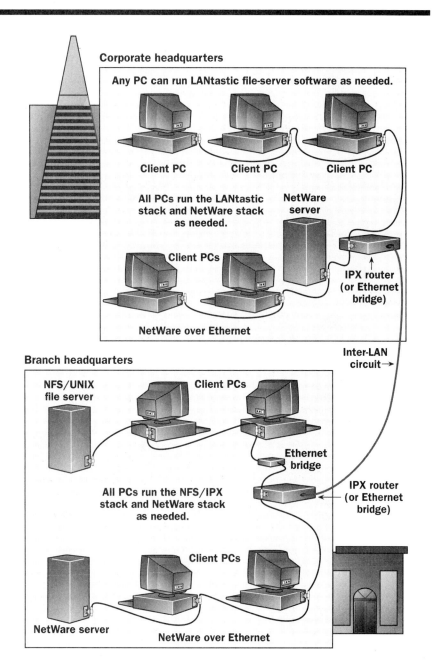

Corporate headquarters

Any PC can run LANtastic file-server software as needed.

Client PC   Client PC   Client PC

All PCs run the LANtastic stack and NetWare stack as needed.

NetWare server

Client PCs

NetWare over Ethernet

IPX router (or Ethernet bridge)

Inter-LAN circuit →

Branch headquarters

NFS/UNIX file server   **Client PCs**

Ethernet bridge

All PCs run the NFS/IPX stack and NetWare stack as needed.

IPX router (or Ethernet bridge)

Client PCs

NetWare server   **NetWare over Ethernet**

Setting up a TCP/IP gateway is the best solution for a homogeneous network of PCs that sometimes need access to a specific TCP/IP network or machine. The PCs on this kind of network do most of their work together, using whatever PC-to-PC communications protocol the network provides. PC applications needing TCP/IP services send data through the gateway. The gateway translates between a PC's network-protocol environment and the TCP/IP environment. The TCP/IP software typically runs on a machine dedicated to the gateway task.

The heart of the IP portion of TCP/IP is a concept called the Internet address. This is a 32-bit number assigned to every node on the network. There are various types of addresses designed for different-size networks, but you can write every address in base 10 using this form: 128.22.5.13. These numbers identify the major network and subnetworks a node is on. The address identifies a particular node and provides a path gateways can use to route information from one machine to another.

Although data delivery systems like Ethernet or X.25 bring their packets to any machine electrically attached to the cable, the IP modules must know each others' Internet addresses to communicate. A machine acting as a gateway between different TCP/IP networks will have a different Internet address on each network. Internal look-up tables and software based on the Address Resolution Protocol are used to route the data between networks through a gateway.

Another piece of software works with the IP-layer programs to move information to the right application on the receiving system. This software follows a standard called the User Datagram Protocol (UDP). It is helpful to think of the UDP software as creating a data address in the TCP/IP message that details exactly what application the data block is supposed to contact at the address described by the IP software. The UDP software provides the final routing for the data within the receiving system.

The TCP or Transmission Control Protocol portion of TCP/IP comes into operation once the packet is delivered to the correct Internet address and application port. Software packages that follow the TCP standard run on each machine, establish a connection to each other, and manage the communications exchanges. A data delivery system like Ethernet makes no promises about successfully delivering a packet. Neither IP nor UDP has the ability to recover packets that aren't successfully delivered. But TCP structures and buffers the data flow, looks for responses, and takes action to replace missing data blocks. This concept of data management is called "reliable stream" service.

Conceptually, software that supports the TCP protocol stands alone. It can work with data received through a serial port, over a packet-switched network, or from a network system like Ethernet. In concept, it doesn't need or even know about IP or UDP, but in practice TCP is an integral part of the TCP/IP equation and is most frequently used with IP and UDP.

■ Novell's NetWare Solution

In NetWare, Version 3.11, Novell delivered a product with many interoperability features, including several optional ways to link to TCP/IP systems. Right out of the box, NetWare 3.11 and later products in the 3.X series provide limited connectivity between computers running TCP/IP software. For example, Unix systems on one NetWare network can send mail and messages to Unix machines attached to the same network or to a remote NetWare server; they can even use printers attached to those machines. But the built-in NetWare TCP/IP functionality does not allow Unix machines to access files stored in other formats on the NetWare server, nor does it allow diverse platforms to exchange files directly.

NetWare 3.X includes a program that runs in a server and allows it to function as a local or remote IP router. The server can look inside the Ethernet or Token-Ring frames it receives, examine the IP address of the destination station, and make decisions about how to send the packet or frame toward the destination. This capability is handy in organizations that have an eclectic base of computers that use the same network cabling scheme, with some using network software that supports Novell's IPX protocol, others using software that conforms to the IP standards.

Figure 12.4 shows a NeXT computer running Unix and using network software that conforms to TCP/IP. If that computer is connected to the same Ethernet cable as a NetWare 3.X server, the NetWare server will transparently allow data from the NeXT machine to move over a long-distance LAN-to-LAN link to another NeXT workstation (also attached to a NetWare server) located on a Unix network in another city. NetWare's router transmits the IP packets to the remote network, allowing the two computers to work as if they were in a Unix-only environment.

The more important method of integrating NetWare with TCP/IP involves invisibly moving NetWare packets across an existing IP-based network. Organizations with IP routers, or with connections to a routing internetwork system, can take advantage of a technique called *IPX tunneling,* which lets NetWare clients and servers interact across existing IP networks. IPX tunneling wraps IPX packets in a TCP/IP envelope so that IP routers can send the packets to different LAN segments. This technique gives NetWare systems the key to the international TCP/IP communications systems already established by many companies, universities, and governmental organizations. Of course, NetWare's ROUTEGEN (misleadingly named BRGEN in earlier versions) is still available to allow IPX packets to be directly transmitted between NetWare networks when a direct link between the two exists.

Figure 12.4

Under NetWare 3.X, a Unix-based NeXT system on a NetWare LAN can communicate with a distant NeXT computer. The two NeXT systems can perform such tasks as exchanging mail and messages. NetWare 3.X also permits wrapping IPX packets in a TCP/IP envelope so that NetWare clients running only IPX can accomplish the same communications through an IP router.

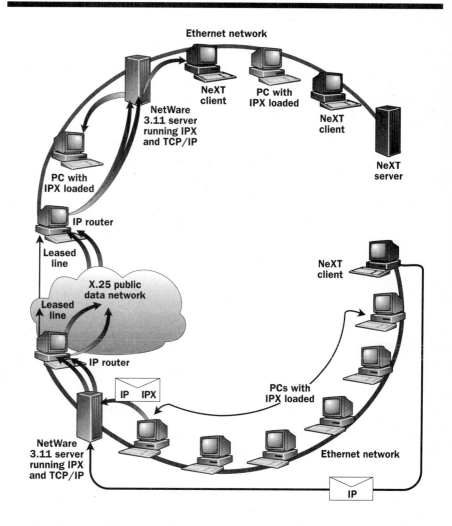

Novell has implemented IP routing functions well, but its router lacks a trusted Routing Information Protocol (RIP) source list, which is found in most dedicated routers. Without this, the router might get incorrect information from another router. Inadvertent and wrong RIP requests, although unlikely, could create never-ending work for the router or even crash the network.

One feature that network managers will appreciate is the Reverse Address Resolution Protocol (RARP). RARP allows you to put the LAN adapter's Ethernet or Token-Ring address and the IP address in a table on the router. Any network node can then query the router for its own IP address.

If an organization with offices in multiple locations already has an IP router or connections to an internetwork routing system, it can take advantage of a NetWare 3.X server's ability to route both IP and IPX packets over inter-LAN connections. Running both protocols over the same network card, the server can route both types of packets simultaneously.

Interestingly, the NetWare 3.X router is both static and dynamic. A *static* router acts on information it reads from its predefined router table. With *dynamic* routing, you put limited information in the router's table. Using the Routing Information Protocol, the router asks other routers how to find addresses not contained in its own table.

In the TCP/IP world, the Simple Network Management Protocol (SNMP) allows many dissimilar hosts such as NeXT, RS/6000, and Sun systems to report statistics to each other. NetWare 3.11 includes an NLM manager—TCPCON—that queries TCP agents on the network cable, requests information about their status, and displays the data on the server console in familiar C-Worthy-style screens. TCPCON is not a robust SNMP manager (it queries only one host at a time), but it provides useful information about network activity.

NetWare NFS is a collection of programs that run in the server and allow Unix users who are attached to the same network cable to access the directory and print services on a NetWare 3.X server. These NLMs run in the server and provide NFS services through Unix *daemons* (routines that run as background processes and perform systemwide public functions) for file sharing, print services, TCP/IP file transfers, file locking, and record locking.

With NetWare NFS running on a NetWare 3.X server, NetWare file and print servers emulate their Unix counterparts as they interact with attached Unix computers. This allows authorized Unix users access to NetWare print queues and file services, and makes volumes on the NetWare server appear just as they would on a native Unix file system. Unix users can also access files stored on the NetWare server from other file systems, including DOS, Macintosh, and OS/2 HPFS.

Because Unix and DOS store data differently, however, sharing files can lead to problems. Unix stores data with only a carriage return (13h) at the end of a line, while DOS uses a carriage return (13h) and a line-feed (10h). NetWare NFS includes two utilities to convert files to and from Unix and

DOS, but they leave you with two copies of a file, and the loss of data integrity could spell trouble. Many people believe the network operating system should solve this problem, but for compatibility and transparency, applications really should handle the conversion themselves. WordPerfect is an excellent example of a program that does.

At PC Magazine LAN Labs we have used NetWare NFS to share Word-Perfect files between WordPerfect running under Unix on a NeXT computer and the DOS version of the program. Since WordPerfect maintains compatibility with its data files across operating systems, on the NeXT workstation we were able to modify a file created with the DOS version and send it to a remote PC workstation's QMS PostScript printer through a NetWare 3.11 print queue. This demonstrates cross-platform computing at its best.

Novell's LAN WorkPlace for DOS lets DOS and Microsoft Windows computers attached to a NetWare 3.X server take advantage of TCP/IP connectivity. Without LAN WorkPlace for DOS, DOS client PCs cannot use the resources available from Unix systems on the same network cable. With it, DOS-based PCs on a NetWare network can act as terminals to the Unix system, exchanging files with it and using other resources attached to it such as CD-ROM drives, modems, printers, and tape backups. LAN WorkPlace for DOS even lets you turn your PC into an FTP (File Transfer Protocol) server, giving Unix computers access to DOS systems' hard disks. With this software in place, Unix systems can access the DOS machines' files, but without NetWare NFS, they cannot use any of the other DOS-based clients' network printers.

To take advantage of this kind of connectivity, you need to select the ODI (Open Data-link Interface) drivers available to NetWare 3.X during the workstation generation process, WSGEN. This selection allows NetWare to use multiple protocol stacks on the same adapter at the same time. With both IPX/SPX and TCP/IP protocols loaded, a PC can talk to both networks simultaneously. More important, you can unload the ODI drivers from memory when you have finished your connection, returning precious RAM to applications.

LAN WorkPlace for DOS works well when you are running either DOS or Windows. In DOS mode, you get a command-line interface. Icons and support for multitasking and dynamic data exchange are characteristics of the Windows version included in the package.

NetWare 3.X now supports Macintosh computers with AppleTalk Filing Protocol (AFP) through optional NLMs on the server. A NetWare 3.X server can even route among LocalTalk, EtherTalk, and TokenTalk in the same server, providing connectivity to several normally isolated LANs. LocalTalk is Apple's network hardware, while EtherTalk and TokenTalk are versions of AppleTalk that run over Ethernet and Token-Ring topology, respectively.

The Macintosh name space provides a native file-storage area on NetWare 3.X servers. Using Apple Computer Corp.'s AppleShare, Macintosh users can access NetWare file servers with Chooser, a built-in menu function on the Mac, and find information stored on the NetWare server by selecting familiar Macintosh icons.

For companies that want maximum compatibility across many platforms now, there's NetWare FTAM. Adhering to the OSI standard, File Transfer Access and Management (FTAM) allows dissimilar Unix computers to communicate at the file level. NetWare FTAM allows systems conforming to the seven-layer OSI model to exchange files with NetWare 3.X servers.

Unlike NetWare NFS, which makes remote files look like an extension to your computer, NetWare FTAM is designed to provide rudimentary file communication between hosts. Users are limited to sending, receiving, renaming, and deleting files from either system. NetWare FTAM is intended for organizations that need to transfer data frequently, not for cross-platform computing.

With add-on products such as LAN WorkPlace for DOS, LAN WorkPlace for OS/2, and LAN WorkPlace for Macintosh, as well as NetWare NFS and Macintosh NLMs, NetWare 3.X provides ways to connect different computing platforms. With these add-on products, dissimilar systems can do more than exchange messages. The computers running LAN WorkPlace (in any of its versions) on the Token-Ring network have direct access not only to the files and resources of the NetWare 3.X server, but also to those of the Unix systems on the Ethernet network and the other computers running LAN WorkPlace on the same Token-Ring network.

■ Links to Unix

There are many other products that work to move packets of data between different protocol streams. In this segment of the chapter I'll describe some products and discuss their capabilities. This outline is not complete or exhaustive; it is intended only to illustrate what mortar is available to help you secure the building blocks of your network.

When you need to link PCs running DOS with networks using IP, you'll usually find some computers running Unix on the IP network. These Unix machines can form a solid platform for interoperability. You can bring DOS's IPX or SMB protocols into the Unix world, or you can bring the Unix protocols into the DOS world. Atlantix Corp.'s Atlantix Axcess, Performance Technology's POWERfusion, NCR's version of Portable NetWare, and AT&T's version of LanMan/X are examples of the former approach, while

Sun's PC/NFS, FTP Software's PC/TCP package, The Wollongong Group's WINTCP, and Crynwr Software's Clarkson Packet Driver Collection are examples of the latter. A third approach is embodied in Locus Computing Corp.'s PC-Interface, which uses its own protocols.

If you have already invested in DOS connectivity, you need a way to add capabilities without detracting from what you have. There are many options, but the question that should be uppermost is how each product works with your installed base. Because Novell is the biggest PC network vendor, there are many products, such as Atlantix Axcess and POWERfusion, that work with NetWare.

Another important approach is to continue to run your current network OS, but to add the services of a Unix computer invisibly. This is not possible with all of the popular PC networking systems, but it is possible for both Net-Ware and LAN Manager through products like NCR's Portable NetWare and AT&T's LanMan/X. These products run special versions of the NetWare or LAN Manager server software over the Unix file system. Performance Technology offers versions of its network operating systems for both DOS and Unix machines. In all cases, the Unix server appears as just another network resource—another DOS drive letter—to the people using the PCs.

These options are most appropriate when you want to run familiar DOS networking standards but also need the flexibility of a Unix host for adding functionality to the network. For example, many organizations have programmers who find it easier to write programs for the LAN using traditional Unix software-development techniques rather than using Novell's difficult NLM and VAP development facilities.

In the peer-to-peer DOS-based network arena, D-Link Systems' LANsmart has the architecture that is most adaptable to running multiple protocols. Since its inception LANsmart has worked with FTP Software's PC/TCP package, and it is also compatible with The Clarkson Packet Driver Collection described above. Artisoft's LANtastic seems to have less inherent internetworking potential, but its large market share has created a market for compatible protocols, and it can be used with the packages from both FTP Software and The Wollongong Group.

FTP Software's PC/TCP Plus offers connectivity with up to ten host Unix and IBM 3270 sessions from DOS and OS/2 PCs. Using PC/TCP's telnet functions, PCs can emulate DEC VT 220 or IBM 3270 terminals over the network cable so they can run Unix or 3270 programs or use resources connected to those types of systems.

In addition, PC/TCP acts as an SNMP (Simple Network Management Protocol) agent, responding to requests for information about network status. If you are using NetWare, you can load PC/TCP on top of NetWare's IPX program to give you connectivity beyond your NetWare network.

One of the most comprehensive visions of network computing comes from Sun Microsystems, which is a major innovator in the Unix marketplace, and which has long promoted the slogan, "The network is the computer." The SunConnect division's PC-NFS software allows DOS PCs to access files on any Unix host that supports NFS. PC-NFS also includes over-the-wire terminal emulation (telnet) and several more specialized utilities. But what Sun really wants to sell is the idea of open network computing (ONC). ONC includes capabilities that go beyond simple file sharing, such as RPCs (Remote Procedure Calls) and NIS (Network Information Services). It also offers a programmers' toolkit, which helps developers create networked applications for both DOS and Unix.

Atlantix Axcess's forte is bringing NetWare, LAN Manager, PC Network, and other PC network protocols to the Unix environment. Any PCs that are already set up for one of these existing PC network systems can easily access files on a Unix system running Atlantix Axcess. And like most other companies that integrate DOS and Unix networks, Atlantix also supplies a terminal emulation program that works over the network. Atlantix's WindowView, which is a Windows 3.X–compatible program, lets you interact with a standard Unix terminal application using the screen and keyboard of your PC.

Locus Computing Corp. has long been active in both the Unix and DOS markets as a supplier of systems software to better-known companies. Its PC-Interface package allows you to access Unix files from a DOS machine. Server software is available for several versions of Unix. Additional utilities allow you to execute programs on a Unix system and to log on to Unix systems over the network. PC-Interface is most appropriate for integrating individual DOS PCs into existing Unix networks.

Another company that provides both Unix file serving and over-the-network terminal emulation is Performance Technology. Its POWERfusion software enables a Unix system to be a file server on a PC LAN. POWERfusion works with various drivers that provide specific PC protocols, such as NetBIOS, ARCnet, or SMB.

On the DOS side, the same company provides POWERworkstation, which is an over-the-network terminal emulator program. An interesting related product is Performance Technology's POWERbridge, which lets you use a PC to bridge a pair of LANs. Despite its name, POWERbridge is not a bridge; I classify it as a NetBIOS router. Performance Technology markets this solution for both X.25 and V.32 (9,600-bps) point-to-point dial-up modem connections. It works on all types of NetBIOS LANs, including LAN Manager and LANtastic and Performance Technology's own POWERlan.

POWERbridge works at the network layer of the OSI stack and routes NetBIOS packets to their destination. As a true NetBIOS dynamic router, it learns the home segments of stations on the networks in real time and properly routes packets, saving money and boosting throughput. Although it routes only NetBIOS packets, it also works on NetWare LANs that run the Novell NetBIOS emulator.

For speeds up to and including 64 kilobits per second, POWERbridge uses a compression algorithm to supply greater throughput. The compression routine works on the fly to reduce the amount of data that goes across the internetwork link. Through multiple virtual circuits, users can establish as many as 254 simultaneous sessions with other networks over a public data network.

You can use a dedicated or nondedicated computer on the network for POWERbridge, but whether you can run other applications on the same computer depends on the amount of network traffic crossing the router, the type of application, and the power and configuration of the computer.

If you are an administrator, you can run a control program from your own PC to monitor traffic, rename resources, and establish new connections. The monitor screen displays many useful pieces of data, including the number of current connections, the amount of traffic for various periods, and information on bad packets. With the proper privileges, you can access this information from any computer on the network.

■ A Pragmatic Future

You cannot afford to be afraid of the challenge of linking different LANs. The problem will appear many times in any organization with a growing computer network system. Establishing rules that mandate conformance to the ISO's open standards is one option many large organizations have taken, but they are paying high front-end costs for long-term returns.

The practical approach that will appeal to most people who use PCs calls for using what works. Fortunately, you have many interoperability options that do work—some of which are also economical. On the bottom line, be pragmatic and go for solutions based on technologies that have broad support.

■ Appendix

Asynchronous Comm Servers

Alloy Computer Products, Inc.
165 Forest Street
Marlboro, MA 01752
508-481-8500

Concept Development Systems, Inc.
PO Box 1988
Kenesaw, GA 30144
404-424-6240
fax: 404-424-8995

Cross Communications Co.
1881 9th St.
Canyon Center Ste. 212
Boulder, CO 80302-5181
303-444-7799
fax: 303-444-4687

Crystal Point, Inc.
22122 20th Ave., SE, Ste. 148
Bothell, WA 98021
206-487-3656
fax: 206-487-3773

Cubix Corp.
2800 Lockheed Way
Carson City, NV 89706
800-829-0550; 702-883-7611
fax: 702-882-2407

David Systems, Inc.
701 E. Evelyn Ave.
Sunnyvale, CA 94086-6527
408-720-8000
fax: 408-720-9485
Tech support: 408-720-6884

Emulex Corp.
3545 Harbor Blvd., PO Box 6725
Costa Mesa, CA 92626
800-854-7112; 714-662-5600
fax: 714-241-0792
Tech support: Use main no.

Gateway Communications, Inc.
2941 Alton Ave.
Irvine, CA 92714
800-367-6555; 714-553-1555
fax: 714-553-1616
Tech support: Use main no.

IBM Corp.
Old Orchard Rd.
Armonk, NY 10504
800-426-2468; 914-765-1900
Tech support: Use toll-free no.

Intercomputer Communications Corp. (ICC)
8230 Montgomery Rd.
Cincinnati, OH 45236
513-745-0500
fax: 513-745-0327

J&L Information Systems, Inc.
9238 Deering Ave.
Chatsworth, CA 91311
818-709-1778

Memsoft Corp.
One Park Place
621 NW 53rd St. #240
Boca Raton, FL 33487
407-997-6655

Microtest, Inc.
3519 E. Shea Blvd.
Phoenix, AZ 85028
800-526-9675; 602-971-6464
fax: 602-971-6963
Tech support: Use main no.

Multi-Tech Systems, Inc.
2205 Woodale Dr.
Mounds View, MN 55112
800-328-9717; 612-785-3500
fax: 612-785-9874
Tech support: Use main no.

Novell, Inc.
122 East 1700 South
Provo, UT 84606-6194
800-453-1267; 801-429-7000
fax: 801-429-5775
Tech support: Use main no.

Penril DataComm Networks
1300 Quince Orchard Blvd.
Gaithersburg, MD 20878
800-4-PENRIL; 301-921-8600
fax: 301-921-8376
Tech support: Use main no.

Shiva Corp.
One Cambridge Center
Cambridge, MA 02142
800-458-3550; 617-252-6300
fax: 617-252-6852
Tech support: 617-252-6400

Softronics, Inc.
5085 List Dr.
Colorado Springs, CO 80919
800-225-8590; 719-593-9540
fax: 719-548-1878

The Software Lifeline, Inc.
Fountain Square
2600 Military Trail #290
Boca Raton, FL 33431
407-994-4466

Star Gate Technologies, Inc.
29300 Aurora Rd.
Solon, OH 44139
800-STAR GATE; 216-349-1860
fax: 216-349-2056
Tech support: Use toll-free no.

Telebit Corp.
1315 Chesapeake Terr.
Sunnyvale, CA 94089
800-835-3248; 408-734-4333
fax: 408-734-3333
Tech support: 408-734-5200

3Com Corp.
PO Box 51845, 5400 Bayfront Plaza
Santa Clara, CA 95052-8145
800-638-3266; 408-764-5000
fax: 408-764-5032
Tech support: 800-876-3266

Xylogics, Inc.
53 Third Ave.
Burlington, MA 01803
800-225-3317; 617-272-8140
fax: 617-273-5392

Bridges

Accton Technology Corp.
46750 Fremont Blvd., Ste. 104
Fremont, CA 94538
510-226-9800
fax: 510-226-9833

Alantec
47800 Westinghouse Dr.
Fremont, CA 94539
800-727-1050; 510-770-1050
fax: 510-770-1054

Allied Telesis, Inc.
575 E. Middlefield Rd.
Mountain View, CA 94043
800-424-4284; 415-964-2771
fax: 415-964-0944
Tech support: Use main no.

Andrew Corp.
2771 Plaza Del Amo
Torrance, CA 90503
800-776-6174; 213-320-7126
fax: 213-618-0386
Tech support: 800-733-0332

Applitek
100 Brickstone Sq.
Andover, MA 01810
800-LAN-CITY; 508-475-4050
fax: 508-475-0550

Artel Communications Corp.
22 Kane Industrial Dr.
Hudson, MA 01749
800-225-0228; 508-562-2100
fax: 508-562-6942

AT&T Computer Systems
1776 On The Green
Morristown, NJ 07960
800-247-1212
fax: 908-644-9768
Tech support: Use main no.

BICC Communications
103 Millbury St.
Auburn, MA 01501
800-447-6526; 508-832-8650
fax: 508-832-8689
Tech support: Use toll-free no.

Cabletron Systems, Inc.
35 Industrial Way, Box 6257
Rochester, NH 03867
603-332-9400
fax: 603-332-4616
Tech support: Use main no.

Caliber Computer Corp.
1500 McCandless Dr.
Milpitas, CA 95035
408-942-1220
fax: 408-942-1345

Canoga-Perkins
21012 Lassen St.
Chatsworth, CA 91311
818-718-6300
fax: 818-718-6312

Chipcom Corp.
118 Turnpike Rd.
Southborough, MA 01772
800-228-9930; 508-460-8900
fax: 508-460-8950

Cisco Systems, Inc.
1525 O'Brien Dr.
Menlo Park, CA 94025
800-553-6387; 415-326-1941
fax: 415-326-1989
Tech support: Use toll-free no.

Clearpoint Research Corp.
35 Parkwood Dr.
Hopkinton, MA 01748-1659
800-253-2778; 508-435-2000
fax: 508-435-7530
Tech support: 800-332-2578

CrossComm Corp.
140 Locke Dr.
Marlboro, MA 01752
508-481-4060
fax: 508-481-4216

David Systems, Inc.
701 E. Evelyn Ave.
Sunnyvale, CA 94086-6527
408-720-8000
fax: 408-720-9485
Tech support: 408-720-6884

Develcon Electronics
515 Consumers Rd., Ste. 500
Willowdale, Ontario M2J 4Z2
Canada
800-667-9333; 416-495-8666
fax: 416-495-9303

Digital Equipment Corp.
146 Main St.
Maynard, MA 01754-2571
508-493-5111
fax: 508-493-8780
Tech support: 800-332-8000

Du Pont Electronics (Electro-Optic Products Group)
3300 Gateway Center Blvd.
Morrisville, NC 27560
800-888-5261; 919-481-5100
fax: 919-481-0753

FiberCom, Inc.
PO Box 11966, 3353 Orange Ave., NE
Roanoke, VA 24022-1966
800-423-1183; 703-342-6700
fax: 703-342-5961

Fibermux Corp.
9310 Topanga Canyon Blvd.
Chatsworth, CA 91311
818-709-6000
fax: 818-709-1556
Tech support: Use main no.

Fibronics International, Inc.
Communications Way
Hyannis, MA 02601-1892
800-456-3279; 508-778-0700
fax: 508-778-0821

Gateway Communications, Inc.
2941 Alton Ave.
Irvine, CA 92714
800-367-6555; 714-553-1555
fax: 714-553-1616
Tech support: Use main no.

General DataComm, Inc.
1579 Straits Tpke.
Middlebury, CT 06762-1299
800-777-4005; 203-574-1118
fax: 203-758-8507
Tech support: 203-598-7526

Hewlett-Packard Co.
3000 Hanover St.
Palo Alto, CA 94304
800-752-0900; 415-857-1501
Tech support: Use toll-free no.

Hughes LAN Systems, Inc.
1225 Charleston Rd.
Mountain View, CA 94043
415-966-7300
fax: 415-960-3738

IBM Corp.
Old Orchard Rd.
Armonk, NY 10504
800-426-2468; 914-765-1900
Tech support: Use toll-free no.

IN-NET Corp.
15150 Avenue of Science, Ste. 100
San Diego, CA 92128-3495
800-283-FDDI; 619-487-3693
fax: 619-487-3697
Tech support: Use toll-free no.

Intellicom, Inc.
20415 Nordhoff St.
Chatsworth, CA 91311
800-992-2882; 818-407-3900
fax: 818-882-2404
Tech support: Use main no.

Kalpana, Inc.
125 Nicholas Lane
San Jose, CA 95134
408-428-1150
fax: 408-428-1161

Lan Technologies, Inc.
2000 Crawford Place, Ste. 210
Mt. Laurel, NJ 08054
800-899-LAN1; 609-234-8777
fax: 609-234-4454

Madge Networks, Inc.
42 Airport Pkwy.
San Jose, CA 95110
800-876-2343; 408-441-1300
fax: 408-441-1335
Tech support: Use toll-free no.

Microcom, Inc.
500 River Ridge Dr.
Norwood, MA 02062
800-822-8224; 617-551-1000

Motorola Codex
20 Cabot Blvd.
Mansfield, MA 02048
800-446-6336; 508-261-4000
fax: 508-261-1203
Tech support: 800-544-0062

Netronix
1372 N. McDowell Blvd.
Petaluma, CA 94954
800-282-2535; 707-762-2703
fax: 707-763-6291

Network Systems Corp.
7600 Boone Ave., N
Minneapolis, MN 55428
612-424-4888
fax: 612-424-2853

Newbridge Networks, Inc.
593 Herndon Pkwy.
Herndon, VA 22070-5421
800-332-1080; 703-834-3600
fax: 703-471-7080

Olicom USA, Inc.
1002 N. Central Expwy., Ste. 239
Richardson, TX 75080
214-680-8131
fax: 214-680-0099
Tech support: Use main no.

Optical Data Systems, Inc.
1101 E. Arapaho Rd.
Richardson, TX 75081-2336
214-234-6400
fax: 214-234-4059
Tech support: Use main no.

Penril DataComm Networks
1300 Quince Orchard Blvd.
Gaithersburg, MD 20878
800-4-PENRIL; 301-921-8600
fax: 301-921-8376
Tech support: Use main no.

Persoft, Inc.
465 Science Dr.
Madison, WI 53711
800-EMU-LATE; 608-273-6000
fax: 608-273-8227

Plexcom
65 Moreland Rd.
Simi Valley, CA 93065
805-522-3333
fax: 805-583-4764

PureData, Inc.
200 W. Beaver Creek Rd.
Richmond Hill, Ontario L4B 1B4
Canada
416-731-6444
fax: 416-731-7017

Racal-Datacom, Inc.
155 Swanson Rd.
Boxborough, MA 01719
800-526-8255; 508-263-9929
fax: 508-263-8655
Tech support: Use main no.

Retix Corp.
2644 30th St.
Santa Monica, CA 90405
800-255-2333; 213-399-2200
fax: 213-458-2685
Tech support: 213-392-6113

SynOptics Communications, Inc.
4401 Great America Pkwy.
PO Box 58185
Santa Clara, CA 95052-8185
408-988-2400
fax: 408-988-5525
Tech support: Use main no.

TCL, Inc.
41829 Albrae St.
Fremont, CA 94538
510-657-3800
fax: 510-490-5814

Teleglobe, Inc.
600 McCaffrey St.
Montreal, Quebec H4T 1N1
Canada
514-738-4781
fax: 514-738-4436

3Com Corp.
PO Box 51845, 5400 Bayfront Plaza
Santa Clara, CA 95052-8145
800-638-3266; 408-764-5000
fax: 408-764-5032
Tech support: 800-876-3266

Timeplex, Inc.
400 Chestnut Ridge Rd.
Woodcliff Lake, NJ 07675
201-391-1111
fax: 201-391-0459

Ungermann-Bass, Inc.
3900 Freedom Circle, PO Box 58030
Santa Clara, CA 95052-8030
800-873-6381; 408-496-0111
fax: 408-970-9300
Tech support: 800-325-5511

Vitalink Communications Corp.
6607 Kaiser Dr.
Fremont, CA 94555
800-443-5740; 510-794-1100
fax: 510-795-1085

Xyplex, Inc.
330 Codman Hill Rd.
Boxborough, MA 01719-1708
800-338-5316; 508-264-9900
fax: 508-264-9930

**Zenith Electronics Corp.
(Communication Products Division)**
1000 Milwaukee Ave.
Glenview, IL 60025-2493
708-391-8000
fax: 708-391-8919

Bulletin Board Systems

**Capital PC User Group Software
Library**
PO Box 1785
Bethesda, MD 20827-1785
301-762-6775

Clark Development Co.
3950 S. 700 East #303
Murray, UT 84107-2173
800-356-1686; 801-261-1686

eSoft, Inc.
15200 E. Girard Ave #2550
Aurora, CO 80014
303-699-6565

Mustang Software, Inc.
PO Box 2264
Bakersfield, CA 93303
800-999-9619; 805-395-0223

Surf Computer Services, Inc.
71-540 Gardess Rd.
Rancho Mirage, CA 92270
619-346-9430

Electronic Mail Gateways

Banyan Systems, Inc.
120 Flanders Rd.
Westboro, MA 01581
508-898-1000

Beyond, Inc.
38 Sidney St.
Cambridge, MA 02139
617-621-0095

Cayman Systems, Inc.
26 Lansdowne St.
Cambridge, MA 02139
617-494-1999
fax: 617-494-9270

cc:Mail, Inc.
2141 Landings Dr.
Mountain View, CA 94043
800-448-2500; 415-961-8800

Datapoint Corp.
8400 Datapoint Dr.
San Antonio, TX 78229-8500
800-733-1500; 512-593-7000
fax: 512-593-7355
Tech support: 512-593-7263

Digital Equipment Corp.
146 Main St.
Maynard, MA 01754-2571
508-493-5111
fax: 508-493-8780
Tech support: 800-332-8000

Enable Software, Inc.
Northway Ten Executive Park
Ballston Lake, NY 12019
800-888-0684; 518-877-8600
fax: 518-877-5225
Tech support: 518-877-8236

Innosoft International, Inc.
250 W. First St., Ste. 240
Claremont, CA 91711
714-624-7907
fax: 714-621-5319

Lotus Development Corp.
55 Cambridge Pkwy.
Cambridge, MA 02142
800-635-6887; 617-577-8500

**Management Systems Designers, Inc.
(Systems Engineering Division)**
131 Park St., NE
Vienna, VA 22180
703-281-7440
fax: 703-281-7636

Microsoft Corp.
One Microsoft Way
Redmond, WA 98052
800-426-9400; 206-882-8080
fax: 206-883-8101
Tech support: 206-454-2030

Retix Corp.
2644 30th St.
Santa Monica, CA 90405
800-255-2333; 213-399-2200
fax: 213-458-2685
Tech support: 213-392-6113

Touch Communications, Inc.
250 E. Hacienda Ave.
Campbell, CA 95008
408-374-2500
fax: 408-374-1680

Walker Richer and Quinn, Inc.
2815 Eastlake Ave., E
Seattle, WA 98102
800-872-2829; 206-324-0350
fax: 206-322-8151
Tech support: 206-325-4357

Frame Relay Systems

Netrix Corp.
13595 Dulles Technology Drive
Herndon, VA 22071
703-742-6000

Interexchange Carriers

Advanced Telecommunications Corp.
1515 S. Federal Highway, #400
Boca Raton, FL 33432
800-226-8888

American Private Line Services Inc.
140 Gould St.
Needham, MA 02194
800-624-9203; 617-455-9000

AT&T (American Telephone & Telegraph Co.)
295 N. Maple Ave.
Basking Ridge, NJ 07920
Contact your local AT&T account
representative:
800-346-3288

Cable & Wireless Communications, Inc.
1919 Gallows Rd.
Vienna, VA 22182
800-969-9998; 703-790-5300

Consolidated Network, Inc.
11701 Borman Dr., #175
St. Louis, MO 63146
314-993-9009

MCI Communications Corp.
c/o Data Marketing Dept. 0172
1650 Tysons Blvd.
McLean, VA 22102
800-888-0800

Southern Pacific Telecommunications Company, Inc.
60 Spear St., #700
San Francisco, CA 94105
415-541-2000

Sprint Data Group
10951 Lakeview Dr.
Lenexa, KS 66215
800-736-1130; 913-541-6876

WilTel
PO Box 21348
Tulsa, OK 74121
800-642-2299; 918-588-3210

Metropolitan Area Network Service Vendors

Bay Area Teleport
1141 Harbor Bay Pkwy., #260
Alameda, CA 94501
415-769-5300

BICC Communications
103 Millbury St.
Auburn, MA 01501
800-447-6526; 508-832-8650
fax: 508-832-8689
Tech support: Use toll-free no.

Diginet Communications Network
51 Monroe St., #507
Rockville, MD 20850
301-217-9672

M/A-Com
7 New England Executive Park
Burlington, MA 01803
617-272-9600

Metropolitan Fiber Systems
1 Tower Ln., #1600
Oakbrook Terr., IL 60181
708-218-7200

Microcom, Inc.
500 River Ridge Dr.
Norwood, MA 02062-5028
800-822-8224; 617-551-1000

Microwave Networks, Inc.
10795 Rockley Rd.
Houston, TX 77099
800-749-2577; 713-495-7123

Raycom Systems, Inc.
16525 Sherman Way, Unit C-8
Van Nuys, CA 91406
800-288-1620; 818-909-4186

Teleport Communications Group
1 Teleport Dr., #301
Staten Island, NY 10311
718-983-2000

TeleSciences
171 N. Covington Dr.
Bloomingdale, IL 60108
800-545-0334; 708-307-5900

Timeplex, Inc.
400 Chestnut Ridge Rd.
Woodcliff Lake, NJ 07675
201-391-1111
fax: 201-391-0459

OSI Software

Frontier Technologies Corp.
10201 N. Port Washington Rd., 13 West
Meguon, WI 53092
414-241-4555
fax: 414-241-7084

Novell, Inc.
122 East 1700 South
Provo, UT 84606-6194
800-453-1267; 801-429-7000
fax: 801-429-5775
Tech support: Use main no.

Retix Corp.
2644 30th St.
Santa Monica, CA 90405
800-255-2333; 213-399-2200
fax: 213-458-2685
Tech support: 213-392-6113

The Wollongong Group, Inc.
1129 San Antonio Rd., PO Box 51860
Palo Alto, CA 94303
800-872-8649; 800-962-8649 (CA);
415-962-7200
fax: 415-969-5547
Tech support: 415-962-7140

Routers

ACC, Inc.
34360 Glendale
Livonia, MI 48150
313-422-4444
fax: 313-422-8891

Amnet, Inc.
1881 Worcester Rd.
Framingham, MA 01701
800-821-0167; 508-879-6306
fax: 508-872-8136

Apple Computer, Inc.
20525 Mariani Ave.
Cupertino, CA 95014
408-996-1010

APT Communications, Inc.
9607 Dr. Perry Rd.
Ijamsville, MD 21754
800-842-0626; 301-831-1182

AT&T Computer Systems
1776 On The Green
Morristown, NJ 07960
800-247-1212
fax: 908-644-9768
Tech support: Use main no.

Cayman Systems, Inc.
26 Lansdowne St.
Cambridge, MA 02139
617-494-1999
fax: 617-494-9270

Chipcom Corp.
118 Turnpike Rd.
Southborough, MA 01772
800-228-9930; 508-460-8900
fax: 508-460-8950

Cisco Systems, Inc.
1525 O'Brien Dr.
Menlo Park, CA 94025
800-553-6387; 415-326-1941
fax: 415-326-1989
Tech support: Use toll-free no.

Compatible Systems Corp.
PO Drawer 17220
Boulder, CO 80308-7220
800-356-0283; 303-444-9532
fax: 303-444-9595

CrossComm Corp.
140 Locke Dr.
Marlboro, MA 01752
508-481-4060
fax: 508-481-4216

Datapoint Corp.
8400 Datapoint Dr.
San Antonio, TX 78229-8500
800-733-1500; 512-593-7000
fax: 512-593-7355
Tech support: 512-593-7263

Data Switch Corp.
One Enterprise Dr.
Shelton, CT 06484
203-926-1801
fax: 203-929-6408

Digital Equipment Corp.
146 Main St.
Maynard, MA 01754-2571
508-493-5111
fax: 508-493-8780
Tech support: 800-332-8000

Eicon Technology Corp.
2196 32nd Ave.
Montreal, Quebec H8T 3H7
Canada
514-631-2592
fax: 514-631-3092
Tech support: Use main no.

Farallon Computing, Inc.
2000 Powell St.
Emeryville, CA 94608
510-596-9000
fax: 510-596-9020
Tech support: Use main no.

Fibronics International, Inc.
Communications Way
Hyannis, MA 02601-1892
800-456-3279; 508-778-0700
fax: 508-778-0821

Frontier Technologies Corp.
10201 N. Port Washington Rd., 13 West
Meguon, WI 53092
414-241-4555
fax: 414-241-7084

Gateway Communications, Inc.
2941 Alton Ave.
Irvine, CA 92714
800-367-6555; 714-553-1555
fax: 714-553-1616
Tech support: Use main no.

Gupta Technologies, Inc.
1040 Marsh Rd.
Menlo Park, CA 94025
800-876-3267; 415-321-9500
fax: 415-321-5471
Tech support: 415-321-4484

Hewlett-Packard Co.
3000 Hanover St.
Palo Alto, CA 94304
800-752-0900; 415-857-1501
Tech support: Use toll-free no.

NEC America, Inc. (Data and Video Communication Systems Division)
110 Rio Robles
San Jose, CA 95134
800-222-4NEC, ext. 1276; 408-433-1250
fax: 408-433-1239

Network Systems Corp.
7600 Boone Ave., N
Minneapolis, MN 55428
612-424-4888
fax: 612-424-2853

Newbridge Networks, Inc.
593 Herndon Pkwy.
Herndon, VA 22070-5421
800-332-1080; 703-834-3600
fax: 703-471-7080

Newport Systems Solutions, Inc.
4019 Westerly Pl. #103
Newport Beach, CA 92660
800-368-6533; 714-752-1511

Novell, Inc.
122 East 1700 South
Provo, UT 84606-6194
800-453-1267; 801-429-7000
fax: 801-429-5775
Tech support: Use main no.

Nuvotech, Inc.
2015 Bridgeway
Sausalito, CA 94965
800-4NUVOTECH; 415-331-7815
fax: 415-331-6445

Penril DataComm Networks
1300 Quince Orchard Blvd.
Gaithersburg, MD 20878
800-4-PENRIL; 301-921-8600
fax: 301-921-8376
Tech support: Use main no.

Performance Technology
800 Lincoln Center
San Antonio, TX 78230
800-722-8649 (UNIX); 800-327-8526
(other products); 512-349-2000

Plexcom
65 Moreland Rd.
Simi Valley, CA 93065
805-522-3333
fax: 805-583-4764

Proteon, Inc.
Two Technology Dr.
Westborough, MA 01581-5008
800-545-7464; 508-898-2800
fax: 508-366-8901
Tech support: Use main no.

Retix Corp.
2644 30th St.
Santa Monica, CA 90405
800-255-2333; 213-399-2200
fax: 213-458-2685
Tech support: 213-392-6113

Shiva Corp.
One Cambridge Center
Cambridge, MA 02142
800-458-3550; 617-252-6300
fax: 617-252-6852
Tech support: 617-252-6400

Sun Microsystems, Inc.
2550 Garcia Ave.
Mountain View, CA 94043
800-821-4643; 800-821-4642 (CA);
415-960-1300
fax: 415-969-9131
Tech support: 800-USA-4SUN

SynOptics Communications, Inc.
4401 Great America Pkwy
PO Box 58185
Santa Clara, CA 95052-8185
408-988-2400
fax: 408-988-5525
Tech support: Use main no.

Syskonnect, Inc.
12930 Saratoga Ave. Ste. DI
Saratoga, CA 95070
800-SK2-FDDI; 415-725-4650
fax: 415-725-4654

Telebit Corp.
1315 Chesapeake Terr.
Sunnyvale, CA 94089
800-835-3248; 408-734-4333
fax: 408-734-3333
Tech support: 408-734-5200

3Com Corp.
PO Box 51845, 5400 Bayfront Plaza
Santa Clara, CA 95052-8145
800-638-3266; 408-764-5000
fax: 408-764-5032
Tech support: 800-876-3266

Timeplex, Inc.
400 Chestnut Ridge Rd.
Woodcliff Lake, NJ 07675
201-391-1111
fax: 201-391-0459

Tri-Data Systems, Inc.
3270 Scott Blvd.
Santa Clara, CA 95054-3011
800-874-3282; 408-727-3270
fax: 408-980-6565
Tech support: Use main no.

Ungermann-Bass, Inc.
3900 Freedom Circle, PO Box 58030
Santa Clara, CA 95052-8030
800-873-6381; 408-496-0111
fax: 408-970-9300
Tech support: 800-325-5511

Vitalink Communications Corp.
6607 Kaiser Dr.
Fremont, CA 94555
800-443-5740; 510-794-1100
fax: 510-795-1085

Wellfleet Communications, Inc.
15 Crosby Dr.
Bedford, MA 01730
617-275-2400
fax: 617-275-5001

Satellite Communications Systems

Alascom
210 E. Bluff Rd.
Anchorage, AK 99519
907-264-7000

AT&T Tridom
840 Franklin Ct.
Marietta, GA 30067
404-426-4261

AvData Systems, Inc.
55 Marietta St. NW
Atlanta, GA 30303
800-476-5915; 404-523-2848

Canadian Satellite Communications, Inc.
50 Burnhamthorpe Rd. West, 10th Floor
Mississauga, Ontario L5B 3C2
Canada
416-272-4960

Computer Power, Inc.
PO Box 2388
Jacksonville, FL 32231
904-350-1400

Comsat General Corp.
950 L'Enfant Pl. SW
Washington, DC 20024
800-888-0077; 202-863-6000

Cylix Communications Corp.
800 Ridge Lake Blvd.
Memphis, TN 38120
901-761-1177

GTE Spacenet Corp.
1801 Research Blvd.
Rockville, MD 20850
800-638-8514; 301-251-8300

Hughes Network Systems, Inc.
11717 Exploration Ln.
Germantown, MD 20876
800-755-4673; 301-428-5840

JFL Communications Inc.
PO Box 1248
Missouri City, TX 77459
713-261-0708

Nova-Net Communications, Inc.
58 Inverness Dr. East
Englewood, CO 80112
303-799-0990

Pittsburgh International Teleport
PO Box 14070
Pittsburgh, PA 15239
800-634-6530; 412-337-1888

Satellite Technology
Management Inc.
3530 Hyland Ave.
Costa Mesa, CA 92626
714-557-2400

Scientific-Atlanta, Inc.
420 N. Wickham Rd.
Melbourne, FL 32935
407-255-3146

Telesat Canada
1601 Telesat Ct.
Gloucester, Ontario K1B 5P4
Canada
613-748-0123; 613-748-8749

SNA Mainframe Gateways

Apple Computer, Inc.
20525 Mariani Ave.
Cupertino, CA 95014
408-996-1010

Attachmate Corp.
13231 Southeast 36th St.
Bellevue, WA 98006
800-426-6283; 206-644-4010
fax: 206-747-9924
Tech support: Use main no.

Avatar Technologies, Inc.
65 South St.
Hopkinton, MA 01748
800-282-3270; 508-435-3000
fax: 508-435-2470
Tech support: Use main no.

Banyan Systems, Inc.
120 Flanders Rd.
Westboro, MA 01581
508-898-1000

Barr Systems, Inc.
4131 Northwest 28 Lane
Gainesville, FL 32606
800-227-7797; 904-371-3050
fax: 904-371-3018
Tech support: Use toll-free no.

Computer Logics, Ltd. (Chi Corp.)
31200 Carter St.
Cleveland, OH 44139
800-828-0311; 216-349-8600
fax: 216-349-8620

Data Switch Corp.
One Enterprise Dr.
Shelton, CT 06484
203-926-1801
fax: 203-929-6408

DCA, Inc. (Digital Communications Associates, Inc.)
1000 Alderman Dr.
Alpharetta, GA 30201-4199
800-348-3221; 404-442-4000
fax: 404-442-4361

Tech support: 404-740-0300 (micro products)

Digital Equipment Corp.
146 Main St.
Maynard, MA 01754-2571
508-493-5111
fax: 508-493-8780
Tech support: 800-332-8000

Eicon Technology Corp.
2196 32nd Ave.
Montreal, Quebec H8T 3H7
Canada
514-631-2592
fax: 514-631-3092
Tech support: Use main no.

Gateway Communications, Inc.
2941 Alton Ave.
Irvine, CA 92714
800-367-6555; 714-553-1555
fax: 714-553-1616
Tech support: Use main no.

Gupta Technologies, Inc.
1040 Marsh Rd.
Menlo Park, CA 94025
800-876-3267; 415-321-9500
fax: 415-321-5471
Tech support: 415-321-4484

IBM Corp.
Old Orchard Rd.
Armonk, NY 10504
800-426-2468; 914-765-1900
Tech support: Use toll-free no.

ICOT Corp.
3801 Zanker Rd., PO Box 5143
San Jose, CA 95150-5143
800-762-3270; 408-433-3300
fax: 408-433-0260
Tech support: Use main no.

Microsoft Corp.
One Microsoft Way
Redmond, WA 98052-6399
800-426-9400; 206-882-8080
fax: 206-883-8101
Tech support: 206-454-2030

Multi-Tech Systems, Inc.
2205 Woodale Dr.
Mounds View, MN 55112
800-328-9717; 612-785-3500
fax: 612-785-9874
Tech support: Use main no.

**National Semiconductor Corp.
(Quadram Products Group)**
219 Perimeter Center Pkwy.
Atlanta, GA 30346
404-551-1000
Tech support: Use main no.

NCR Corp.
1700 S. Patterson Blvd.
Dayton, OH 45479
800-225-5627; 513-445-5000
fax: 513-445-2008
Tech support: 800-CALL-NCR

NDC Communications, Inc.
2860 Zanker Rd., Ste. 118
San Jose, CA 95134
408-428-9108
fax: 408-428-9109

Network Software Associates, Inc.
39 Argonaut
Laguna Hills, CA 92656
714-768-4013
fax: 714-768-5049
Tech support: Use main no.

Novell, Inc.
122 East 1700 South
Provo, UT 84606-6194
800-453-1267; 801-429-7000
fax: 801-429-5775
Tech support: Use main no.

Phaser Systems, Inc.
651 Gateway Blvd., Ste. 400
South San Francisco, CA 94080
800-234-5799; 415-952-6300
fax: 415-952-1239

Rabbit Software Corp.
7 Great Valley Pkwy., E
Malvern, PA 19355
800-RABBITC; 215-647-0440
fax: 215-640-1379
Tech support: 800-445-4357

Sun Microsystems, Inc.
2550 Garcia Ave.
Mountain View, CA 94043
800-821-4643; 800-821-4642 (CA);
415-960-1300
fax: 415-969-9131
Tech support: 800-USA-4SUN

Tri-Data Systems, Inc.
3270 Scott Blvd.
Santa Clara, CA 95054-3011
800-874-3282; 408-727-3270
fax: 408-980-6565
Tech support: Use main no.

TCP/IP Software

Apple Computer, Inc.
20525 Mariani Ave.
Cupertino, CA 95014
408-996-1010

Banyan Systems, Inc.
120 Flanders Rd.
Westboro, MA 01581
508-898-1000

Beame & Whiteside Software, Ltd.
259 Fiddler's Green Rd.
Ancaster, Ontario L9G 1W9
Canada
416-648-6556
fax: 416-648-6558

Datapoint Corp.
8400 Datapoint Dr.
San Antonio, TX 78229-8500
800-733-1500; 512-593-7000
fax: 512-593-7355
Tech support: 512-593-7263

Distinct Corp.
14082 Loma Rio Dr.
Saratoga, CA 95070
408-741-0781
fax: 408-741-0795

Fibronics International, Inc.
Communications Way
Hyannis, MA 02601-1892
800-456-3279; 508-778-0700
fax: 508-778-0821

Frontier Technologies Corp.
10201 N. Port Washington Rd., 13 West
Meguon, WI 53092
414-241-4555
fax: 414-241-7084

FTP Software, Inc.
26 Princess St.
Wakefield, MA 01880
617-246-0900
fax: 617-246-0901
Tech support: 617-246-2920

Hughes LAN Systems, Inc.
1225 Charleston Rd.
Mountain View, CA 94043
415-966-7300
fax: 415-960-3738

IBM Corp.
Old Orchard Rd.
Armonk, NY 10504
800-426-2468; 914-765-1900
Tech support: Use toll-free no.

IN-NET Corp.
15150 Avenue of Science, Ste. 100
San Diego, CA 92128-3495
800-283-FDDI; 619-487-3693
fax: 619-487-3697
Tech support: Use toll-free no.

Network Research
2380 N. Rose Ave.
Oxnard, CA 93030
800-541-9508; 805-485-2700
fax: 805-485-8204

Novell, Inc.
122 East 1700 South
Provo, UT 84606-6194
800-453-1267; 801-429-7000
fax: 801-429-5775
Tech support: Use main no.

Racal-Datacom, Inc.
155 Swanson Rd.
Boxborough, MA 01719
800-526-8255; 508-263-9929
fax: 508-263-8655
Tech support: Use main no.

Sun Microsystems, Inc.
2550 Garcia Ave.
Mountain View, CA 94043
800-821-4643; 800-821-4642 (CA);
415-960-1300
fax: 415-969-9131
Tech support: 800-USA-4SUN

TGV, Inc.
603 Mission St.
Santa Cruz, CA 95060
800-TGV-3440; 408-427-4366
fax: 408-427-4365

Unisys Corp.
PO Box 500
Blue Bell, PA 19424-0001
215-542-4011
Tech support: 800-448-1424

Walker Richer and Quinn, Inc.
2815 Eastlake Ave., E
Seattle, WA 98102
800-872-2829; 206-324-0350
fax: 206-322-8151
Tech support: 206-325-4357

The Wollongong Group, Inc.
PO Box 51860, 1129 San Antonio Rd.
Palo Alto, CA 94303
800-872-8649; 800-962-8649 (CA)
415-962-7200
fax: 415-969-5547
Tech support: 415-962-7140

X.25 and Frame Relay Carriers

Datapac (Telecom Canada)
160 Elgin St., Rm. 1080
Ottawa, Ontario K1G 3J4
Canada
613-781-6798

IBM Information Network (IBM Corp.)
3405 W. Martin Luther King Jr. Blvd.
Tampa, FL 33607
800-727-2222; 813-878-3000

Infonet (Infonet Services Corp.)
2100 East Grand Ave.
El Segundo, CA 90245
800-342-5272; 213-335-2600

Mark Net (GE Information Services)
401 N. Washington St.
Rockville, MD 20850
800-433-3683; 301-251-6510

SprintNet Data Network (U.S. Sprint Communications Co.)
12490 Sunrise Valley Dr.
Reston, VA 22096
800-736-1130; 703-689-6000

Tymnet Global Network (BT North America, Inc.)
2560 N. First St.
San Jose, CA 95161-9019
800-872-7654; 408-922-0250

X.25 Gateways

Amnet, Inc.
1881 Worcester Rd.
Framingham, MA 01701
800-821-0167; 508-879-6306
fax: 508-872-8136

Apple Computer, Inc.
20525 Mariani Ave.
Cupertino, CA 95014
408-996-1010

Banyan Systems, Inc.
120 Flanders Rd.
Westboro, MA 01581
508-898-1000

Datapoint Corp.
8400 Datapoint Dr.
San Antonio, TX 78229-8500
800-733-1500; 512-593-7000
fax: 512-593-7355
Tech support: 512-593-7263

David Systems, Inc.
701 E. Evelyn Ave.
Sunnyvale, CA 94086-6527
408-720-8000
fax: 408-720-9485
Tech support: 408-720-6884

Eicon Technology Corp.
2196 32nd Ave.
Montreal, Quebec H8T 3H7
Canada
514-631-2592
fax: 514-631-3092
Tech support: Use main no.

Frontier Technologies Corp.
10201 N. Port Washington Rd., 13 West
Meguon, WI 53092
414-241-4555
fax: 414-241-7084

Gateway Communications, Inc.
2941 Alton Ave.
Irvine, CA 92714
800-367-6555; 714-553-1555
fax: 714-553-1616
Tech support: Use main no.

IBM Corp.
Old Orchard Rd.
Armonk, NY 10504
800-426-2468; 914-765-1900
Tech support: Use toll-free no.

ICOT Corp.
3801 Zanker Rd., PO Box 5143
San Jose, CA 95150-5143
800-762-3270; 408-433-3300
fax: 408-433-0260
Tech support: Use main no.

J&L Information Systems, Inc.
9238 Deering Ave.
Chatsworth, CA 91311
818-709-1778

Netrix Corp.
13595 Dulles Technology Dr.
Herndon, VA 22071
703-742-6000

Novell, Inc.
122 East 1700 South
Provo, UT 84606-6194
800-453-1267; 801-429-7000
fax: 801-429-5775
Tech support: Use main no.

Sun Microsystems, Inc.
2550 Garcia Ave.
Mountain View, CA 94043
800-821-4643; 800-821-4642 (CA)
415-960-1300
fax: 415-969-9131
Tech support: 800-USA-4SUN

3Com Corp.
PO Box 51845, 5400 Bayfront Plaza
Santa Clara, CA 95052-8145
800-638-3266; 408-764-5000
fax: 408-764-5032
Tech support: 800-876-3266

Xyplex, Inc.
330 Codman Hill Rd.
Boxborough, MA 01719-1708
800-338-5316; 508-264-9900
fax: 508-264-9930

WAITS

SofNet, Inc.
380 Interstate North Pkwy., Ste. 150
Atlanta, GA 30339
404-984-8088
fax: 404-984-9956
Tech support: Use main no.

XcelleNet, Inc.
5 Concourse Pkwy., Ste. 200
Atlanta, GA 30328
404-804-8100
fax: 404-804-8102

■ Glossary

access method   A protocol that determines which device in a local area network has access to the transmission media at any instant. CSMA/CD is an example of an access method. IBM uses the same term for specific kinds of communications software that include protocols for exchanging data, constructing files, and other functions.

access protocol   The traffic rules that LAN workstations abide by to avoid data collisions when sending signals over shared network media; also referred to as the *media-access control (MAC) protocol.* Common examples are carrier sense multiple access (CSMA) and token passing.

access server   A networked PC that is available for remote control by distant computers calling over telephone lines and modems. Access servers provide a way to run any application on the LAN remotely.

ACK   A positive acknowledgment control character. This character is exchanged between system components when data has been received without error. The control character is also used as an affirmative response for setting up a communications exchange. ACK is also used as the name of a message containing an acknowledgment.

acoustic coupler   The portion of a modem that physically holds a telephone handset in two rubber cups. The cups house a small microphone and speaker that "talk" and "listen" to the telephone handset.

ADCCP (Advanced Data Communications Control Procedures)   A bit-oriented ANSI-standard communications protocol. It is a link-layer protocol.

A/D converter   A device that converts analog signals to digital.

address   A unique memory location. Network interface cards and CPUs often use shared addresses in RAM to move data from each card to the PC's processor. The term can also refer to the unique identifier for a particular node in a network.

Address Resolution Protocol (ARP)   A protocol within the Transmission Control Protocol/Internet Protocol (TCP/IP) suite that "maps" IP addresses to Ethernet addresses. TCP/IP requires ARP for use with Ethernet.

Advanced Communications Function (ACF)   An IBM program package to allow sharing computer resources through communications links. It supports SNA.

Advanced Communications Service   A large data communications network developed by AT&T.

AFP (AppleTalk File Protocol)   Apple's network protocol, used to provide access between file servers and clients in an AppleShare network. AFP is also used by Novell's products for the Macintosh.

alphanumeric   Characters made up of letters and numbers; usually contrasted with graphics characters made up of dots in terminal emulation.

analog   Commonly refers to transmission methods developed to transmit voice signals. These methods were designed only for the bandwidth of the human voice (up to about 3 kHz); this limits their capability to pass high-speed digital signals.

ANSI (American National Standards Institute)   An organization that develops and publishes standards for codes, alphabets, and signaling schemes.

API (application program interface)   A set of standard software interrupts, calls, and data formats that application programs use to initiate contact with network services, mainframe communications programs, or other program-to-program communications. For example, applications use APIs to call services that transport data across a network.

APPC (Advanced Program-to-Program Communications)   An IBM protocol analogous to the OSI model's session layer; it sets up the necessary conditions that enable application programs to send data to each other through the network.

APPC/PC   An IBM product that implements APPC on a PC.

AppleTalk   An Apple networking system that can transfer data at a rate of 230 kilobytes per second over shielded twisted-pair wire. Superseded by the term *LocalTalk*.

application layer   The highest (seventh) level of the OSI model. It describes the way that application programs interact with the network operating system.

applications processor   A special-purpose computer that enables a telephone system to furnish special services such as voice mail, messaging services, and electronic mail.

ARCnet (Attached Resources Computing Networks) A networking architecture (marketed by Datapoint Corp. and other vendors) using a token-passing bus architecture, usually on coaxial cable.

ARPANET (Advanced Research Projects Agency Network) A network originally sponsored by the Defense Advanced Research Projects Agency (DARPA) to link universities and government research centers. The TCP/IP protocols were pioneered on ARPANET.

ARQ A control code that calls for the retransmission of a block of data.

ASCII (American Standard Code for Information Interchange) The data alphabet used in the IBM PC to determine the composition of the 7-bit string of 0's and 1's that represents each character (alphabetic, numeric, or special).

ASR (automatic send/receive) A term left over from teleprinters that punched messages on paper tape. Now, it is sometimes used to indicate any terminal that has a storage capability.

asynchronous A method of transmission in which the time intervals between characters do not have to be equal. Start and stop bits are added to coordinate the transfer of characters.

asynchronous communications server Another name for a network modem server. Modem servers make a group of modems available to the client workstations on a first-come-first-served basis.

attenuation The decrease in power of a signal transmitted over a wire, measured in decibels. As attenuation increases, the signal decreases.

automatic number identification (ANI) A feature that passes a caller's ten-digit telephone number over the network to the customer's premises so that the caller can be identified.

background program (background mode) A program that performs its functions while the user is working with a different program. Communications programs often operate in background mode. They can receive messages while the user works with other programs. The messages are stored for later display.

balun (BALanced UNbalanced) An impedance-matching device that connects a balanced line (such as a twisted-pair line) and an unbalanced line (such as a coaxial cable).

bandwidth   The range of frequencies a circuit will pass. Analog circuits typically have a bandwidth limited to that of the human voice (about 300 Hz to 3 kHz). The square waves of a digital signal require a higher bandwidth. The higher the transmission rate, the greater the bandwidth requirement. Fiber-optic and coaxial cables have excellent bandwidths. Also, in common usage, *bandwidth* refers to the upper limit of the rate that information can be transferred over a network.

base address   The first address in a series of addresses in memory, often used to describe the beginning of a network interface card's I/O space.

baseband   A network that transmits signals as a direct-current pulse rather than as variations in a radio-frequency signal.

basic-rate interface (BRI)   The ISDN standard governing how a customer's desktop terminals and telephones can connect to the ISDN switch. It specifies two B-channels that allow 64-kilobit-per-second simultaneous voice and data service, and one D-channel that carries call information and customer data at 16 kbps.

baud   A measure of transmission speed; the reciprocal of the time duration of the shortest signal element in a transmission. In RS-232C ASCII, the signaling element is 1 bit.

BBS (bulletin board system)   An electronic message system that provides tightly controlled network access over modems and telephone lines.

BCD (binary-coded decimal)   A coding scheme using a 6-bit (six-level) code.

B-channel   A "bearer" channel that carries voice or data at 64 kilobits per second in either direction and is circuit-switched.

benchmark test   A program used to measure system speed or throughput.

Bindery   A database maintained by Novell's NetWare operating system that holds information on users, servers, and other elements of the network.

Bisynchronous Communications   Also abbreviated as BSC, this protocol is one of the two commonly used methods of encoding data for transmission between devices in IBM mainframe computer systems. Data characters are gathered in a package called a *frame*, which is marked by 2 synchronization bits (bisync). The more modern protocol is SDLC.

bit   The smallest unit of information. In digital signaling, this commonly refers to a 0 or a 1.

block   A number of characters transmitted as a group.

BNC connector   A small coaxial connector with a half-twist locking shell.

boot ROM   A read-only memory chip allowing a workstation to communicate with the file server and to read a DOS boot program from the server. Stations can thus operate on the network without having a disk drive.

bps   Bits per second.

bridge   An interconnection device, sometimes working within a PC and sometimes within a special-purpose computer, that can connect LANs using similar or dissimilar data links such as Ethernet, Token-Ring, and X.25. Bridges link LANs at the data-link layer of the OSI model. Modern bridges read and filter data packets and frames, and they pass traffic only if the address is on the same segment of the network cable as the originating station.

broadband   Refers to a network that carries information riding on carrier waves rather than directly as pulses, providing greater capacity at the cost of higher complexity.

broadcast   To send a message to all stations or an entire class of stations connected to the network.

brouter   A device that combines the functions of a bridge and a router. Brouters can route one or more protocols, such as TCP/IP and XNS, and bridge all other traffic. Contrast with *bridge*, *router*, and *gateway*.

buffer   A temporary storage space. Data may be stored in a buffer as it is received, before or after transmission. A buffer may be used to compensate for the differences between the speed of transmission and the speed of processing.

buffered repeater   A device that amplifies and regenerates signals so they can travel farther along a cable. This type of repeater also controls the flow of messages to prevent collisions.

bus topology   A "broadcast" arrangement in which all network stations receive the same message through the cable at the same time.

byte   A group of 8 bits.

C   A programming language used predominantly by professional programmers to write applications software.

cache   An amount of RAM set aside to hold data that is expected to be accessed again. The second access, which finds the data in RAM, is very fast.

call packet   A block of data carrying addressing and other information that is needed to establish an X.25 switched virtual circuit (SVC).

carrier signal   A tone or radio signal modulated by data, usually for long-distance transmission.

CCITT X.25 Recommendation   An international standard defining packet-switched communication protocols for a public or private network. The recommendation is prepared by the Comité Consultatif International Télégraphique et Téléphonique (CCITT). Along with other CCITT recommendations, the X.25 Recommendation defines the physical-, data-link-, and network-layer protocols necessary to interface with X.25 networks. The CCITT X.25 Recommendation is supported by most X.25 equipment vendors, but a new CCITT X.25 Recommendation is published every four years.

CCS 7   A network signaling standard for ISDN that incorporates information from databases in order to offer advanced network services.

central office (CO)   The telephone-switching location nearest to the customer's premises. It serves the businesses and residences connected to its loop lines.

channel   A path between sender and receiver that carries one stream of information (a two-way path is a *circuit*).

character   One letter, number, or special code.

CICS (Customer Information Control System)   This IBM software runs on a mainframe and makes a variety of services available for application programs. It furnishes easy ways for programs to enter mainframe files and find data within them.

circuit switching   A method of communicating in which a dedicated communications path is established between two devices, the bandwidth is guaranteed, and the delay is essentially limited to propagation time. The telephone system uses circuit switching.

clear packet   A block of data containing a command that performs the equivalent of hanging up the telephone.

client/server computing   A computing system in which processing can be distributed among "clients" on the network that request information and one or more network "servers" that store data, let clients share data and programs, help in printing operations, and so on. The system can accommodate standalone applications (word processing), applications requiring data from the server (spreadsheets), applications that use server capabilities to exchange information among users (electronic mail), and applications providing true client/server teamwork (databases, especially those based on Structured Query Language, or SQL). Before client/server computing, a server would download an entire database to a client machine for processing. SQL database applications divide the work between machines, letting the database stay on the server.

cluster controller   A computer that sits between a group of terminals and the mainframe, gathering messages and multiplexing over a single link to the mainframe.

CMIP (Common Management Information Protocol)   An OSI-based structure for formatting messages and for transmitting information between data-collection programs and reporting devices. This was developed by the International Standards Organization and designated as ISO 9596.

CMOT (CMIP Over TCP/IP)   An Internet standard defining the use of CMIP for managing TCP/IP networks.

coax or coaxial cable   A type of network media. Coaxial cable contains a copper inner conductor surrounded by plastic insulation and then a woven copper or foil shield.

codec (coder/decoder)   A device that transforms analog voice signals into a digital bit stream (coder) and digital signals into analog voice (decoder) using pulse-code modulation.

collision   An attempt by two units to send a message at one time on a single channel. In some networks, the detection of a collision causes all senders to stop transmissions, while in others the collision is noticed when the receiving station fails to acknowledge the data.

common carrier   A transmission company (such as a telephone company) that serves the general public.

communications controller   A programmable computer dedicated to data communications and serving as the "front end" in the IBM SNA network.

concentrator   See *wiring hub*.

contention   The condition when two or more stations attempt to use the same channel at the same time.

control character　A character used for special signaling; often not printed or displayed, but causing special functions such as the movement of paper in a printer, the blanking of a display screen, or "handshaking" between communicating devices to control the flow of data.

COW interface (character-oriented Windows interface)　An SAA-compatible user interface for OS/2 applications.

cps　Characters per second.

CPU (central processing unit)　The functional "brain" of a computer; the element that does the actual adding and subtracting of 0's and 1's that is essential to computing.

CRC (cyclic redundancy check)　A numeric value derived from the bits in a message. The transmitting station uses one of several formulas to produce a number that is attached to the message. The receiving station applies the same formula and should derive the same number. If the numbers are not the same, an error condition is declared.

crosstalk　The spillover of a signal from one channel to another. In data communications it is very disruptive. Usually, careful adjustment of the circuits will eliminate crosstalk.

CRT (cathode ray tube)　A video screen.

CSMA (carrier sense multiple access)　A media-sharing scheme in which stations listen in to what's happening on the network media; if the cable is not in use, a station is permitted to transmit its message. CSMA is often combined with a means of performing collision detection, hence *CSMA/CD*.

CSU (channel service unit)　Hardware responsible for terminating the digitized T-1 signal, performing diagnostics, and allowing that signal to be read by the attached data-communication equipment and the network.

current loop　An electrical interface that is sensitive to current changes rather than voltage swings; used with older teleprinter equipment.

cursor　The symbol indicating the place on the video screen where the next character will appear.

customer premises equipment (CPE)　A general term for the telephones, computers, private branch exchanges, and other hardware located on the end user's side of the network boundary, established by the Computer Inquiry II action of the Federal Communications Commission.

D/A converter   A device that changes digital pulses into analog signals.

Data Access Protocol   A specialized protocol used by Digital Equipment Corp.

data compression   A technique that can move more data through the circuit than the signaling system would otherwise allow by transforming a set of data into a smaller representation of that data.

datagram   A packet of computer-generated information that includes a complete destination address provided by the user, not the network, along with whatever data the packet carries.

data-link control   A communications layer in SNA that manages the physical data circuits.

data-link layer   The second layer of the OSI model. Protocols functioning in this layer manage the flow of data leaving a network device and work with the receiving station to ensure that the data arrives safely.

data packet   In X.25, a block of data that transports full-duplex information via an X.25 switched virtual circuit (SVC) or permanent virtual circuit (PVC). X.25 data packets may contain up to 1,024 bytes of user data, but the most common size is 128 bytes (the X.25 default).

data set   1. A file, a "set" of data. 2. The name the telephone company often uses for a modem.

DB-25   The designation of a standard plug-and-jack set used in RS-232C wiring: 25-pin connectors, with 13 pins in one row and 12 in the other row.

DCE (data communications equipment)   Refers to any X.25 network component that implements the CCITT X.25 standard.

D-channel   The "data" channel of an ISDN interface, used to carry control signals and customer call data in a packet-switched mode. In the basic-rate interface (BRI), the D-channel operates at 16 kilobits per second; in the primary-rate interface (PRI), the D-channel is used at 64 kbps.

DDCMP (Digital Data Communications Message Protocol)   A byte-oriented, link-layer protocol from Digital Equipment Corp., used to transmit messages over a communications line.

DDD (direct distance dialing)   Use of the common long-distance telephone system.

DECnet   A communications protocol and line of networking products from Digital Equipment Corp., compatible with Ethernet and a wide range of systems.

delay   Commonly, a pause in activity. Delay can also be a kind of distortion on a communications circuit. Specifically, it is the property of an electrical circuit that slows down and distorts high-frequency signals. Devices called *equalizers* slow down the lower frequencies and "equalize" the signal.

demodulation   The process of retrieving data from a modulated carrier wave; the reverse of modulation.

dial-up line   A communications circuit established by dialing a destination over a commercial telephone system. Network switches create a temporary point-to-point connection that is broken down and relocated when the call ends.

digital   In common use, on/off signaling; signals consist of 0's and 1's instead of a great multitude of analog-modulated frequencies.

digital service levels   Classifications of circuits based on the digital signaling speed the circuits are configured to carry.

disk duplexing   A fault-tolerant technique that writes simultaneously to two hard disks using different controllers.

disk mirroring   A fault-tolerant technique that writes data simultaneously to two hard disks using the same controller.

DISOSS (Distributed Office Supported System)   An integrated package of electronic-mail and document-preparation programs from IBM, designed for IBM mainframe computer systems.

distance-vector routing   A relatively old set of routing protocols that send a packet off in the general direction of its destination.

distortion   Any change to the transmitted signal. Distortion can be caused by crosstalk, delay, attenuation, or other factors.

Distributed Systems Architecture (DSA)   A Honeywell architecture that conforms to the Open Systems Interconnection model proposed by the ISO. It supports X.25 for packet switching and X.21 for packet-switched and circuit-switched network protocols.

DQDB (Distributed Queue Dual Bus)   A proposed IEEE 802.6 standard for metropolitan-area networks (MANs).

driver   A software program that interfaces between portions of the LAN software and the hardware on the network interface card.

DS-0   A CCITT standard that describes a service providing 64-kilobit-per-second channels.

DS-1   A CCITT standard that describes a service transmitting 2,048 kilobits per second, equivalent to 30 DS-0 channels.

DSU (digital service unit)   The hardware device that actually transmits the digitized data over a DS-1 signal or line.

DSX-1 (digital signal cross-connect level 1)   A set of standards and parameters for cross-connecting DS-1 signals.

DTE (data terminal equipment)   Refers to any end-user device that can access an X.25 network using the CCITT X.25 standard, LAP/LAB, and X.25 PAP.

duplex   1. In communications circuits, the ability to transmit and receive at the same time; also referred to as *full duplex*. Half-duplex circuits can receive only or transmit only. 2. In terminals, a choice between displaying locally generated characters and echoed characters.

dynamic routers   Sophisticated routers that make packet-by-packet decisions, based on the information they glean from other routers and network devices about the efficiency and reliability of different routes between the source and destination nodes.

EBCDIC (Extended Binary Coded Decimal Interchange Code)   The data alphabet used in all IBM computers except the PC; it determines the composition of the 8-bit string of 0's and 1's representing each character (alphabetic, numeric, or special).

echoplex   A method of transmission in which characters are echoed from the distant end and the echoes are presented on the terminal; this provides a constant check of the communications circuit to the user.

echo suppressor   A device used to eliminate the echo effect of long-distance voice transmission circuits. This suppressor must be disabled for full-duplex data transmission; the modem answer tones turn the suppressor off automatically.

ECMA (European Computer Manufacturers' Association)   A trade association that provides input to international standards-forming organizations.

EDI (electronic data interchange)   The communication of orders, invoices, and similar transactions electronically between organizations.

EIA (Electronic Industries Association)   A body of U.S. electronics manufacturers that works closely with international organizations like the CCITT to establish standards for the interconnection of data-processing and communications equipment.

802.X   The Institute of Electrical and Electronics Engineers (IEEE) committee that developed a set of standards describing the cabling, electrical topology, physical topology, and access scheme of network products; in other words, the 802.X standards define the physical and data-link layers of LAN architectures. IEEE 802.3 is the work of an 802 subcommittee that describes the cabling and signaling for a system nearly identical to classic Ethernet. IEEE 802.5 comes from another subcommittee and similarly describes IBM's Token-Ring architecture.

EISA (Extended Industry Standard Architecture)   A PC bus system that serves as an alternative to IBM's Micro Channel Architecture (MCA). The EISA architecture, backed by an industry consortium headed by Compaq, is compatible with the IBM AT bus; MCA is not.

electronic-mail gateway   A device that moves messages and attached files between dissimilar or identical LANs. E-mail gateways fall into two different categories: *proprietary* (operating only within a certain group of products) and *open* or nonproprietary.

elevator seeking   A method of optimizing the movement of the heads on the hard disk in a file server.

EMA (Enterprise Management Architecture)   Digital Equipment Corp.'s company-specific architecture, conforming to ISO's CMIP.

emulation   Simulation of a system, function, or program.

equalization   Balancing of a circuit so that it passes all frequencies with equal efficiency.

Ethernet   A network cable and access protocol scheme originally developed by Xerox, now marketed mainly by Digital Equipment Corp. and 3Com.

EtherTalk   1. The Apple Ethernet adapter for the Macintosh II computer. 2. The software driver used by the Macintosh to communicate with Ethernet adapters.

facsimile (fax)   The transmission of page images by a system that is concerned with patterns of light and dark rather than with specific characters. Older systems use analog signals; newer devices use digital signals and may interact with computers and other digital devices.

fault   A physical or logical break in a communications link.

fault management   One of the five basic categories of network management defined by the International Standards Organization (ISO). Fault management is used for the detection, isolation, and correction of faults on the network.

fault tolerance   A method of ensuring continued operation through redundancy and diversity.

FCC   Federal Communications Commission.

FDDI (Fiber Distributed Data Interface)   A specification for fiber-optic networks operating at 100 megabits per second. FDDI uses wiring hubs, and the hubs are prime candidates to serve as network monitoring and control devices.

FEP (front-end processor)   A computer that sits between groups of cluster controllers and the mainframe, concentrating signals before they are transmitted to the mainframe.

fiber optics   A data-transmission method that uses light pulses sent over glass cables.

field   A particular position within a message frame. Positions are labeled as the control field, flag field, and so on. Bits in each message have a meaning for stations on the network.

file lock   See *locking*.

file server   A type of server that holds files in private and shared directories for LAN users. See *server*.

firmware   Frequently called software programs that are burned into a chip. The software contained in the firmware controls the functions of a system's hardware.

flow control   A convention used to regulate communications between two nodes. Hardware and software techniques are available.

foreign exchange   A telephone line that represents a local number in a calling area quite removed from the telephone's actual termination. If your office is in the suburbs but many of your customers are in the city, you might have a foreign-exchange line with a city telephone office.

four-wire circuit   A transmission arrangement where two half-duplex circuits (two wires each) are combined to make one full-duplex circuit.

fractional T-1   Individual DS-0 circuits sold to companies via the long-distance companies.

frame   A data packet on a Token-Ring network. Also denotes a data packet on other networks such as X.25 or SNA.

frame relay   A method of packet switching that depends on high-quality connections. Frame-relay packets do not include many of the error-control features of X.25 packets, so they are smaller and generate less overhead, but frame relay and X.25 packets can coexist on the same network.

frequency-agile modem   A modem used on some broadband systems that can shift frequencies to communicate with stations in different dedicated bands.

frequency converter   In broadband cable systems, the device that translates between the transmitting and receiving frequencies.

frequency-division multiplexing   A technique for combining many signals on one circuit by separating them in frequency.

frequency-shift keying   A transmission method using two different frequencies that are shifted to represent the digital 0's and 1's; used in some common modems.

FTAM (File Transfer Access and Management)   An OSI protocol that provides access to files stored on dissimilar systems.

FTP (File Transfer Protocol)   A protocol that describes how one computer can host other computers to allow transferring files in either direction. Users can see directories of either computer on the host and perform limited file-management functions. Software for the FTP client function is usually a part of TCP/IP packages for the PC; some vendors also provide FTP host software for the PC. See *TFTP*.

full duplex   The ability for communications to flow both ways over a communications link at the same time.

functional-management layer   A communications layer in SNA that formats presentations.

gateway   A device that serves as a shared point of entry from a local area network into a larger information resource such as a large packet-switched information network or a mainframe computer.

GOSIP (Government OSI Profile)   The U.S. government's version of the OSI protocols. GOSIP compliance is typically a requirement in government networking purchases.

ground   An electrically neutral contact point.

half duplex   1. Alternating transmissions; each station can either transmit or receive, not both simultaneously. 2. In terminals, describes the condition when a terminal displays its own transmissions instead of a remote-end echo. 3. The configuration option in some modems allowing local character echo.

handshaking   Exchange of control codes or specific characters to control data flow.

HDLC (High-level Data Link Control)   A comprehensive standard developed by the International Standards Organization (ISO). It is a bit-oriented link-layer protocol.

high-speed modem   A modem operating at speeds from 2,400 to 9,600 bits per second.

HLLAPI (High-Level-Language Application Program Interface)   A scripting language (that is, a set of verbs) that allows programmers to build transparent interfaces between 3270 terminals and applications on IBM mainframes.

HotFix   A Novell program that dynamically marks defective blocks on the hard disk so they will not be used.

Hz (hertz)   Cycles per second.

ICMP (Internet Control Message Protocol)   The TCP/IP process that provides the set of functions used for network-layer management and control.

IEEE 802   A large family of standards for the physical and electrical connections in local area networks, developed by the IEEE (Institute of Electrical and Electronics Engineers).

IEEE 802.1D   An IEEE media-access-control-level standard for inter-LAN bridges linking IEEE 802.3, 802.4, and 802.5 networks.

IEEE 802.2   An IEEE standard for data-link-layer software and firmware for use with IEEE 802.3, 802.4, and 802.5 networks.

IEEE 802.3 1Base5   An IEEE specification matching the older AT&T StarLAN product. It designates a 1-megabit-per-second signaling rate, a baseband signaling technique, and a maximum cable-segment distance of 500 meters.

IEEE 802.3 10Base2   This IEEE specification matches the thin Ethernet cabling. It designates a 10-megabit-per-second signaling rate, a baseband signaling technique, and a maximum cable-segment distance of 185 (nearly 200) meters.

IEEE 802.3 10BaseT   An IEEE standard describing 10-megabit-per-second twisted-pair Ethernet wiring using baseband signaling. This system requires a wiring hub.

IEEE 802.3 10Broad36   This IEEE specification describes a long-distance type of Ethernet cabling with a 10-megabit-per-second signaling rate, a broadband signaling technique, and a maximum cable-segment distance of 3,600 meters.

IEEE 802.4   This IEEE specification describes a LAN using 10-megabit-per-second signaling, token-passing media-access control, and a physical bus topology. It is typically used as part of networks following the Manufacturing Automation Protocol (MAP) developed by General Motors. This is sometimes confused with ARCnet, but it is not the same.

IEEE 802.5   This IEEE specification describes a LAN using 4- or 16-megabit-per-second signaling, token-passing media-access control, and a physical ring topology. It is used by IBM's Token-Ring systems.

IEEE 802.6   This IEEE standard for metropolitan-area networks (MANs) describes what is called a Distributed Queue Dual Bus (DQDB). The DQDB topology includes two parallel runs of cable—typically fiber-optic cable—linking each node (typically a router for a LAN segment) using signaling rates in the range of 100 megabits per second.

IGRP (Interior Gateway Routing Protocol)   A TCP/IP protocol created by Cisco Systems and adopted by a number of vendors. It is a distance-vector routing protocol.

impedance   An electrical property of a cable, combining capacitance, inductance, and resistance, and measured in ohms.

IND$FILE   A mainframe editing utility, commonly used to make PC-to-mainframe file transfers; a logical unit in an SNA network that addresses and interacts with the host.

interface   An interconnection point, usually between pieces of equipment.

internal   Refers to devices installed within a PC.

Internet   A collection of networks and gateways including ARPAnet, MILnet, and NSFnet (National Science Foundation net). Internet uses TCP/IP protocols.

interrupt   A signal that suspends a program temporarily, transferring control to the operating system when input or output is required. Interrupts may have priority levels, and higher-priority interrupts take precedence in processing.

I/O   Input/output.

I/O bound   A condition where the operation of the I/O port is the limiting factor in program execution.

IP (Internet Protocol)   A standard describing software that keeps track of the Internet address for different nodes, routes outgoing messages, and recognizes incoming messages.

IPX (Internet Packet Exchange)   NetWare's native LAN communications protocol, used to move data between server and/or workstation programs running on different network nodes. IPX packets are encapsulated and carried by the packets used in Ethernet and the similar frames used in Token-Ring networks.

IRQ (interrupt request)   A computer instruction that causes an interruption of a program for an I/O task.

ISDN (Integrated Services Digital Network)   As officially defined by CCITT, "a limited set of standard interfaces to a digital communications network." The result is a network that supplies end users with voice, data, and certain image services on end-to-end digital circuits. The plan is to provide two 64-kilobit-per-second channels over digital telephone lines to desktops worldwide.

IS-IS (Intermediate System to Intermediate System)   A protocol designed specifically to the ISO's OSI Model. IS-IS routers have the same kinds of criteria defined under *OSPF*, but many vendors feel the IS-IS protocol will offer more interoperability than OSPF thanks to its implementation by the ISO.

ISO (International Standards Organization)   A Paris-based organization that developed the Open Systems Interconnection (OSI) model.

IXC (interexchange carrier)   A long-distance telephone company.

jam signal   A signal generated by a card to ensure that other cards know that a packet collision has taken place.

jumper   A plastic-and-metal shorting bar that slides over two or more electrical contacts to set certain conditions for operation.

k   Used in this book to represent a kilobyte (1,024 bytes).

kernel   The heart of an operating system, containing the basic scheduling and interrupt handling but not the higher-level services, such as the file system.

LAN Manager   The multiuser network operating system codeveloped by Microsoft and 3Com. LAN Manager offers a wide range of network-management and control capabilities.

LAN Manager/X (LM/X)   LAN Manager for the Unix environment.

LAN Server   IBM's proprietary OS/2-based network operating system. LAN Server is compatible with LAN Manager, codeveloped by Microsoft and 3Com. LAP-B Link access procedure (balanced), the most common data-link control protocol used to interface X.25 DTEs with X.25 DCEs. X.25 also specifies a *LAP*, or link access procedure (not balanced). Both LAP and LAP-B are full-duplex, point-to-point bit-synchronous protocols. The unit of data transmission is called a *frame*; frames may contain one or more X.25 packets.

learning bridge   A bridge that learns and remembers the identities of nodes on either LAN segment.

leased line   A communications circuit reserved for the permanent use of a customer; also called a *private line*. Leased lines typically involve high front-end installation costs.

LEC (local exchange carrier)   One of the companies providing local telephone service in the United States.

light-wave communications   Usually, communications using fiber-optic cables and light generated by lasers or light-emitting diodes (LEDs). The phrase can also refer to systems using modulated light beams passing through the air between buildings or other adjacent locations.

link layer   The second layer in the OSI architecture. This layer performs the function of taking data from the higher layers, creating packets, and sending them accurately out through the physical layer.

local   Refers to programs, files, peripherals, and computational power accessed directly in the user's own machine rather than through the network.

local area network (LAN)   A computer communications system limited to no more than a few miles and using high-speed connections (2 to 100 megabits per second).

local area transport (LAT)   A DECnet protocol used for terminal-to-host communications.

local loop   The connection between a customer's premises and the telephone company's central office.

LocalTalk   The 230.4-kilobit-per-second media-access method developed by Apple Computer for use with its MacIntosh computer.

locking   A method of protecting shared data. When an application program opens a file, *file locking* either prevents simultaneous access by a second program or limits such access to "read only." DOS Versions 3.0 and higher allow an application to lock a range of bytes in a file for various purposes. Since DBMS programs interpret this range of bytes as a record, this is called *record locking*.

low-speed modem   A modem operating at speeds up to 600 bits per second.

LU 6.2 (Logical Unit 6.2)   In IBM's SNA scheme, a software product that implements the session-layer conversation specified in the Advanced Program-to-Program Communications (APPC) protocol.

MAC (media-access control)   See *access protocol*.

mainframe   A large centralized computer.

MAN (metropolitan-area network)   A public high-speed network (100 megabits per second or more) capable of voice and data transmission over a range of 25 to 50 miles (40 to 80 kilometers).

MAP (Manufacturing Automation Protocol)   A token-passing bus LAN originally designed by General Motors and now adopted as a subset of the IEEE 802.3 standards.

mark   A signaling condition equal to a binary 1.

MAU   See *medium attachment unit* and *Multistation Access Unit*.

MCA (Micro Channel Architecture)   The basis for IBM Micro Channel bus, used in high-end models of IBM's PS/2 series of personal computers.

media   Plural of *medium*; the cabling or wiring used to carry network signals. Typical examples are coax, fiber-optic, and twisted-pair wire.

media-sharing LAN   A network in which all nodes share the cable using a media-access control (MAC) scheme. Contrast with *circuit switching* or *packet switching*.

medium attachment unit (MAU)   A transceiver that attaches to the AUI port on an Ethernet adapter and provides electrical and mechanical attachments to fiber-optic, twisted-pair, or other media.

medium-speed modem   A modem operating between 600 and 2,400 bits per second.

message switching   A routing technique using a message store-and-forward system. No dedicated path is established. Rather, each message contains a destination address and is passed from source to destination through intermediate nodes. At each node, the entire message is received, stored briefly, and then passed on to the next node.

MHS (Message Handling Service)   A program developed by Action Technologies and marketed by that firm and Novell to exchange files with other programs and send files out through gateways to other computers and networks. It is used particularly to link dissimilar electronic-mail systems.

MIB (management information base)   A directory listing the logical names of all information resources residing in a network and pertinent to the network's management.

midsplit   A type of broadband cable system in which the available frequencies are split into two groups, one for transmission and one for reception. This requires a frequency converter.

MNP (Microcom Network Protocol)   A standard developed by Microcom for providing asynchronous-data error control for modem products.

modem (modulator/demodulator)   A device that translates between electrical signals and some other means of signaling. Typically a modem translates between direct-current signals from a computer or terminal and analog signals sent over telephone lines. Other modems handle radio frequencies and light waves.

modem eliminator   A wiring device designed to replace two modems; it connects equipment over a distance of up to several hundred feet. In asynchronous systems, this is a simple cable.

modem remote control   A network access technique using remote-control software running on a remote PC to control a networked PC through a modem connection.

modulation   A process of varying signals to represent intelligent information. The frequency, amplitude, or phase of a signal may be modulated to represent an analog or digital signal.

multiple name spaces   The association of several names or other pieces of information with the same file. This allows renaming files and designating them for dissimilar computer systems such as the PC and the Mac.

multiplexer   A device that provides a way for many other devices to share a single long-distance connection.

multipoint line   A single communications link for two or more devices shared by one computer and more than one terminal. Use of this line requires a polling mechanism. It is also called a *multidrop line*.

Multistation Access Unit (MAU)   IBM's name for a Token-Ring wiring concentrator.

NAK   A control code indicating that a character or block of data was not properly received. The name stands for *negative acknowledgment*. See *ACK*.

Named Pipes   A technique used for communications between applications operating on the same computer or across the network. It includes a relatively easy-to-use API, providing application programmers with a simple way to create interprogram communications using routines similar to disk-file opening, reading, and writing.

N-connector   The large-diameter connector used with thick Ethernet cable.

NCP   1. (NetWare Core Protocol) The data format of the requests NetWare uses to access files. 2. (Network Control Program) Special IBM software that runs in a front-end processor and works with VTAM on the host computer to link the application programs and terminal controllers.

NDIS (Network Driver Interface Specification)   A device driver specification codeveloped by Microsoft and 3Com. Besides providing hardware and protocol independence for network drivers, NDIS supports both DOS and OS/2, and it offers protocol multiplexing so that multiple protocol stacks can coexist in the same host.

NetBIOS (Network Basic Input/Output System)   A layer of software originally developed by IBM and Sytek to link a network operating system with specific hardware. It can also open communications between workstations on a network at the transport layer. Today, many vendors either provide a version of NetBIOS to interface with their hardware or emulate its transport-layer communications services in their network products.

NetVIEW   IBM's company-specific network-management and control architecture. This architecture relies heavily on mainframe data-collection programs and also incorporates PC-level products running under OS/2.

NetWare   A popular series of network operating systems and related products made by Novell.

network   A continuing connection between two or more computers that facilitates sharing files and resources.

network access   The actual local or remote network connection or interface of a PC to the network via a NIC or some other device.

network-addressable unit (NAU)   In SNA, a device that can be the source and destination of messages.

network layer   The third level of the OSI model, containing the logic and rules that determine the path to be taken by data flowing through a network; not important in small LANs.

NFS (Network File System)   One of many distributed-file-system protocols that allow a computer on a network to use the files and peripherals of another networked computer as if they were local. This protocol was developed by Sun Microsystems and adopted by other vendors.

NIC (network interface card)   A LAN adapter; a printed circuit board that goes into an expansion slot on a computer to make the electrical and mechanical connection between the computer and the network cable.

NLMs (NetWare Loadable Modules)   Applications and drivers that run in a server under Novell's NetWare 386 and can be loaded or unloaded on the fly. In other networks, such applications could require dedicated PCs.

NMP (Network Management Protocol)   An AT&T-developed set of protocols designed to exchange information with and control the devices that govern various components of a network, including modems and T1 multiplexers.

NNTP (Network News Transport Protocol)   An extension of the TCP/IP protocol that provides a network news transport service.

node   A connection or switching point on the network.

ODI   (Open Data-link Interface) A standard interface for transport protocols, allowing them to share a single network card without any conflicts.

OfficeVision   IBM's set of applications designed to bring a uniform user interface to the company's various lines of computing products. OfficeVision works in conjunction with IBM's Systems Application Architecture.

OMI (Open Messaging Interface)   A standard for a messaging application interface, developed in the fall of 1991 by a consortium of companies including Apple, IBM, and Lotus Development Corp. This new electronic-messaging standard will be incorporated into Apple, IBM, and Lotus software.

on-line   Connected to a network or a host computer system.

ONMS (Open Network Management System)   Digital Communications Associates' architecture for products conforming to ISO's CMIP.

Open Systems Interconnection (OSI) reference model   A model for networks developed by the International Standards Organization, dividing the network functions into seven connected layers. Each layer builds on the services provided by those under it.

OpenView   Hewlett-Packard's suite of a network-management application, a server platform, and support services. OpenView is based on HP-UX, which complies with AT&T's Unix system.

OPT (Open Protocol Technology)   Novell's strategy for complete protocol independence. NetWare supports multivendor hardware with this approach.

OSF (Open Software Foundation)   A consortium of industry leaders working to standardize the Unix operating system.

OSI   See *Open Systems Interconnection*.

OSPF (open shortest path first)   A routing protocol that enables routers to make decisions based on traffic load, throughput, circuit cost, and the service priority assigned to packets originating from or going to a specific location.

OS/2 (Operating System/2)   An operating system developed by IBM and Microsoft for use with Intel's microprocessors. Unlike its predecessor, DOS, OS/2 is a multitasking operating system.

OS/2 Extended Edition   IBM's proprietary version of OS/2; it includes built-in communications and database-management facilities.

OverVIEW   Proteon's architecture for products conforming to SNMP.

packet   A block of data sent over the network transmitting the identities of the sending and receiving stations, error-control information, and a message.

packet filter   A feature of a bridge that compares each packet received with specifications set by the network administrator. If the packet matches the specifications, the bridge can either forward or reject it. Packet filters let the administrator limit protocol-specific traffic to one network segment, isolate electronic-mail domains, and perform many other traffic-control functions.

packet switching   A transmission technique that maximizes the use of digital transmission facilities by transmitting packets of digital data from many customers simultaneously on a single communications channel.

packet-switched networks   Networks containing switches that examine each packet and can choose among alternative redundant routes. They potentially offer reliability unmatched by other inter-LAN alternatives.

PAD (packet assembler/disassembler)   An X.25 PAD. A hardware-and-software device, sometimes inside a PC, that provides users access to an X.25 network. CCITT Recommendations X.3, X.28, and X.29 define the PAD parameters, terminal-to-PAD interface, and PAD-to-X.25 host interface.

PAP (packet-level procedure)   A protocol for the transfer of packets between an X.25 DTE and an X.25 DCE. X.25 PAP is a full-duplex protocol that supports data sequencing, flow control, accountability, and error detection and recovery.

parallel transmission   Simultaneous transmission of bits down parallel wires; for example, *byte parallel transmission* requires eight wires. See *serial transmission*.

parity   In ASCII, a check of the total number of 1 bits (as opposed to 0's) in a character's binary representation. A final eighth bit is set so that the count, when transmitted, is always even or always odd. This even or odd state can easily be checked at the receiving end; an incorrect parity bit can help reveal errors in the transmission.

passive head end   A device that connects the two broadband cables of a dual-cable system. It does not provide frequency translation.

PBX (private branch exchange)   A telephone system serving a specific location. Many PBX systems can carry computer data without the use of modems.

PDS (Premise Distribution System)   AT&T's proprietary building-wide telecommunications cabling system.

peer-to-peer resource sharing   An architecture that lets any station contribute resources to the network while still running local application programs.

physical layer   The lowest layer of the OSI model. It consists of network wiring and cable and the interface hardware that sends and receives signals over the network.

PING (Packet Internet Groper)   An exercise program associated with TCP/IP and used to test the Internet communications channel between stations.

pipe   A communications process within the operating system that acts as an interface between a computer's devices (keyboard, disk drives, memory, and so on) and an applications program. A pipe simplifies the development of application programs by "buffering" a program from the intricacies of the hardware or the software that controls the hardware; the application developer writes code to a single pipe, not to several individual devices. A pipe is also used for program-to-program communications.

polling   A method of controlling the transmission sequence of communicating devices on a shared circuit by sending an inquiry to each device asking whether it wishes to transmit.

PPP (Point-to-Point Protocol)   One of two TCP/IP routing protocols for communications over serial communications lines without intervening adapters such as modems or other types of terminating equipment. The other TCP/IP protocol is called SLIP or *Serial Line Internet Protocol.*

presentation layer   The sixth layer of the OSI model, which formats data for screen presentation and translates incompatible file formats.

Presentation Manager   The portion of the operating system OS/2 providing users with a graphics-based rather than character-based interface. The screens are similar to those of Microsoft Windows.

primary-rate interface (PRI)   In ISDN, the specification for the interface at each end of the high-volume trunks linking PBX and central-office facilities or connecting network switches to each other. The primary rate consists of 23 B or "bearer" channels (operating at 64 kilobits per second) and a D or "data" channel (also functioning at 64 kbps). The combined signal-carrying capacity is 1.544 megabits per second—equivalent to that of a type T1 channel.

print server   A computer on the network that makes one or more attached printers available to other users. The server usually requires a hard disk to spool the print jobs while they wait in a queue for the printer.

print spooler   The software that holds print jobs sent to a shared printer over a network when the printer is busy. Each file is saved in temporary storage and then printed when the shared printer is available.

PROFS (Professional Office System)   Interactive productivity software developed by IBM that runs under the VM/CMS mainframe system. PROFS is frequently used for electronic mail.

propagation delay   The delay between the time a signal enters a channel and the time it is received. This is normally insignificant in local area networks, but it becomes a major factor in satellite communications.

protocol   A specification that describes the rules and procedures that products should follow to perform activities on a network, such as transmitting data. If they use the same protocols, products from different vendors can communicate on the same network.

protocol-independent router   A device that uses some of the same techniques developed for learning bridges but applies them to all routed and some nonrouted protocols.

PSDN   Packet-switched data network.

PU (physical unit)   In an SNA network, usually a terminal or printer connected to the controller.

PVC (permanent virtual circuit)   See *VC*.

public data network   A commercially owned or national-monopoly packet-switched network, publicly available as a service to data-processing users.

pulse-code modulation (PCM)   A common method for digitizing voice signals. The bandwidth required for a single digitized voice channel is 64 kilobits per second.

query language   A programming language designed to make it easier to specify what information a user wants to retrieve from a database.

queue   A list formed by items in a system waiting for service. An example is a print queue of documents to be printed in a network print server.

RAM (random access memory)   Also known as *read-write memory*; the memory used to execute application programs.

record locking   A feature that excludes other users from accessing (or sometimes just writing to) a record in a file while the first user is accessing that record.

redirector   A software module loaded into every network workstation; it captures application programs' requests for file- and equipment-sharing services and routes them through the network for action.

remote client   A form of remote network access where a remote PC uses redirection software just like a client PC on the LAN. The remote PC uses a modem instead of a LAN adapter card, establishing a very slow network interface.

repeater   A device that amplifies and regenerates signals so they can travel farther on a cable. The capacity of repeaters lies between approximately 500 and 1,500 meters of cable.

restart packet   A block of data that notifies X.25 DTEs that an irrecoverable error exists within the X.25 network. Restart packets clear all existing SVCs and resynchronize all existing PVCs between an X.25 DTE and X.25 DCE.

reverse channel   An answer-back channel provided during half-duplex operation. It allows the receiving modem to send low-speed acknowledgments to the transmitting modem without breaking the half-duplex mode. This is also used to arrange the turnaround between modems so that one ceases transmitting and the other can begin.

RF (radio frequency)   A generic term referring to the technology used in cable television and broadband networks. It uses electromagnetic waveforms, usually in the megahertz (MHz) range, for transmission.

RFS (Remote File Service)   One of the many distributed-file-system network protocols that allows one computer to use the files and peripherals of another as if they were local. Developed by AT&T and adopted by other vendors as a part of Unix V.

ring   A network connection method that routes messages through each station on the network in turn. Most ring networks use a token-passing protocol, which allows any station to put a message on the network when it receives a special bit pattern.

RIP (Routing Information Protocol)   One of the first routing protocols, still found today in many inter-LAN systems. It was developed in the early 1980s and uses distant-vector logic.

RJE (Remote Job Entry)   A method of submitting work to an IBM mainframe in a batch format. Though superseded by the 3270 system, it is still widely used in some installations.

RJ-11, RJ-45   Designations for commonly used modular telephone connectors. RJ-11 is the 8-pin connector used in most voice connections. RJ-45 is the 8-pin connector used for data transmission over twisted-pair telephone wire.

RO (receive-only)   Refers to a one-way device such as a printer, plotter, or graphics display.

ROM (read-only memory)   Memory containing preloaded programs that cannot be rewritten or changed by the CPU.

router   An interconnection device that is similar to a bridge but serves packets or frames containing certain protocols. Routers link LANs at the network layer of the OSI model. Modern routers handle multiple protocol stacks simultaneously and move packets or frames onto the right links for their destinations. For example, an X.25 router will wrap an Ethernet packet back into an Ethernet system.

RPC (Remote Procedure Call)   A set of software tools developed by a consortium of manufacturers and designed to assist developers in creating distributed applications. These tools automatically generate the code for both sides of the program (client and server) and let the programmer concentrate on other portions of the application.

RS-232C   An electrical standard for the interconnection of equipment established by the Electrical Industries Association; the same as the CCITT code V.24. RS-232C is used for serial ports.

RS-449   An EIA standard that applies to binary, serial synchronous, or asynchronous communications systems.

RU (request unit or response unit)   A message that makes a request or responds to one during a session.

SAA (Systems Application Architecture)   A set of specifications written by IBM, describing how users, application programs, and communications programs interface. SAA represents an attempt to standardize the look and feel of applications and the methods they use to communicate.

SAP (Service Advertising Protocol)   A format for NetWare servers and routers to use in sending out messages in order to find each other. It uses a short data field, contained within IPX. Each NetWare server sends out a SAP message every 60 seconds.

SDLC (synchronous data link control)   The data-link layer of SNA, SDLC is a more efficient method than the older bisync protocol when it comes to packaging data for transmission between computers. Packets of data are sent over the line without the overhead created by synchronization and other padding bits.

serial port   An I/O port that transmits data 1 bit at a time; contrasted with a *parallel port*, which transmits multiple bits (usually 8) simultaneously. RS-232C is a common serial signaling protocol.

server   1. A computer with a large power supply and cabinet capacity. 2. Any computer on a network that makes file, print, or communications services available to other network stations.

session   The name for the connection between a mainframe terminal (or a PC emulating a mainframe terminal) and the mainframe itself when they are communicating. The number of sessions that can be run simultaneously through a LAN gateway is limited by the gateway software and the hardware configuration.

session layer   The fifth layer of the OSI model, which sets up the conditions whereby individual nodes on the network can communicate or send data to each other. The functions of this layer are used for many purposes, including determining which side may transmit during half-duplex communications.

SFT (system fault tolerance)   The capability to recover from or avoid a system crash. Novell uses a Transaction Tracking System (TTS), disk mirroring, and disk duplexing as its system recovery methods.

SLIP (Serial Line Internet Protocol)   See *PPP*.

SMB (Server Message Block)   A distributed-file-system network protocol that allows one computer to use the files and peripherals of another as if they were local. Developed by Microsoft and adopted by IBM and many other vendors.

SMDS (switched multimegabit data service)   A service that will be offered by the long distance companies at the rate T-1 (1.544 megabits per second) and higher.

SMF (Standard Message Format)   A standard used by MHS. Each message includes a header section with addressing information, the ASCII message, and attachments.

SMTP (Simple Mail Transfer Protocol)   A protocol that describes an electronic-mail system with both host and user sections. Many companies sell host software (usually for Unix) that will exchange SMTP mail with proprietary mail systems, such as IBM's PROFS. The user software is often included as a utility in TCP/IP packages for the PC.

SNA (Systems Network Architecture)   IBM's scheme for connecting its computerized products so that they can communicate and share data.

SNADS (SNA Distribution Services)   An IBM protocol that allows the distribution of electronic mail and attached documents through an SNA network.

SNMP (Simple Network Management Protocol)   A structure for formatting messages and for transmitting information between reporting devices and data-collection programs; developed jointly by the Department of Defense, industry, and the academic community as part of the TCP/IP protocol suite.

space   The signal condition that equals a binary 0.

SPX (Sequenced Packet Exchange)   An enhanced set of commands implemented on top of IPX to create a true transport-layer interface. SPX provides more functions than IPX, including guaranteed packet delivery.

SQL (Structured Query Language)   A formal data sublanguage for specifying common database operations such as retrieving, adding, changing, or deleting records. SQL is pronounced "sequel."

STA (Spanning Tree Algorithm)   A technique based on an IEEE 802.1 standard that detects and eliminates logical loops in a bridged network. When multiple paths exist, STA lets a bridge use only the most efficient one. If that path fails, STA automatically reconfigures the network so that another path becomes active, sustaining network operations.

StarLAN   A networking system developed by AT&T that uses CSMA protocols on twisted-pair telephone wire; a subset of 802.3.

start bit   A data bit used in asynchronous transmission to signal the beginning of a character and indicate that the channel is in use. It is a space signal lasting only for the duration of 1 bit.

star topology   A network connection method that hooks up all links to a central node.

static router   A router pre-programmed with a fixed set of routes that does not change dynamically.

statistical time-division multiplexing   The ability of a multiplexer to have an aggregate throughput rate greater than the composite speed.

stop bit   A data bit used in asynchronous transmission to signal the end of a character and indicate that the channel is idle. It is a mark signal lasting at least for the duration of 1 bit.

store and forward   See *message switching*.

Streams   An architecture introduced with Unix System V, Release 3.2, that provides for flexible and layered communication paths between processes (programs) and device drivers. Many companies market applications and devices that can integrate through Streams protocols.

strobe   An electrical pulse used to call for the transfer of information.

SVC (switched virtual circuit)   See *VC*.

Switched 56   A service offered by both local and long-distance telephone companies, providing 56-kilobit-per-second data transfer over dial-up telephone lines.

sync character   A character (two or more in bisync) sent from a transmitting station for synchronizing the clocks in transmitting and receiving stations.

synchronous   Refers to a transmission system in which characters are synchronized by the transmission of initial sync characters and a common clock signal. No stop or start bits are used.

T1   A 1.544-megabit-per-second communications circuit provided by long-distance communications carriers for voice or data transmission. T1 lines are typically divided into 24 64-kilobit channels.

tap   A connector that couples to a cable without blocking the passage of signals down the cable.

TCAM (Telecommunications Access Method)   An IBM system for controlling communications.

T-connector   A coaxial connector, shaped like a T, that connects two thin Ethernet cables while supplying an additional connector for a network interface card.

TCP (Transmission Control Protocol)   A specification for software that bundles and unbundles sent and received data into packets, manages the transmission of packets on a network, and checks for errors.

TCP/IP (Transmission Control Protocol/Internet Protocol)   A set of communications protocols that has evolved since the late 1970s, when it was first developed by the Department of Defense (DoD). Because programs supporting these protocols are available on so many different computer systems, they have become an excellent way to connect different types of computers over networks.

Telex   An international messaging service, marketed in the United States by Western Union.

TELNET   A terminal-emulation protocol. Software supporting TELNET usually comes as a utility in a TCP/IP package, and all TELNET programs provide DEC VT-100 terminal emulation. Many companies either provide or allow other add-in emulators.

10Base2   IEEE's specifications for running Ethernet over thin coaxial cable.

10Base5   IEEE's specifications for running Ethernet over thick coaxial cable.

10BaseT   IEEE's specifications for running Ethernet over unshielded twisted-pair wiring.

terminal adapter (TA)   An ISDN phone or a PC card that emulates one. Devices on the end of a basic-rate interface line are known as terminals.

terminator   A resistor used at each end of an Ethernet cable to ensure that signals do not reflect back and cause errors. It is usually attached to an electrical ground at one end.

TFTP (Trivial File Transfer Protocol)   A simplified version of FTP that transfers files but does not provide password protection or user-directory capability. It is associated with the TCP/IP family of protocols.

thick Ethernet A cabling system using relatively stiff, large-diameter cable to connect transceivers. The transceivers connect to the nodes through flexible multi-wire cable.

thin Ethernet A cabling system using a thin and flexible coaxial cable to connect each node to the next node in line.

3174, 3270, and so on Appear at the end of the alphabet in this glossary.

3+Open A family of 3Com networking products built around the LAN Manager file/print server. 3+Open includes connectivity, messaging, and network management services.

TIC (Token-Ring Interface Coupler) An IBM device that allows a controller or processor to attach directly to a Token-Ring network. This is an optional part of several IBM terminal cluster controllers and front-end processors.

time-division multiplexing (TDM) A method of placing a number of signals on one communications circuit by allocating the available time among competing stations. Allocations may be on a microsecond basis.

time domain reflectometry (TDR) A method of sending a radio pulse down a wire or cable to detect a shorted or open condition. High-priced devices can pinpoint a fault within inches; lower-priced devices often provide widely varying results when they try to pinpoint the distance to a fault.

T interface A standard basic-rate interface using four copper wires.

token passing An access protocol in which a special message (token) circulates among the network nodes, giving them permission to transmit.

Token-Ring The wire and the access protocol scheme whereby stations relay packets in a logical ring configuration. This architecture, pioneered by IBM, is described in the IEEE 802.5 standards.

TOP (Technical and Office Protocol) An implementation of OSI standards in office and engineering environments. TOP, developed by Boeing and other firms, employs Ethernet specifications.

topology The map or plan of the network. The physical topology describes how the wires or cables are laid out, and the logical or electrical topology describes how the messages flow.

TP-4 (Transport Protocol 4) An OSI layer-4 protocol developed by the National Bureau of Standards.

transceiver A communicating device capable of transmitting and receiving.

transmission control The layer in SNA that controls sessions and manages communications.

transport layer The fourth layer of the OSI model. Software in this layer checks the integrity of and formats the data carried by the physical layer (1), managed by the data layer (2), and perhaps routed by the network layer (3).

tree Refers to a network arrangement in which the stations are attached to a common branch or data bus.

TTS (Transaction Tracking System) A log of all file activity in NetWare.

twisted-pair Ethernet See *IEEE 802.3 10BaseT*.

twisted-pair wiring Cable comprised of two wires twisted together at six turns per inch to provide electrical self-shielding. Some telephone wire—but by no means all—is twisted-pair.

Type 3 cable An unshielded twisted-pair wire that meets IBM specifications for use in 4-megabit-per-second Token-Ring networks.

UDP (User Datagram Protocol) A TCP/IP protocol describing how messages reach application programs within a destination computer. This protocol is normally bundled with IP-layer software.

U interface A standard basic-rate interface using two copper wires.

Unix A multitasking, multiuser operating system for minicomputers that was developed by AT&T and has enjoyed popularity among engineering and technical professionals. Unix is finding new uses as the basis of file-server operating systems for networks of PCs.

UNMA (Unified Network Management Architecture) AT&T's company-specific architecture conforming to the ISO's CMIP.

UUCP (Unix-to-Unix Copy Program) A standard Unix utility used for information exchange between two Unix nodes.

V.32   A CCITT standard that describes how modems should talk to each other using two-way signaling at 4,800 and 9,600 bps over dial-up telephone lines. A newer version, V.32bis, adds 7,200-, 12,000-, and 14,400-bps transfer rates.

V.32bis   See *V.32*.

V.35   A CCITT interface standard describing the types of connectors, cables, and electrical signals used on the interconnecting links.

V.42   A CCITT hardware-implemented asynchronous error-control standard.

V.42bis   A CCITT-standard method of implementing data compression on the fly in hardware.

VAN (value-added network)   A privately owned packet-switched network whose services are sold to the public. See *PDN*.

VC (virtual circuit)   A temporary connection path, set up between two points by software and packet switching, that appears to the user to be available as a dedicated circuit. This "phantom" circuit can be maintained indefinitely or can be ended at will.

An X.25 VC is a PAP logical connection between an X.25 DTE and an X.25 DCE. X.25 supports both switched VCs (SVCs) and permanent VCs (PVCs). SVCs are analogous to dial-up lines; that is, they allow a particular X.25 DTE to establish a connection with different X.25 DTEs on a per-call basis. By contrast, PVCs are analogous to leased lines because they always connect two X.25 DTEs.

VINES (VIrtual NEtworking Software)   A Unix-based network operating system from Banyan Systems.

virtual circuit   See *VC*.

voice channel   A transmission path usually limited to passing the bandwidth of the human voice.

VPDN (virtual private data networks)   Subscriber services available through long-distance telephone companies that offer services equivalent to full-time leased lines at a lower cost.

VSAT (very small aperture terminal)   A system that combines a ground station with a digital transponder in an orbiting geostationary satellite to provide flexible inter-LAN circuits across short or long distances.

VTAM (Virtual Telecommunications Access Method)   An IBM standard for software that runs on the host mainframe computer and works with the Network Control Program to establish communications between the host and the cluster controllers. Among other things, VTAM sets the pacing and LU characteristics.

WAITS (wide area information transfer systems)   Networked computers running software that automates the tasks of moving files between networks. Computers running WAITS software can satisfy all the LAN-to-LAN connectivity needs for many organizations.

WAN (wide-area network)   A type of network that connects computers over areas potentially as wide as the entire world.

wideband   Refers to a channel or transmission medium capable of passing more frequencies than a standard 3 kHz voice channel.

wideband modem   A modem that operates at over 9,600 bits per second.

wiring hub   A cabinet, usually mounted in a wiring closet, that holds connection modules for various kinds of cabling. The hub contains electronic circuits that retime and repeat the signals on the cable. The hub may also contain a microprocessor board that monitors and reports on network activity.

X.25   A CCITT standard that describes how data is handled in and how computers can access a packet-switched network.

X.400   The CCITT designation for an international electronic-mail distribution system.

X.402   A CCITT standard for X.400 architecture.

X.403   A CCITT standard for testing compliance with the 1984 X.400 standards.

X.420   A CCITT standard for message-content specification.

X.435   A CCITT standard called "Message Handling Systems: EDI Messaging Systems" that provides a standard way to handle bills, invoices, contracts, and other business documents over electronic mail.

X.500   The CCITT designation for a directory standard to coordinate the dispersed file directories of different systems.

XNS (Xerox Network Services)   A multilayer protocol system developed by Xerox and adopted, at least in part, by Novell and other vendors. XNS is one of the many distributed-file-system protocols that allows network stations to use other computers' files and peripherals as if they were local.

X/Open   A consortium of computer-industry vendors, chartered to specify an open system platform based on the Unix operating system.

X Window   A network-based windowing system that provides a programmatic interface for graphic window displays. X Window permits graphics produced on one networked workstation to be displayed on another.

3174   A new version of the 3274 terminal cluster controller.

3270   The generic name for the family of interoperable IBM system components—terminals, printers, and terminal cluster controllers—that can be used to communicate with a mainframe by means of the SNA or bisync protocols. All of these components have four-digit names, some of which begin with the digits 327.

3274/3276   The most commonly used cluster controller. This device links as many as 32 3270-type terminals and printers to a mainframe front-end processor.

3278   The most commonly used terminal in the 3270 family. It features a monochrome display and offers a limited graphics set.

3279   A color terminal that is part of the 3270 family.

3287   The current series of printers in the 3270 equipment family.

3705   A common front-end processor, typically used to link several 3274s to a mainframe.

3725   A common front-end processor, intended for linking groups of cluster controllers to a mainframe.

3745   A new communications controller that combines the functions of a cluster controller and a front-end processor. The 3745 can interface simultaneously with as many as 8 Token-Ring networks, 512 terminals or printers, and 16 1.544-megabit-per-second communications lines.

■ Index

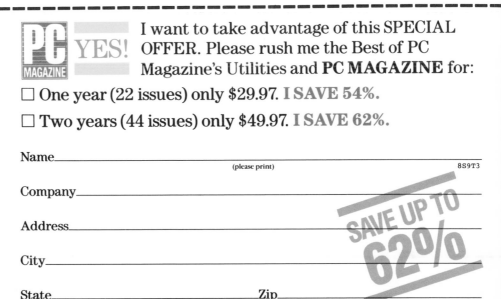

ACROSS THE MILES: BUILDING CONNECTIONS AMONG LAN SEGMENTS

This diagram illustrates a rather atypical LAN segment, endowed with practically every type of network interconnection device: bridges (B), routers (R), BBS software, access and modem servers (A/M), and e-mail gateways (G). The diagram also shows various communications circuits that can be used to carry data to other LAN segments: leased lines, VSATs, and public data networks, among others. In this book, you'll find in-depth coverage of all these device and media options: how much they cost, when they are most appropriate, and how you can put them to work to make the most effective use of your LAN-to-LAN links (and LAN-to-LAN-to-LAN links!).

In practice, you are not likely to employ all of the indicated network interconnection device options on the same segment; the same is true of the media circuits. The diagram simply points up the multitude of network devices and transport media available. Keep in mind that you can structure an

internetwork system with many combinations of network devices and communications circuits.

While this diagram shows routers connected through a public data network, note that a bridge, an access server, or even a BBS could also take advantage of PDN service. Typically, most users will rely on dial-up lines when internetwork communication is accomplished through access servers (including those with modem-server capabilities for outgoing communications) or BBS software. For users who need to transfer large files or update remote databases, the leased line connecting two bridges on different LAN segments would benefit from a 1.544-megabit-per-second T1 service, which could have subchannels broken out for an access server or even voice PBX connections.

If your primary means of internetwork communications is via an e-mail gateway, chances are that high-speed throughput is not the main concern; in that case, leased lines operating at a slower 19.2 kilobits per second or even public dial-up lines may be a more cost-effective investment. Your needs may simply call for the proprietary gateway module to link two LANs running the same e-mail software, or you may need to make use of MHS gateways to connect distant LANs running diverse e-mail packages.

Outfitting your business with VSATs (very small aperture terminals) makes sense when you have multiple locations—generally at least ten, though a case could be made for fewer—that are 500 miles or more from each other. VSATs

can operate at speeds comparable to those of T1 links, but they make better back-up devices since they are not prey to the same problems that can strike land-based systems, such as natural disasters.

If you need to link LANs in metropolitan areas, options as diverse as FDDI, ISDN, and even wideband microwave radio links are available. FDDI, which uses fiber-optic cables, eliminates the problems of electrical noise and interference that can occur when copper cables are used, and ISDN provides the benefit of fast digital service. Microwave radio links are an interesting option, but are practical only when a line of sight exists between the two locations.

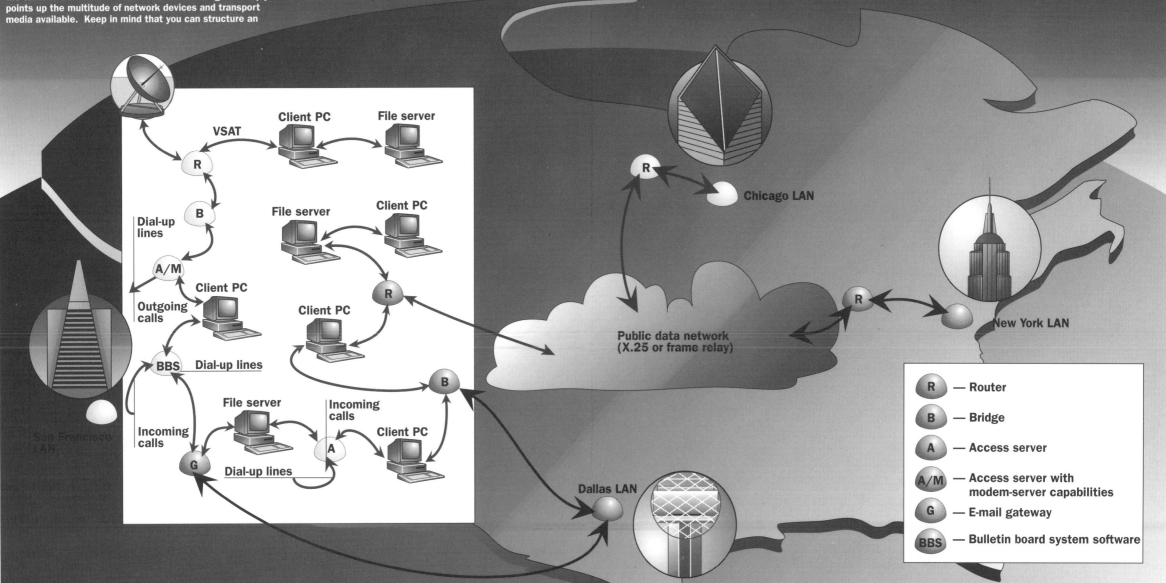